IMAGES
of America

AROUND LIMA

On the cover: Civil War veterans pose for a photograph after a dinner presented in their honor by the Daughters of the American Revolution on May 30, 1913.

IMAGES
of America

AROUND LIMA

Michael Leavy

ARCADIA
PUBLISHING

ISBN 978-0-7385-0983-9

Published by Arcadia Publishing
Charleston, South Carolina

Printed in the United States of America

Library of Congress Catalog Card Number: 2001098961

For all general information contact Arcadia Publishing at:
Telephone 843-853-2070
Fax 843-853-0044
E-mail sales@arcadiapublishing.com
For customer service and orders:
Toll-Free 1-888-313-2665

Visit us on the Internet at www.arcadiapublishing.com

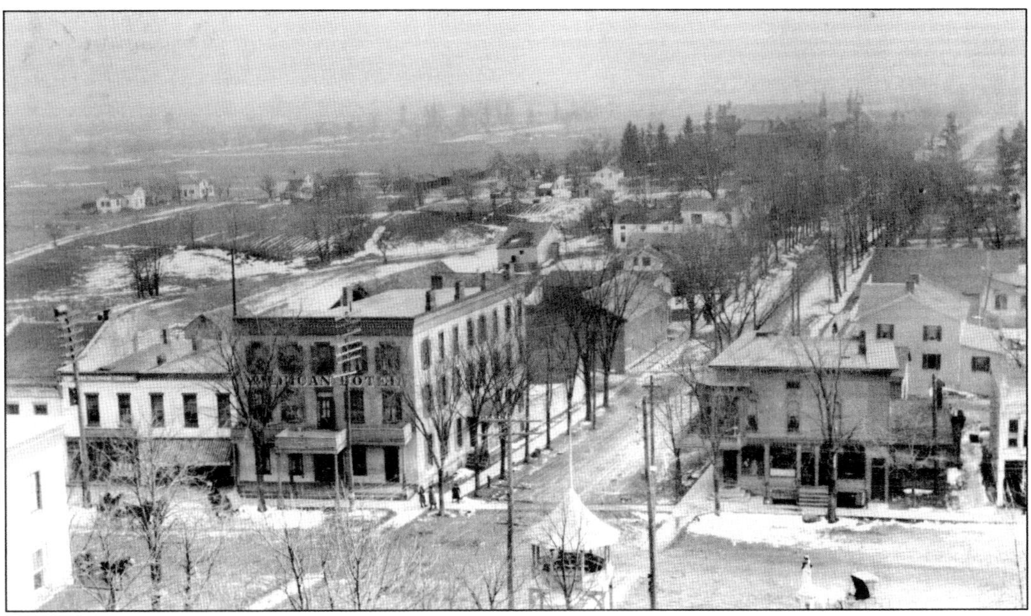

The location of the original Lima crossroads was not far from this spot. Primary Seneca trails intersected here. Over those trails the Seneca carried on trade with other tribes of the Iroquois Confederacy. They also used the trails to hunt and to make war. Prior to the Senecas, evidence of human occupation dates back 4,000 to 5,000 years. Within the township of Lima, there may have been as many as 30 longhouses at the various villages. With white settlement the east–west trail became vital to westward immigration. Today, it is designated as Routes 5 & 20 and takes us through old land grants, or preemptions, past the mansions of land agents and the shacks of pioneers. In short, it takes us though one of the most historic regions of America.

Contents

Acknowledgments

I would like to express my gratitude to all those who enthusiastically provided me with information and resources and who, through their very generosity, contributed to a project that should deepen your appreciation for this region: Cathy Gardner, for providing the Corby photograph collection; Fran Gotcsik; Diane Ham-Mendon, town historian; Anne Bullock, Honeoye Falls village historian; Margaret Parshall, Historical Society of the Town of East Bloomfield; Sandra Schlenker, president of West Bloomfield Historical Society; Noeme Panke, for processing glass plates; Maureen Kingston, historian of the town of Avon; Jeanne Wenrich, chairwoman of the Avon Historical and Preservation Society; *Avon—Heart of the Genesee County*, by Marie C. Preston; Charles and Sheila Thomas; and Pat Reynolds. Special thanks go to members of the Lima Historical Society for their support and for providing the bulk of the photographs used.

—Michael Leavy
Lima, New York

INTRODUCTION

Prior to the American War of Independence, Gen. George Washington traveled far westward to observe a land he had been told much about. At that time the Genesee Valley was the frontier. A few pioneer settlements struggled for survival within what was still the land of Iroquois. Washington secretly viewed Indian plantations and was stunned by their magnificence: acres of corn with stalks up to 18 feet tall, pumpkins, squash, and orchards with bows bent in fruitful harvest. The villages were comprised of sturdy wooden houses—some with glass windows. The network of primary and secondary trails was remarkable. This was hardly the primitive culture Washington had been told it was. It was a proud and resourceful agricultural society whose citizens lived, in many cases, better than most whites.

When he left, Washington resolved to acquire the region for the new nation he hoped to establish. The Iroquois had allied with the British in the ongoing battle for North America. That would be reason enough. Combined Indian-Tory attacks on American settlements, launched from the British stronghold at Niagara, would provide suitable justification to pick a fight. However, eventual peace would mean little with only 13 puny colonies as the nucleus for a new nation. Washington wanted to secure as much land to the west as he could lay hands on. Thus, in 1779, he sent the Sullivan Expedition into Pennsylvania and New York's Genesee Country. Some 5,000 highly trained soldiers systematically destroyed villages and razed crops until they had wrested the region from the Indians and placed it under American control.

Many of the soldiers were from New England. Accustomed to rocky soil, they marveled at the vast richness of this land; many decided, on the spot, to return here after the war. One of them was Paul Davison, who came west with his brother-in-law, Jonathan Gould, in 1788. They started a small farm and then returned for their families. Their rugged endeavor established the foundation of Lima, known variously as Migell's Gore and the admittedly more appealing Charleston. In 1808, it became fixed as Lima.

The Genesee Turnpike (State Road) brought a ceaseless westward flow of pioneers. As many as six inns sprang up in Lima alone. Bloomfield, Avon, and Honeoye Falls were among the towns that came into existence and prospered; yet, it is amazing how towns so close could be so diversified.

Along the State Road and down Clover and Rochester Streets, conductors on the Underground Railroad hurried fugitive slaves to Rochester ports and eventual freedom.

The mills came and, by 1820, this area was the breadbasket of America. Canals and railroads arrived bringing continued economic prosperity.

In 1830, a singular event transformed Lima from a rustic pioneer village into one of the most important educational centers in New York. The Conference of the Methodist Church selected Lima for its establishment of Genesee Wesleyan Seminary. The construction of a magnificent campus on a hilltop in the village set Lima apart from similar small towns. Elegant homes and stores appeared; important people came to speak. Moreover, it produced a list of glittering alumnae, among them Sen. Kenneth Keating; Belva Lockwood, the first woman to run for president; and Henry Raymond, publisher of the *New York Times*. Elim Bible Institute acquired the property in 1950 and began classes in 1951 as a bible and missionary school. The institute continues a long tradition of coeducational excellence.

Today, Lima still has its busy crossroads. Bypassed by railroads and canals, and lacking any dynamic water systems to power mills, the town prospered—moderately—and still does. One radio commercial refers to Lima as "the center of the universe." The locals laugh. Yet, when they consider the rich neighbors that orbit it—towns connected by schools, roads, traditions, churches, and most importantly family—Lima fulfills the message of that ad.

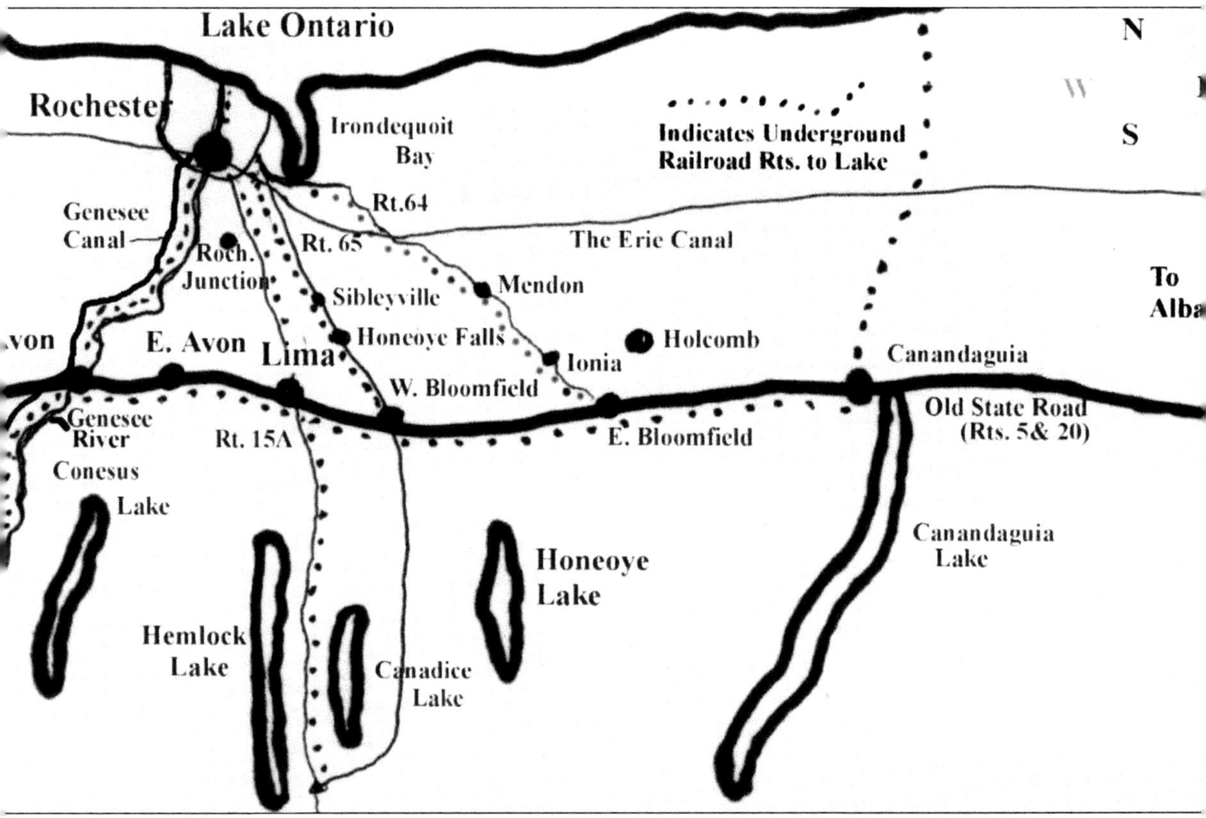

Situated within both the Genesee Region and the Finger Lakes, the area around Lima is gloriously endowed with natural beauty. The old State Road (Routes 5 & 20) was built from Albany to Buffalo, and it brought a flood of settlers into this rich agricultural region. Many of them saw no reason to travel farther, and so they stayed.

One

Lima Early On

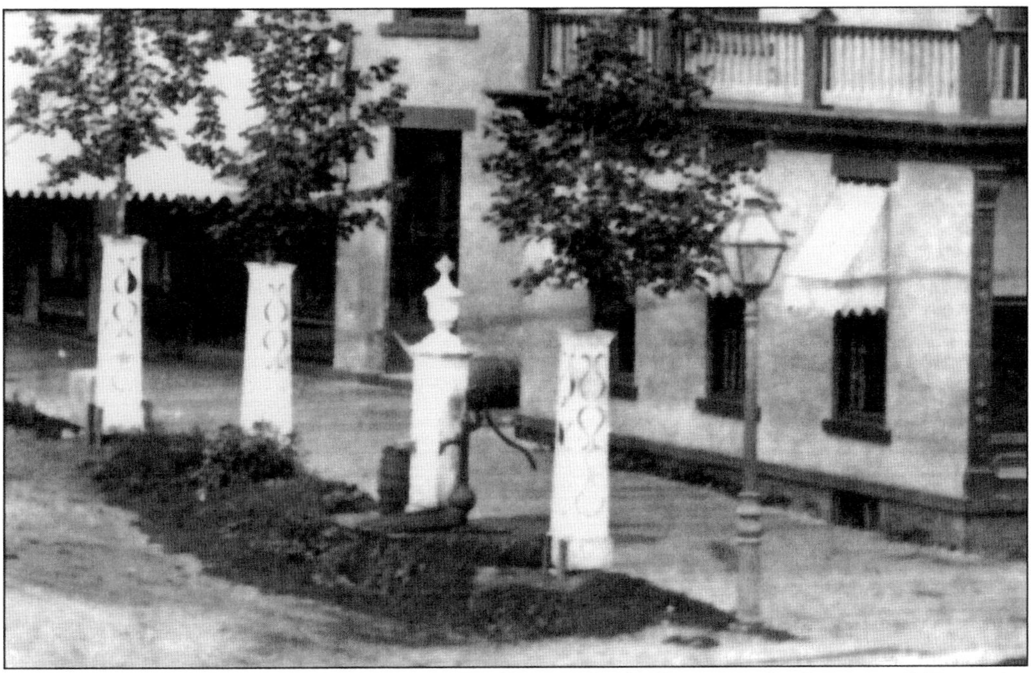

A fanciful town pump beside the Masonic Hall offered refreshment to both man and beast. An iron hand pump drew water for horses and cattle. Beside it a more elaborate affair, adorned with a classical urn, side arm, and spigot, allowed more dignified usage. Prior to the Civil War, this pump, in the dead of night, would prove an oasis to fugitive slaves coming up from Hemlock and then north on Rochester Street to freedom at a Lake Ontario port.

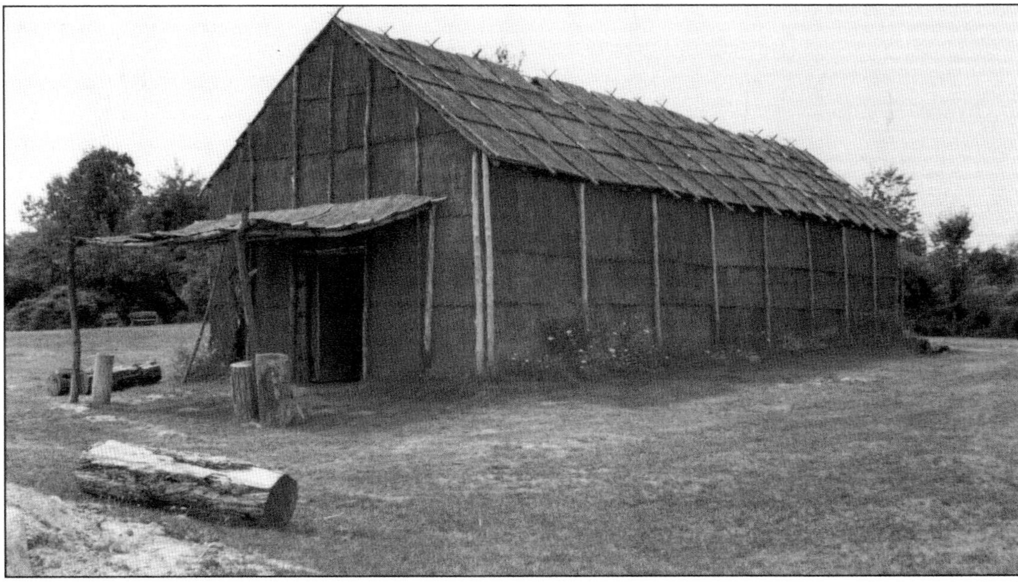

Longhouses were the mainstay of the Seneca. A village of these efficient and cleverly built structures could last 15 to 30 years. After that, the men would be sent ahead to build a new village, usually over two-year period, and the rest of the village would follow upon completion. Around Lima, many footprints of longhouses have been excavated over the years. Some are over 100 feet long. This remarkable reconstruction is at the Ganondagan historical site in the nearby town of Victor.

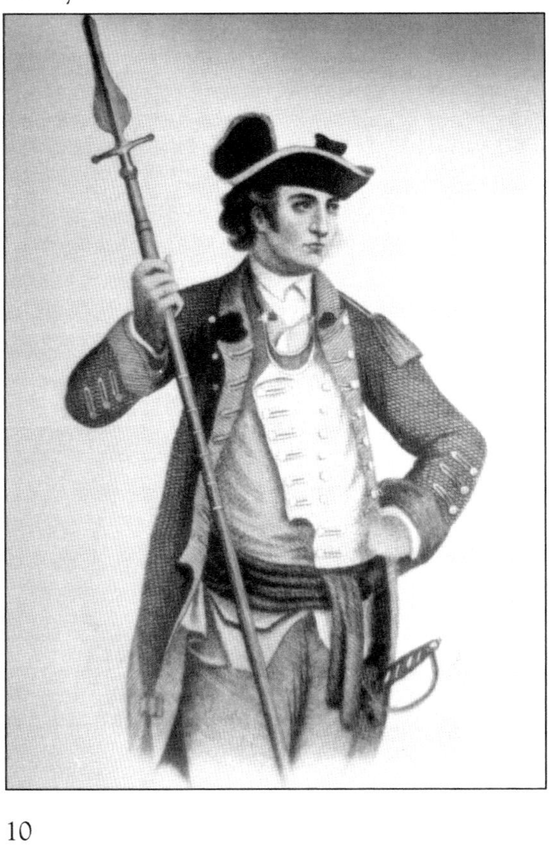

Longhouses were long gone when Gen. John Sullivan led his brigades into the Finger Lakes and Genesee Country in 1779. He burned villages and crops in a scorched-earth policy which, during the Civil War, Gen. William Tecumseh Sherman reviewed while planning his march to the sea. The Sullivan Expedition was about many things: ancient hatreds, ill-considered alliances, brutal massacres, and bold-faced land grabs. Sullivan brilliantly executed the plan on behalf of the Americans.

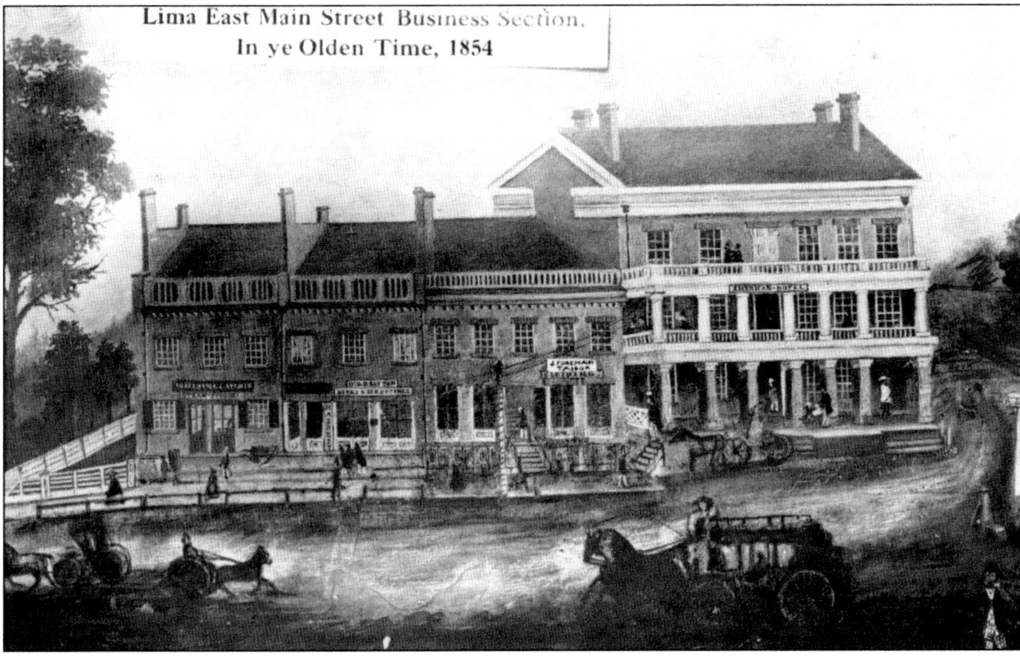

A postcard rendering depicts the early flourish of activity at the crossroads. Stagecoaches, buggies, and a two-wheeled chaise hurry along. An earlier American Hotel, with columned verandas, is doing a brisk business. This block remains intact today.

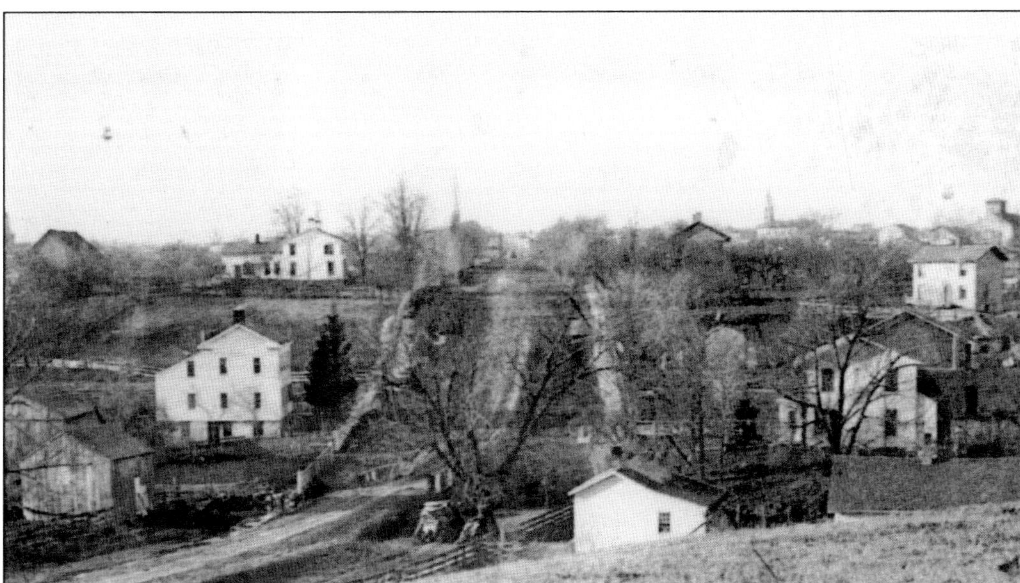

A view looking west from the Wemett farm, just east of the village, offers an idea of what Lima looked like *c.* the mid-1800s. At the lower left is the State Road. Stagecoach drivers, some wearing straw hats and flamboyant calico jackets, had to drive their teams hard to get up the hill. They blew their tin horns to alert taverns to prepare meals for arriving passengers.

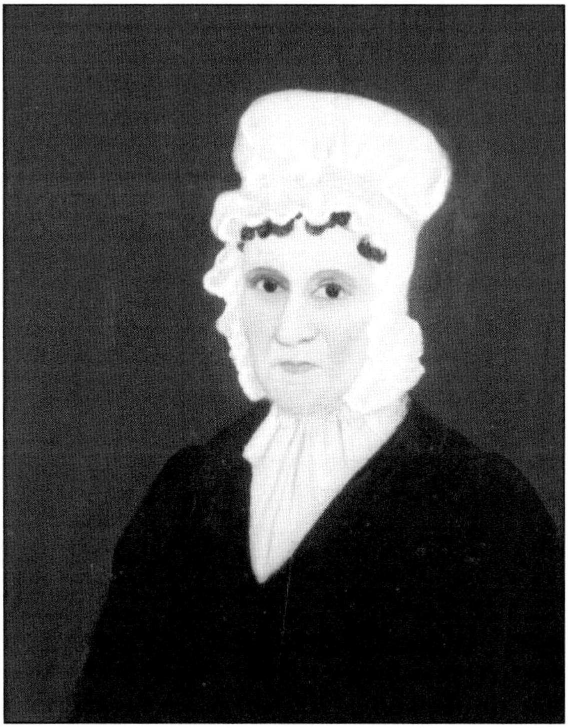

Typical of the stalwart pioneer was Judith Lyon who, with her husband, Wakeman, arrived in Charleston (Lima) in 1812. They had a farm on the site of the present Presbyterian church, which they helped organize. Widowed in 1815, Judith Lyon courageously raised her six small children well. She lived to the age of 90, dying in 1870.

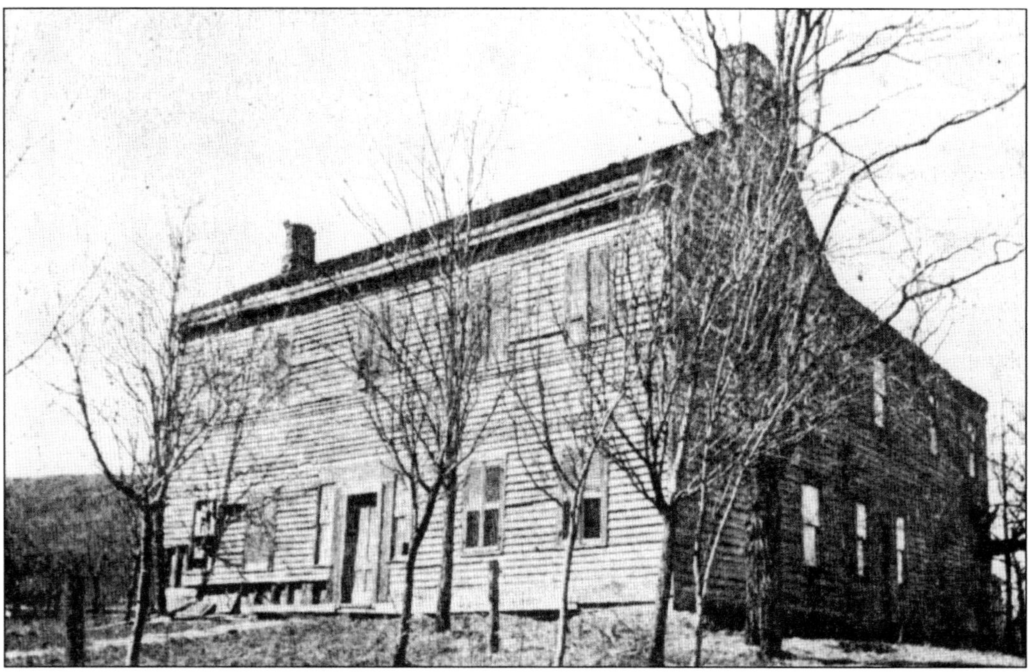

The State Road, laid along the original Indian trail, was completed in 1809. It connected the Hudson and Niagara Rivers. A favorite of travelers was the Nash House, built in 1796. In 1816, the house was painted a vivid yellow and renamed the Yellow Wasp. The second-floor ballroom had 24 huge springs beneath its planks. The inn was a center of social gatherings and had its share of brawls. It is a sad wreck in this 1906 image and was demolished that same year.

The Charleston Congregational Society—later Lima Presbyterian Church—erected this handsome church in 1816. It was 40 feet long. A stately iron fence surrounded the yard. There were large stables in back for worshipers' horses, and a small churchyard cemetery was built on the north rise of the property.

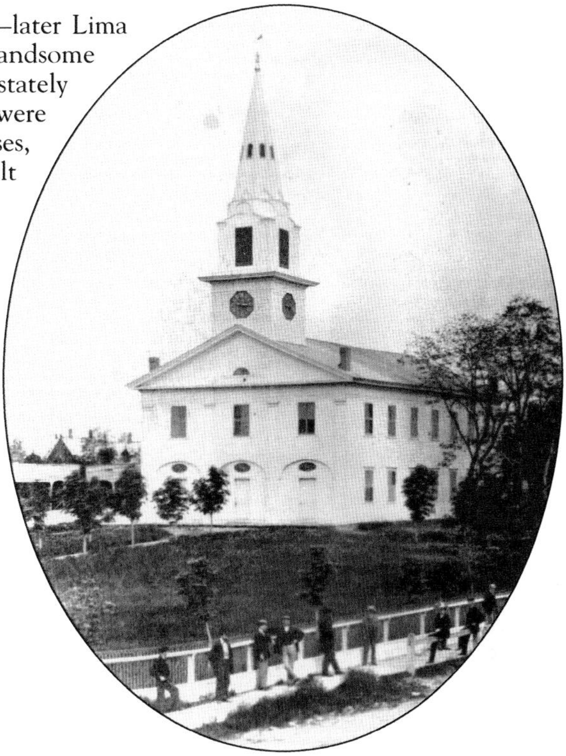

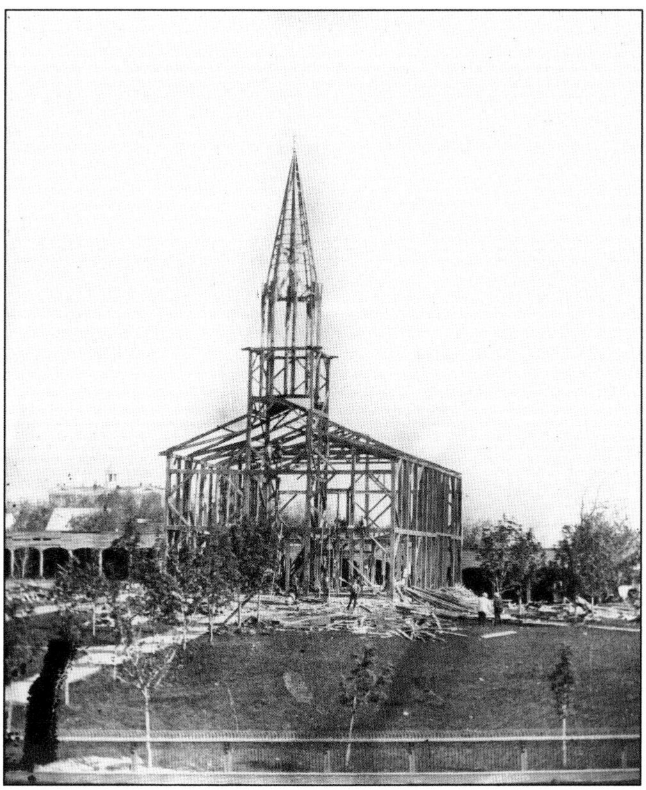

The church is being dismantled to make way for a more substantial brick structure to be built in 1874. This rare image provides a look at early construction techniques. It would be reasonable to assume that much of this wood ended up in surrounding structures.

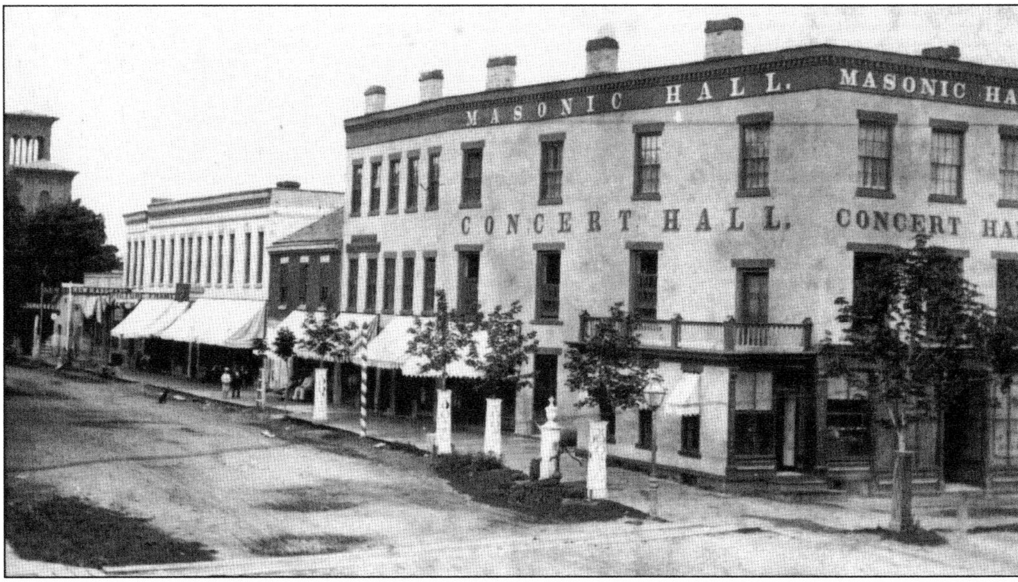

The Masons were often cruelly victimized during the Anti-Masonic Movement, an irrational, often violent assault against Freemasonry. In one instance clothes from a Lima smallpox victim were left on a porch where Masons were meeting. The members brushed the clothes aside when they left the meeting and, in the process, became infected with smallpox and eventually died from the disease.

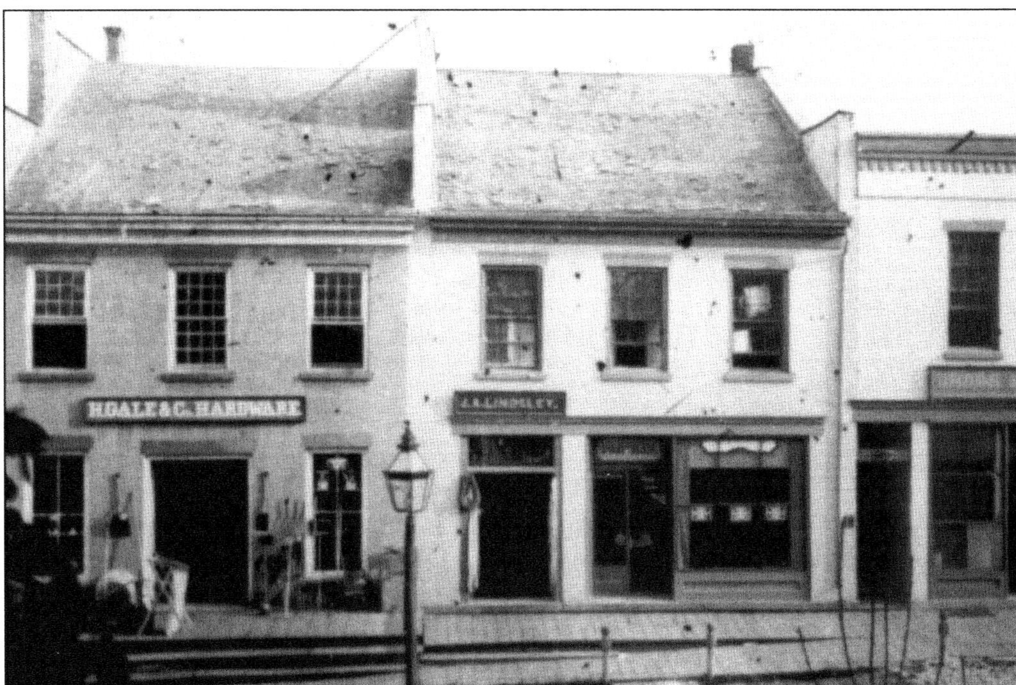

One of the earliest views of Lima shows the south side of East Main Street. On the left is H. Gale & Company Hardware. Next to the hardware store is J.A. Lindsley. A wooden crosswalk, wooden sidewalks, and an oil lamppost indicate that the photograph dates from the mid-1800s.

The richly appointed interior of the third-floor Masonic lodge sparkles in this glass plate image. In the center is a marble altar. The master would sit in the dais, between the columns. The chairs were arranged for the deacons and wardens. The original 1866 carpet remains in use today, and the lodge looks pretty much as it does in this photograph.

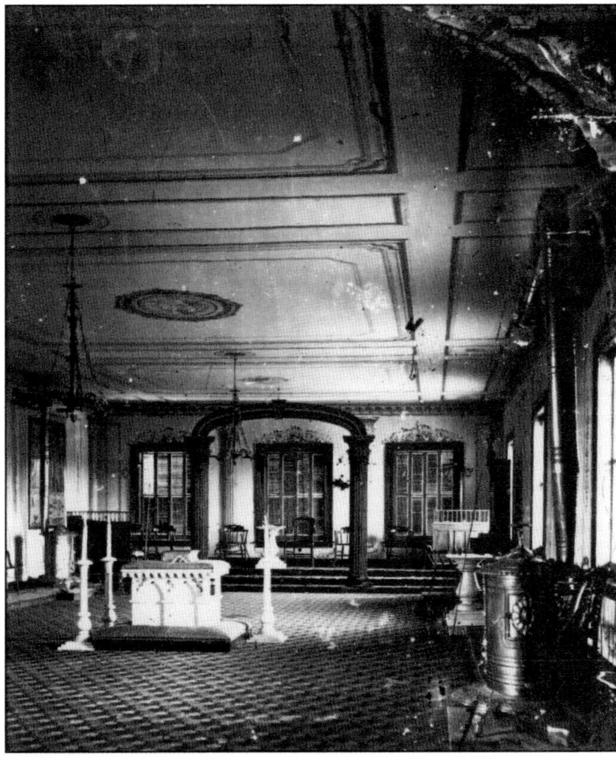

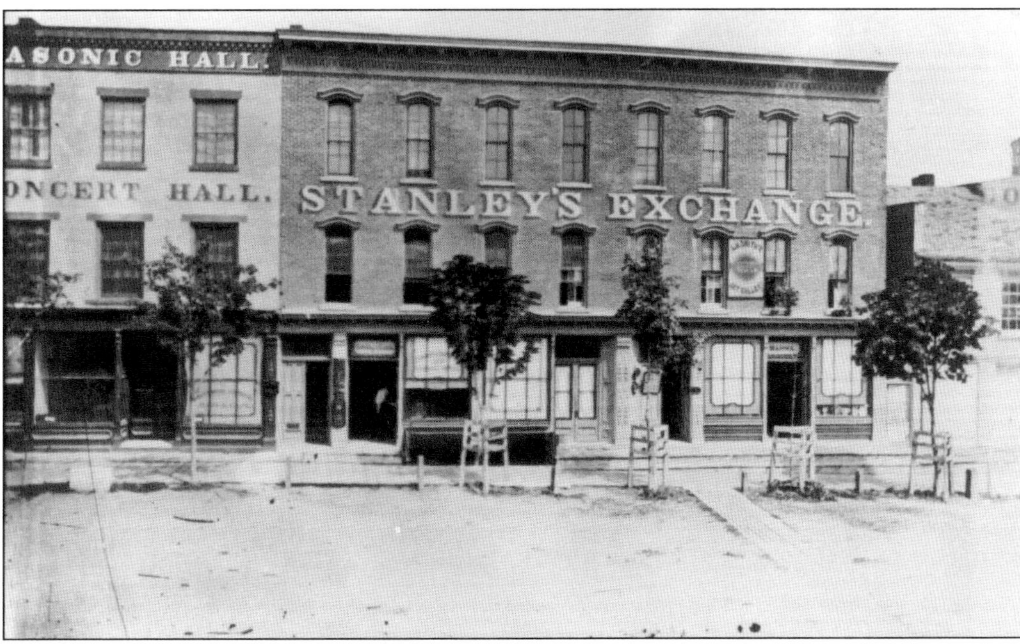

The Stanley Exchange was a block of buildings similar to those directly across the street from it; a more substantial storefront was added later. Daniel Stanley owned the bank, or exchange, as well as other businesses in the block. He was also a landowner, having several farms, and records refer to him as "Banker/Gentleman." The Exchange still has an upper-story dance hall and, in the cellar, remnants of an oyster bar.

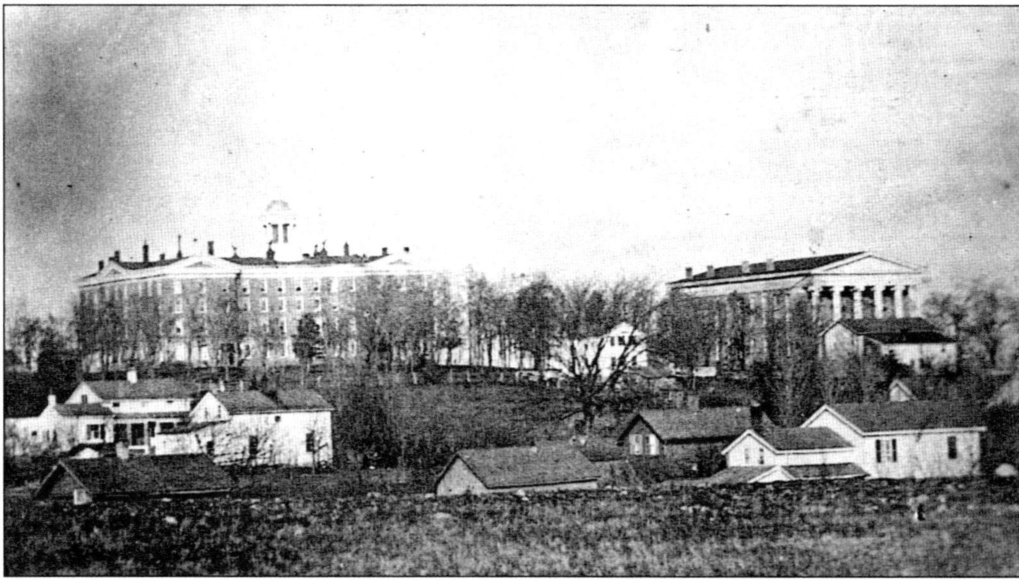

Few upstate New York towns had anything to rival this. Genesee Wesleyan Seminary sits majestically atop Seminary Hill. Its influence on the history of Lima was formative and profound. In 1849, Genesee College was founded on the same campus. In 1870, it moved to Syracuse and evolved into Syracuse University. In 1950, Elim Bible Institute acquired the property and began classes in 1951.

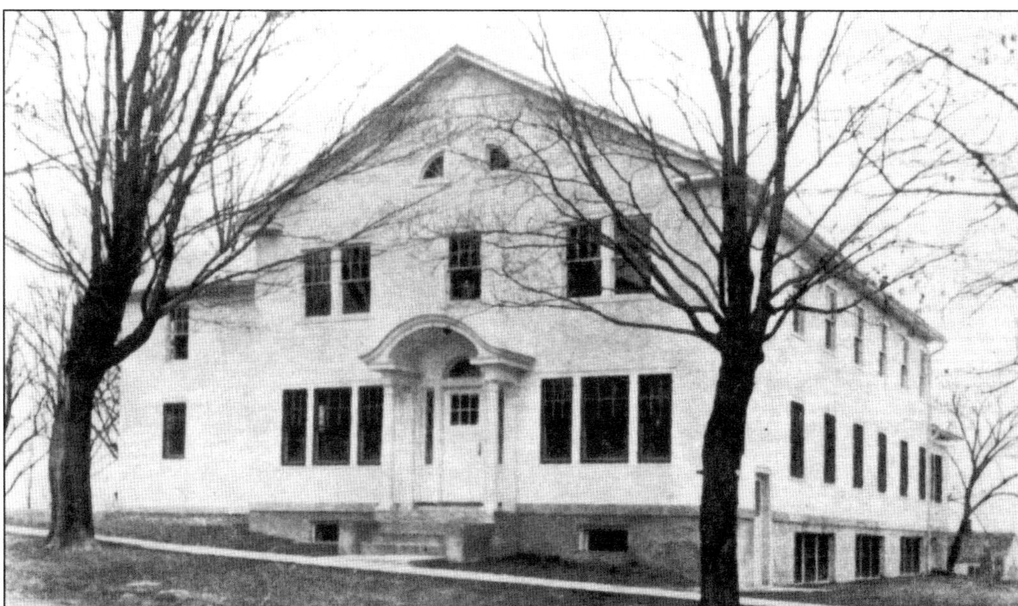

The new music studio of Genesee Wesleyan Seminary was located across the street from College Hall.

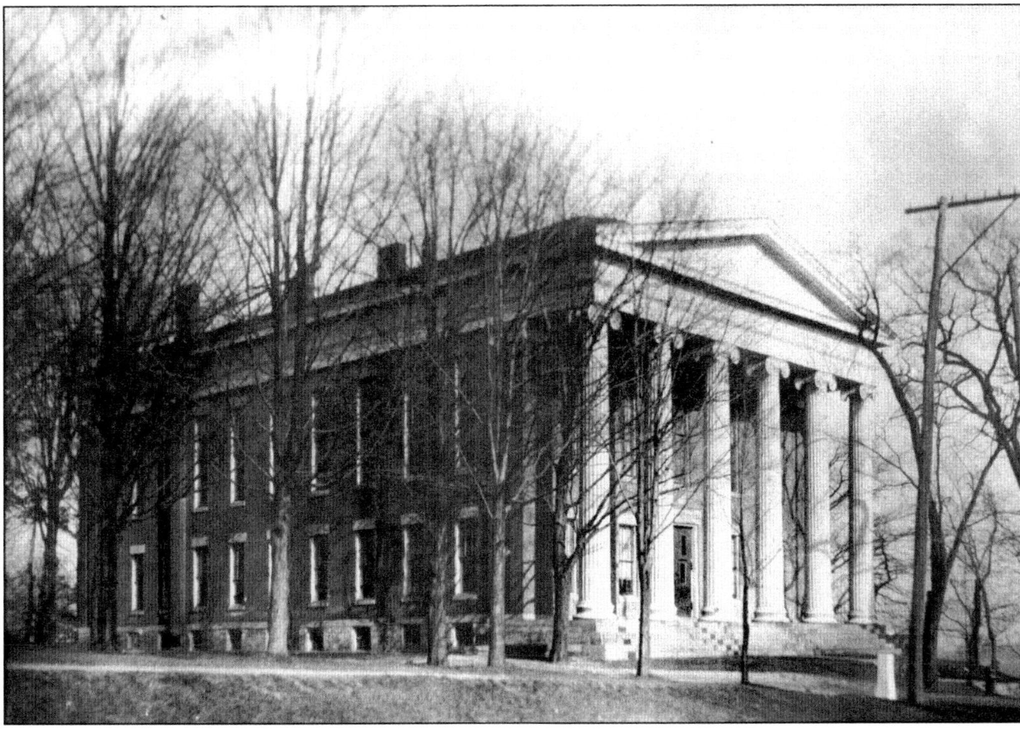

Founded in 1849, College Hall received its charter and endowment in 1850. This handsome building was then constructed. Eventually, conflicts arose over the operation of both the college and the seminary, and the college was moved to Syracuse *c.* 1870. This photograph was taken *c.* 1914 by student George Corby, who bicycled to class from his farm on Corby Road.

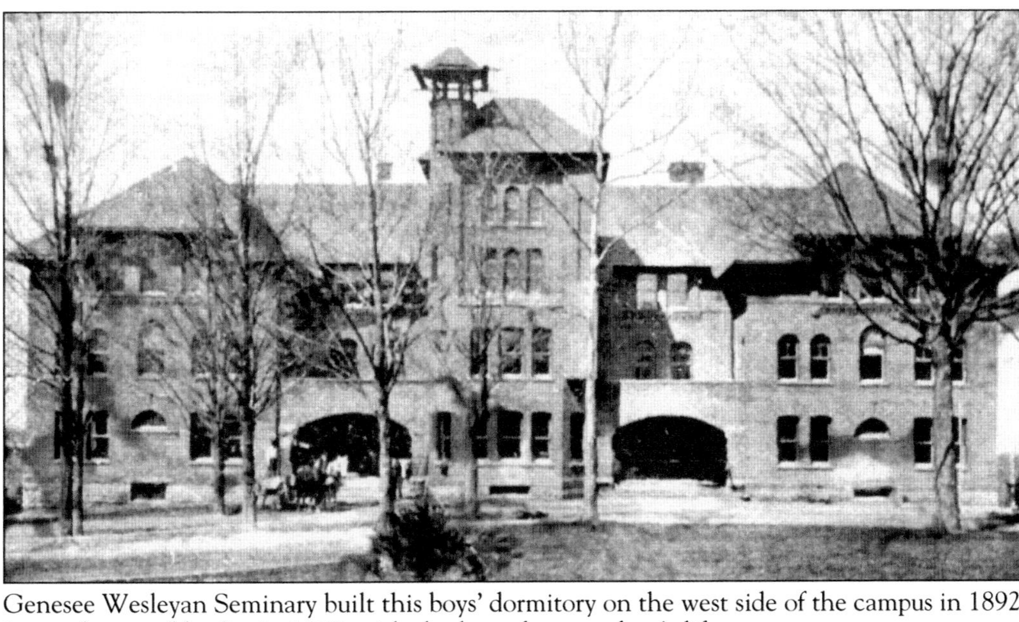

Genesee Wesleyan Seminary built this boys' dormitory on the west side of the campus in 1892. It was destroyed by fire in 1897, with the loss of one student's life.

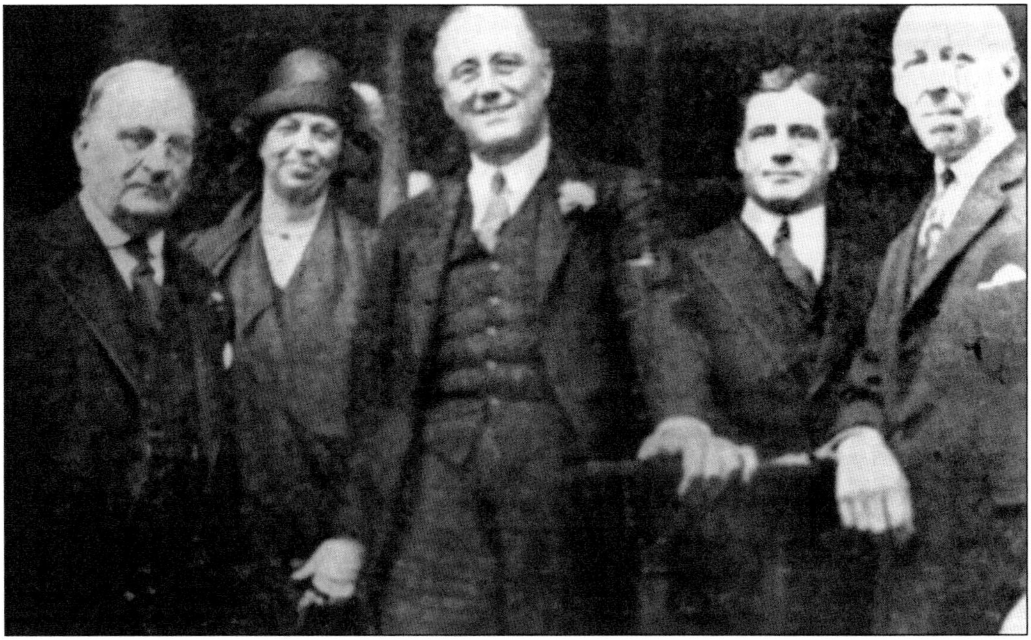

Gov. and Mrs. Franklin Delano Roosevelt (third and second from the left) are greeted by Dr. Frank MacDaniel (left), president of Genesee Wesleyan Seminary, and other officials under the veranda of the seminary on June 12, 1930. Trains from surrounding towns and cars brought a crowd of some 2,000 to hear the governor's address, given on the campus lawn.

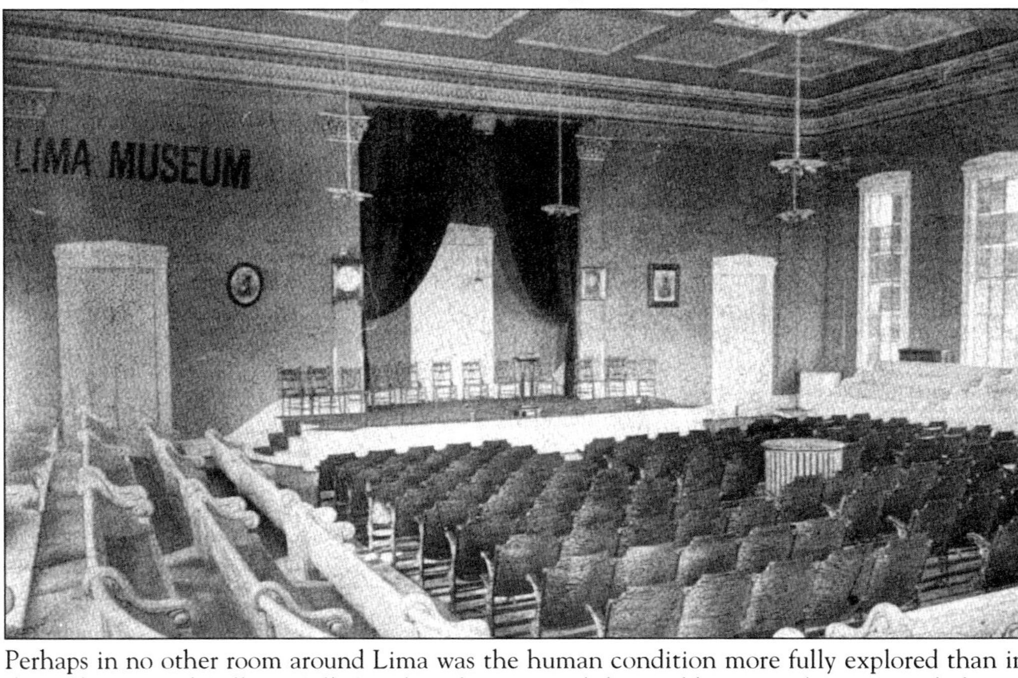

Perhaps in no other room around Lima was the human condition more fully explored than in the auditorium of College Hall. Speakers from around the world came to lecture on abolition, women's rights, prohibition, and so on. Debates and plays were well attended and, before the age of radio and television, concerts were popular, whether held here, on the campus lawn, at the Masonic Concert Hall, or on the bandstand.

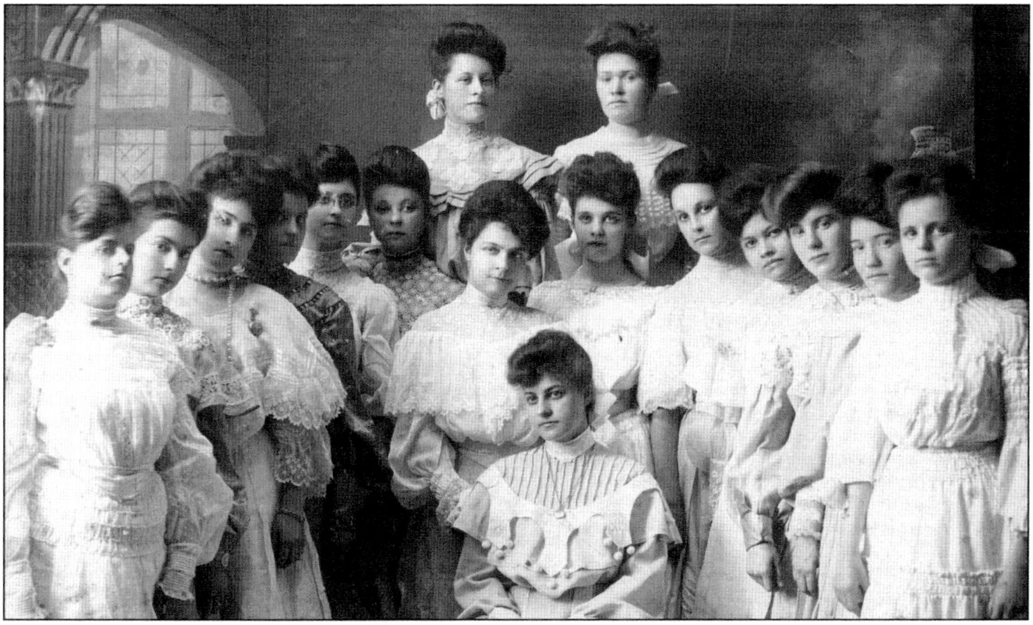

The Ingelow Cabinet, formerly the Genesee Wesleyan Seminary Ladies' Literary Society, poses for this Bronson Studio plate, taken in 1904. Pictured, from left to right, are the following: (front row) Mabel Fulmer, president; (middle row) Esther Taylor, Pearl Hall, Beatrice Edwards, Mildred Parker, Marion Grenolds, Alice Harris, Laura Robinson, Mabel Dutton, Elizabeth Dibble, Molly Jemmison, Isabelle Shepherd, Nellie Hendrick, and Florence Talmadge; (back row) Ruby Hunt and Anna Burr.

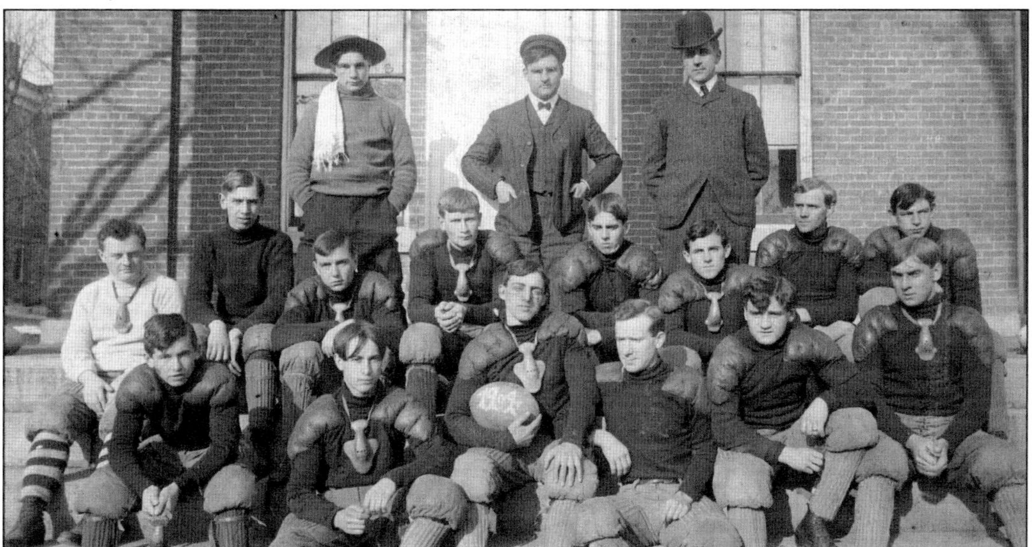

In this 1904 Bronson Studio plate, the Genesee Wesleyan Seminary football team poses beneath the soaring columns of College Hall. In those days, when the game was over, you folded your leather helmet and stuck it in your back pocket. Identified by last name, from left to right, are the following: (first row) Lynn, Lindsay, and Loughrey; (second row) Martin Bristol, Smith, Vail, Beeney, and Godfrey; (third row) Salmon, Rodgers, Parker, Hart, and Sutton; (fourth row) trainer Coe, Professor Tilroe, and Coach Purdy.

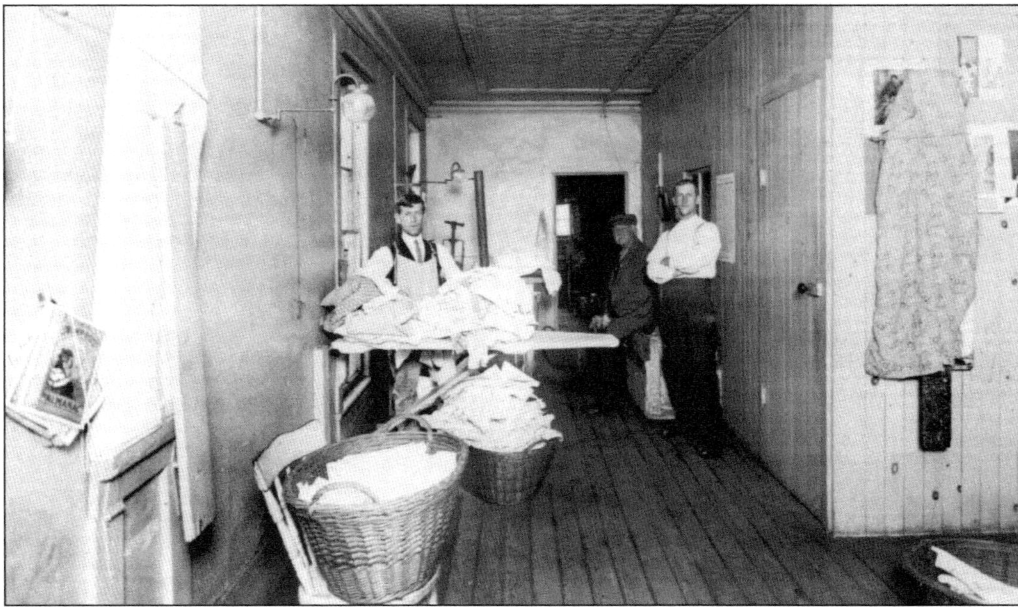

The Learys were an industrious family, having several businesses downtown. This second-floor establishment, over the Lima Recorder print shop on Rochester Street, is Leary Brothers Laundry. Bill Leary is behind the ironing board; across from him, arms folded, is Jack Leary. Ben Ollerenshaw is in the background.

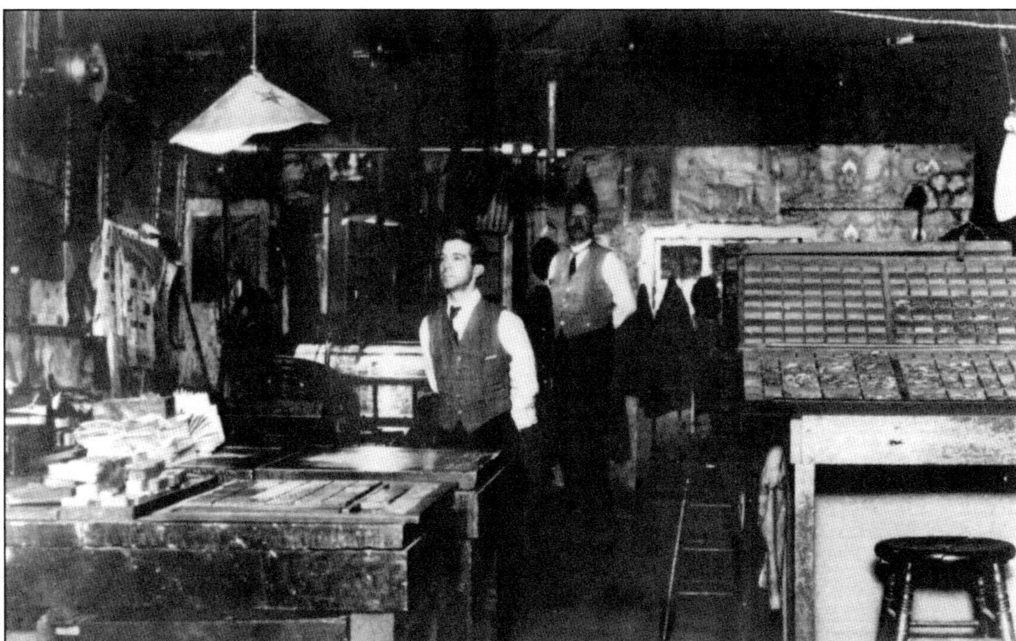

This c. 1915 photograph shows the Lima Recorder printing office, located on Rochester Street beneath Leary Brothers Laundry. The proprietor, Fred Van Geller, is in front, and his father, Charles Van Geller, is in the back. Today, a service station operates where this structure once stood.

Two

Lima Village Scenes

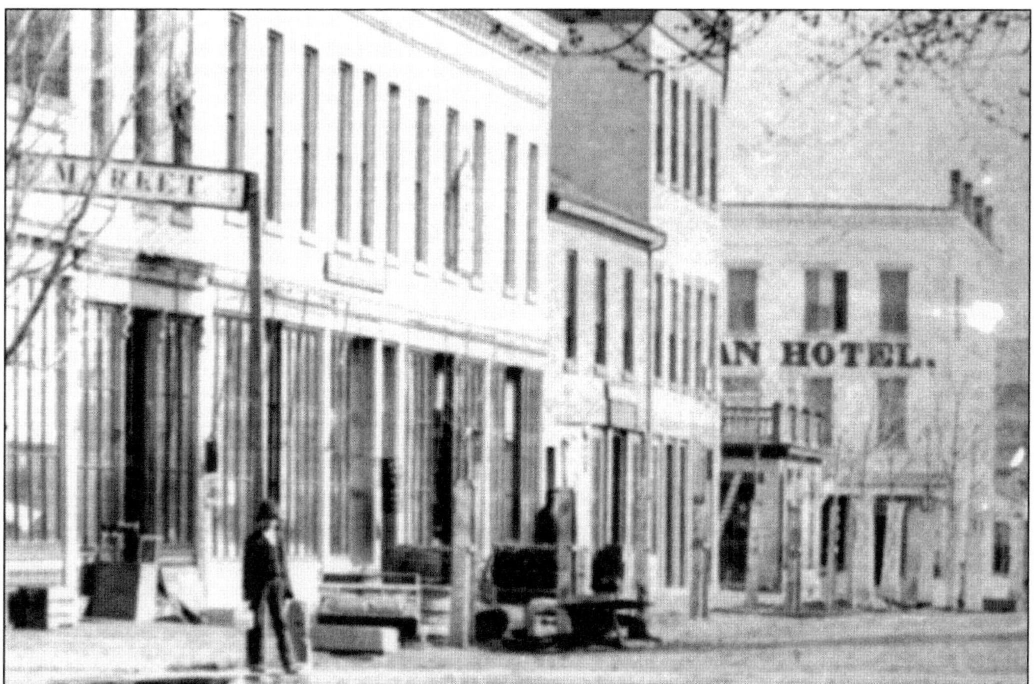

This 1860s view of the Rochester Street mercantile district was taken during a cold month. Awnings have been removed and the frames retracted so that sunlight can help warm the buildings. The smaller structure behind the Masonic Hall burned in the 1920s.

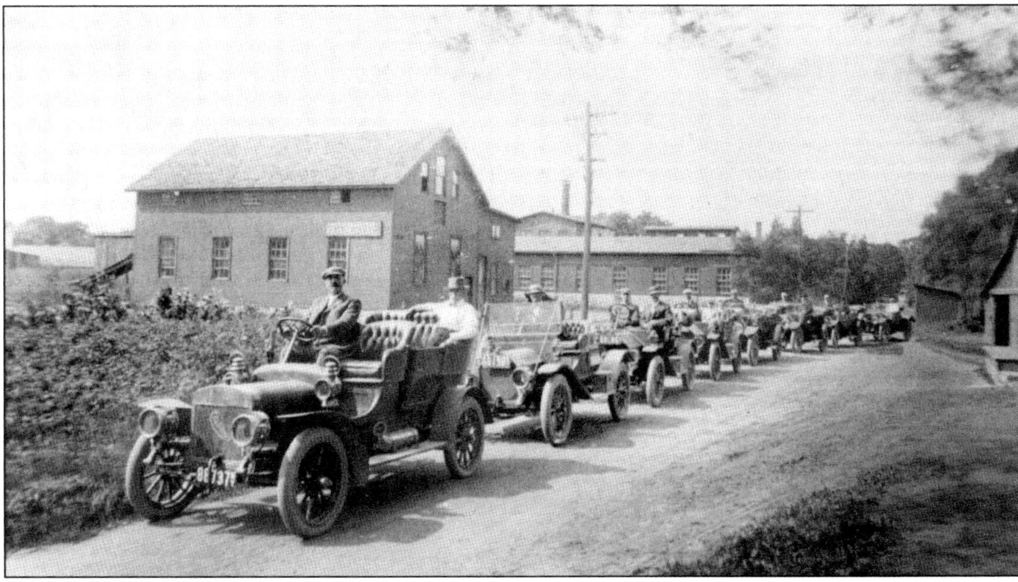

These sporty runabouts lined up on Livingston Street are Carters, an off-brand probably taken over by a larger maker. Behind the garage is Papec Machine Company. Across the street was Gillette Bottling Works, a *c.* 1858 cider mill that developed into soda making. The company sold as far away as New York City and Chicago. When Schuyler Gillette died unexpectedly, he took his pop recipes with him and the company had to close. Livingston Street was often called "Pop Alley."

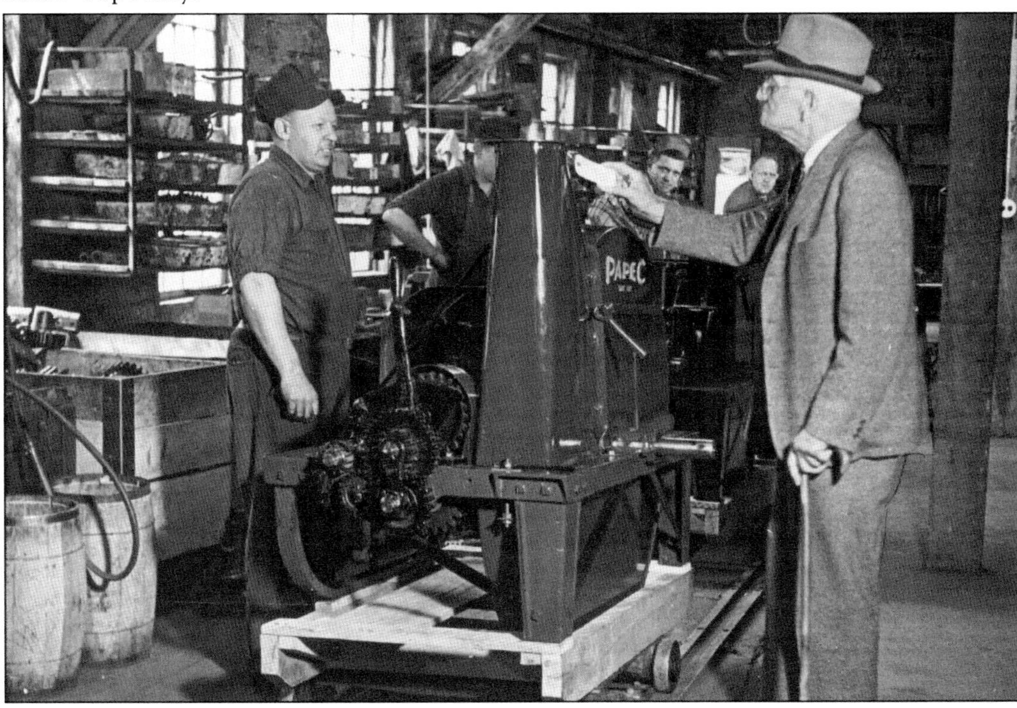

Ward Preston looks on proudly as a potential client inspects a tooling machine. Papec Machine Shop was located on Livingston Street. Also housed in this building was a rubber air plant that manufactured solid rubber tires.

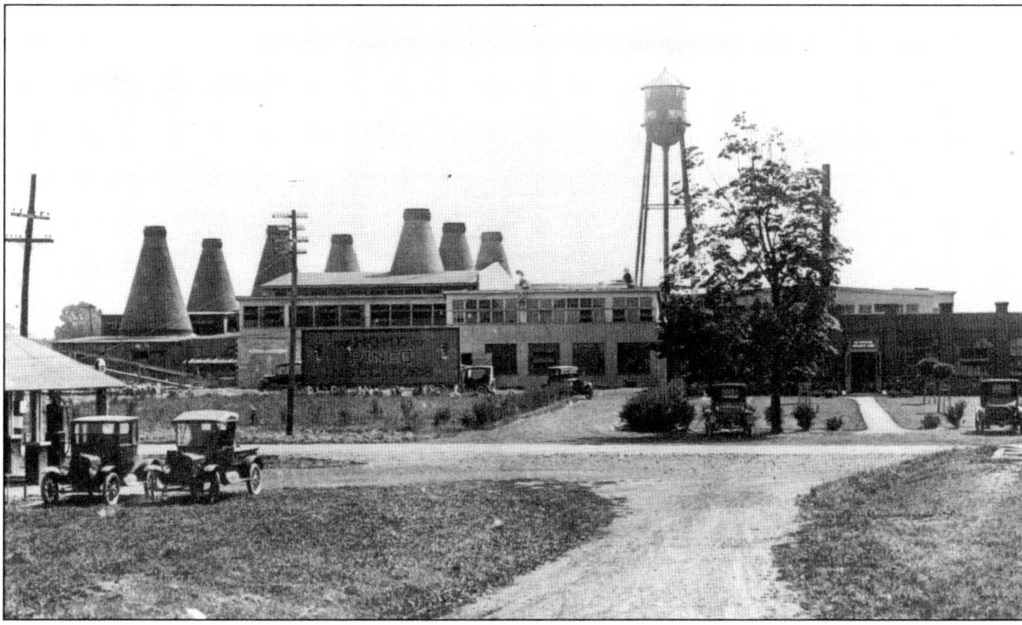

The "Home of Pinco Insulators" was to Lima's financial prosperity what Genesee Wesleyan Seminary was to its spiritual well-being. Shown in this 1912 photograph are the massive beehive kilns used to bake the insulators. They were fired in succession, each being brought to the right temperature for baking. When one cooled down, production moved to the next—like crop rotation.

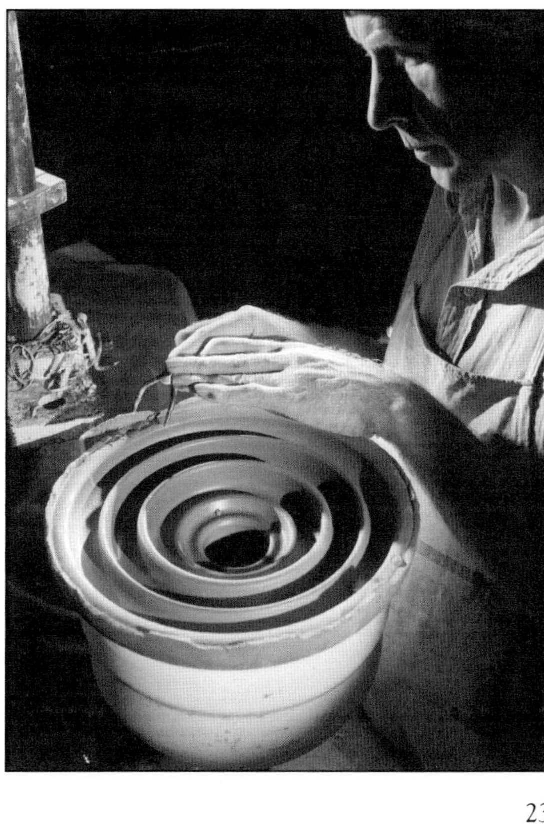

A worker skillfully trims a large ceramic insulator before it is sent to the kilns. Clearly craftsmanship and pride are captured in this 1950s photograph.

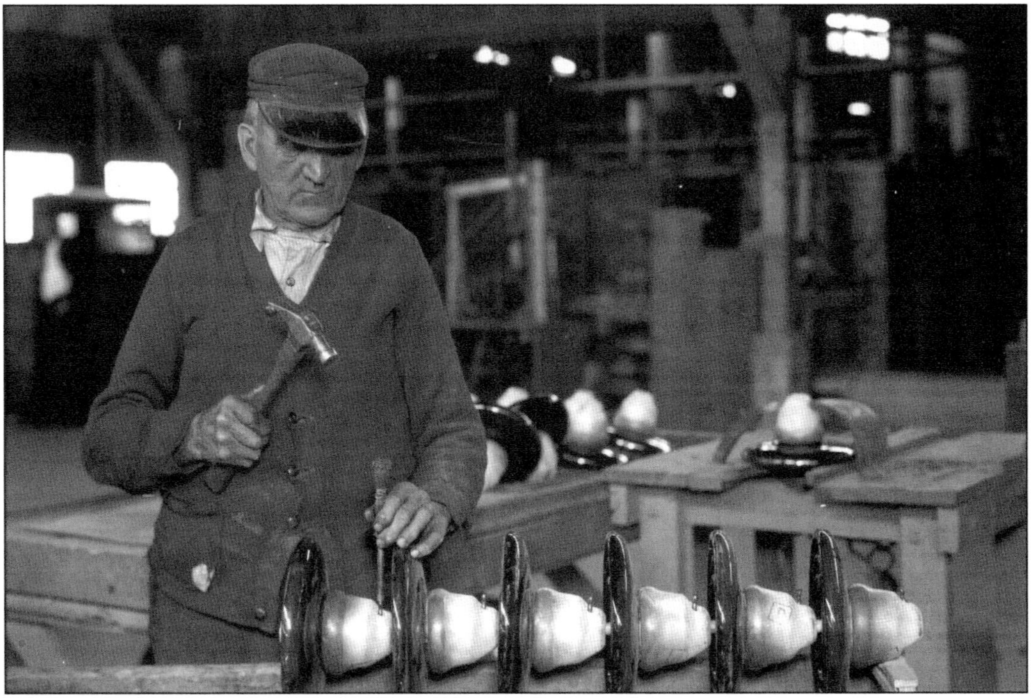

With work clothes frayed and stained from factory labor, a seasoned employee exhibits dedication and craftsmanship as he puts the finishing touches on an insulator assembly.

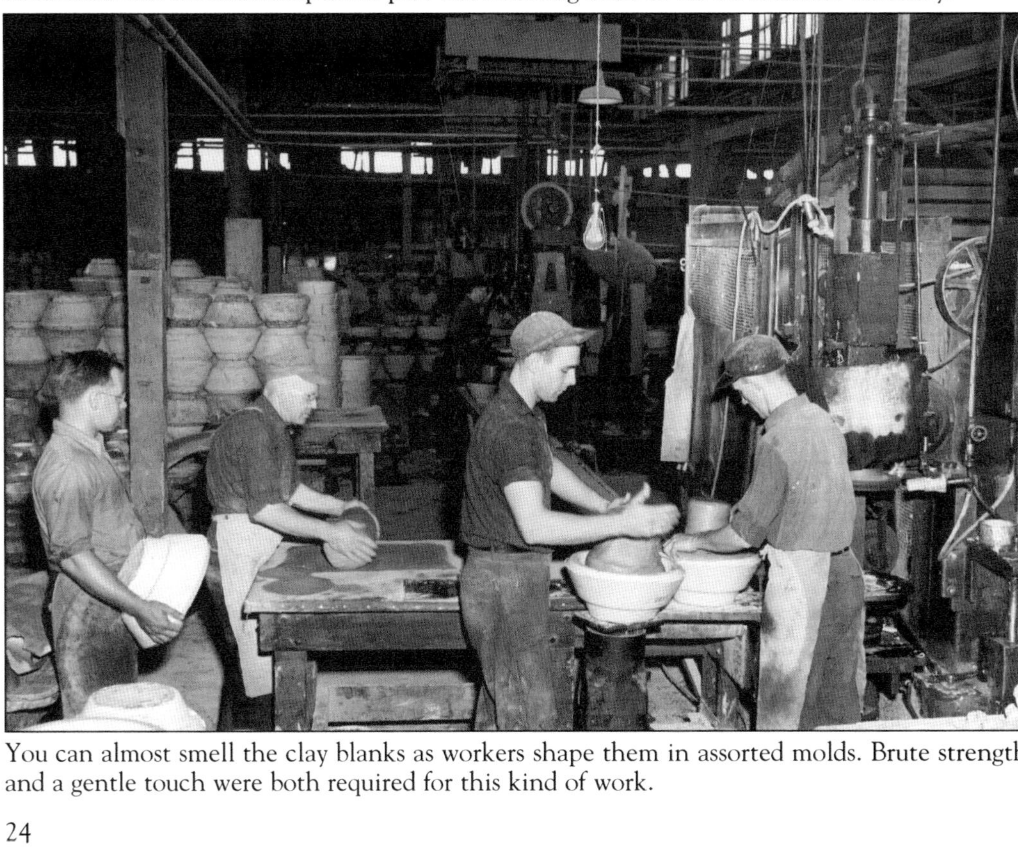

You can almost smell the clay blanks as workers shape them in assorted molds. Brute strength and a gentle touch were both required for this kind of work.

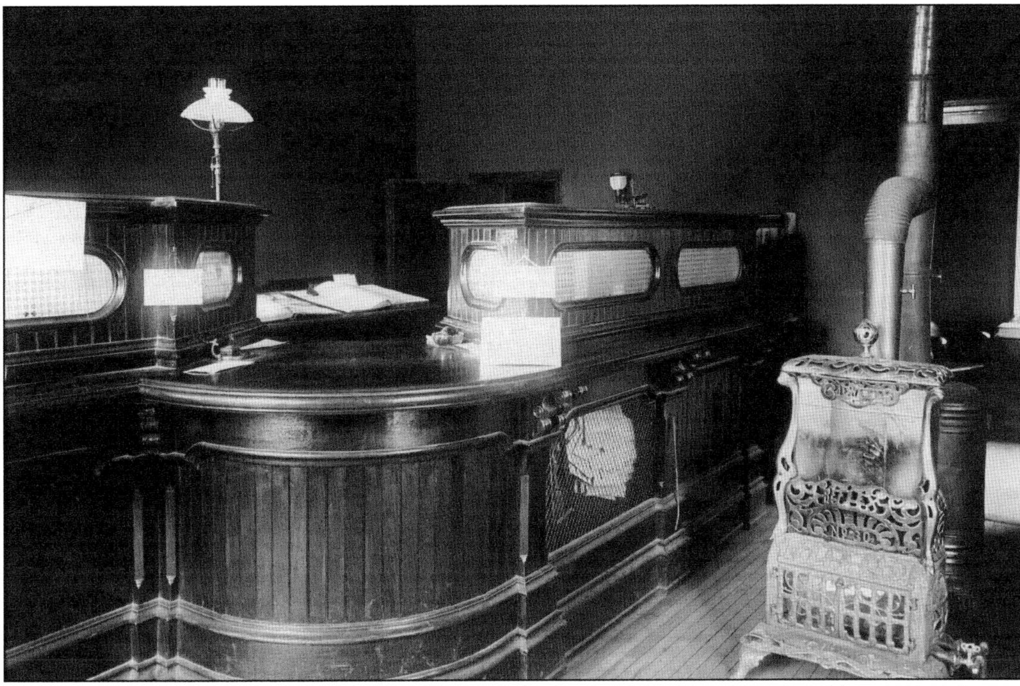

This picture was taken on February 5, 1915, at the time of the Lima Bank robbery. This famous whodunit remains unsolved. The robber or robbers netted $9,960.78 in what was described as "one of the boldest bank robberies in Western New York history." One positive outcome of the affair was that investigators photographed nearly every street in Lima, giving the town a remarkable visual history of that time.

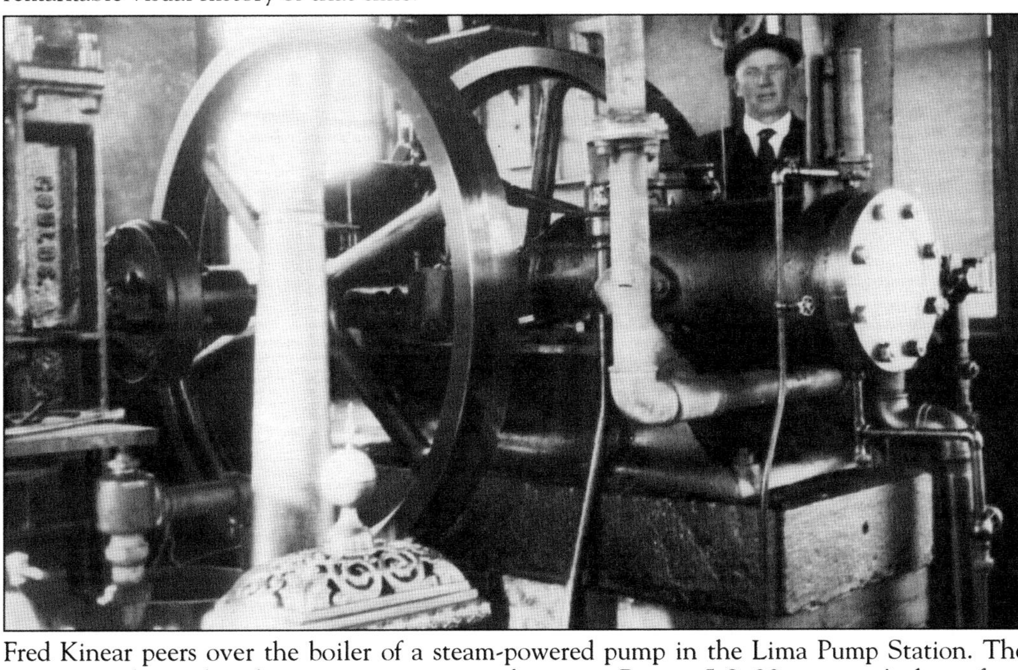

Fred Kinear peers over the boiler of a steam-powered pump in the Lima Pump Station. The station was located at the reservoir just west of town on Routes 5 & 20—a stone's throw from where the Yellow Wasp once stood. The photograph dates from c. 1905.

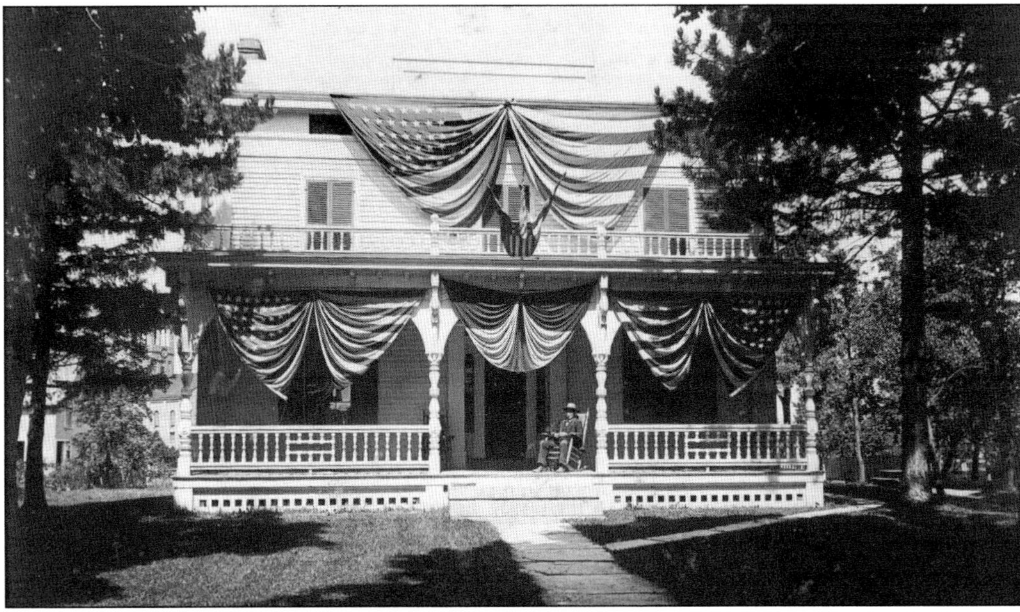

Much of downtown Lima was gloriously regaled in bunting and banners, as the Peck house on East Main Street was, when the Livingston County Firemen's Convention was held here in 1894. Mr. Peck, a wool merchant, built the house at a time when flocks of sheep were so extensive in this area that the world price for wool was set here. At the time of this photograph, the house was owned by George Atwell III. The decorations came from a Rochester company.

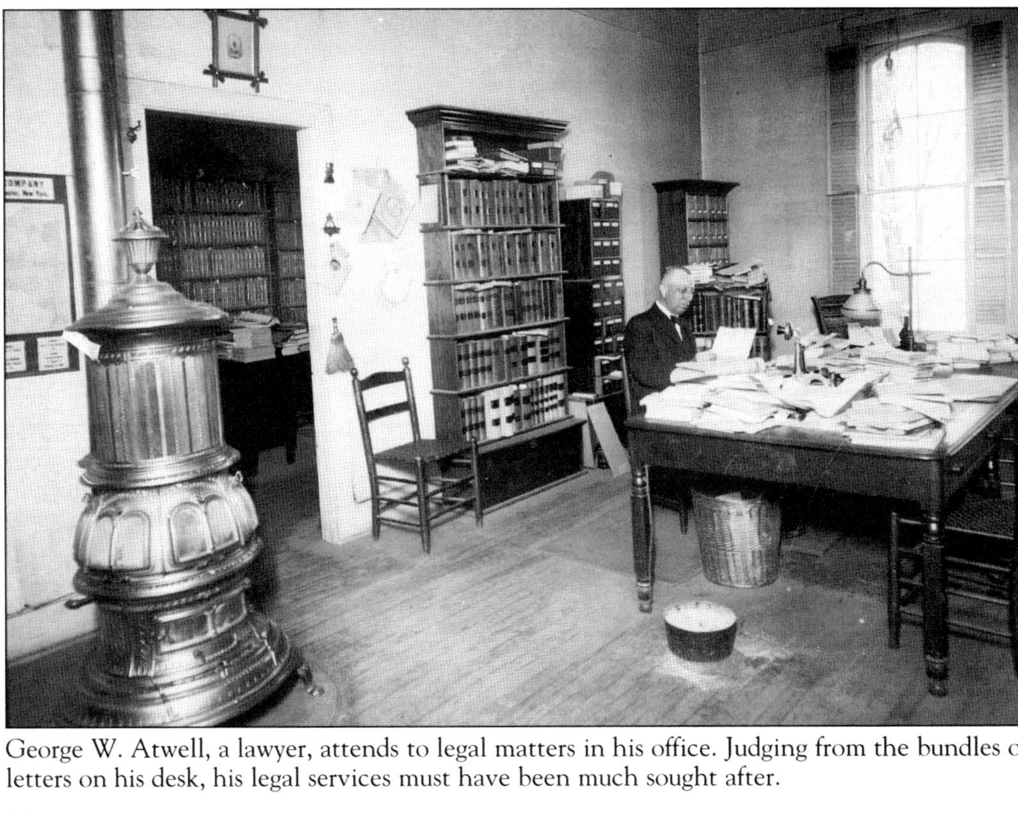

George W. Atwell, a lawyer, attends to legal matters in his office. Judging from the bundles of letters on his desk, his legal services must have been much sought after.

Dr. John Bennett Jr. was one of Lima's first doctors. He lived in the former inn built by Ruben Thayer in 1793. The Wemett family later owned the property.

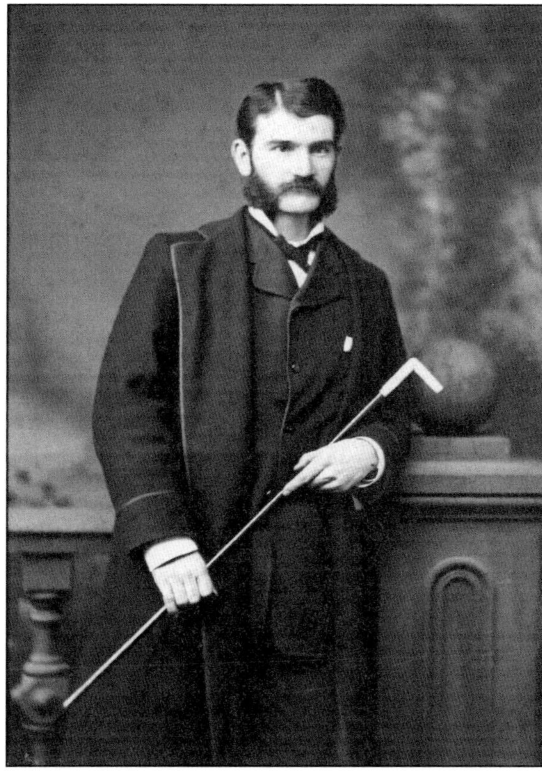

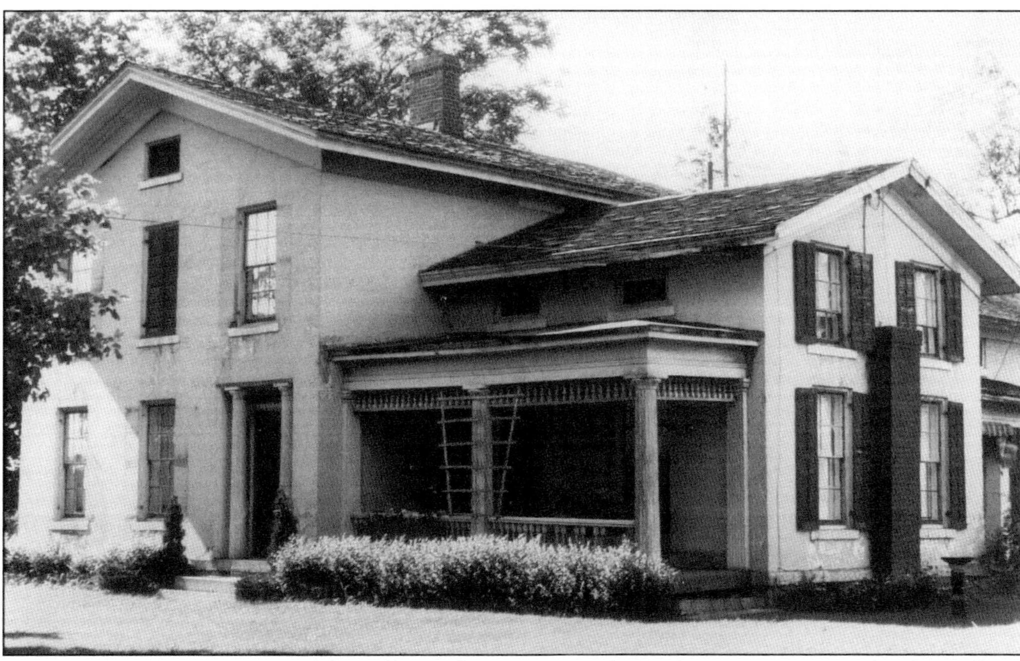

Situated on a hill just east of the village, the *c.* 1793 Ruben Thayer tavern was the first official inn in town. Stagecoach drivers changed their horses here. The Thayer brickyard, located on a nearby creek, produced bricks for the tavern, as well as for the 1806 Warner inn (Hennessy house), the Seminary campus buildings, and other noted landmarks.

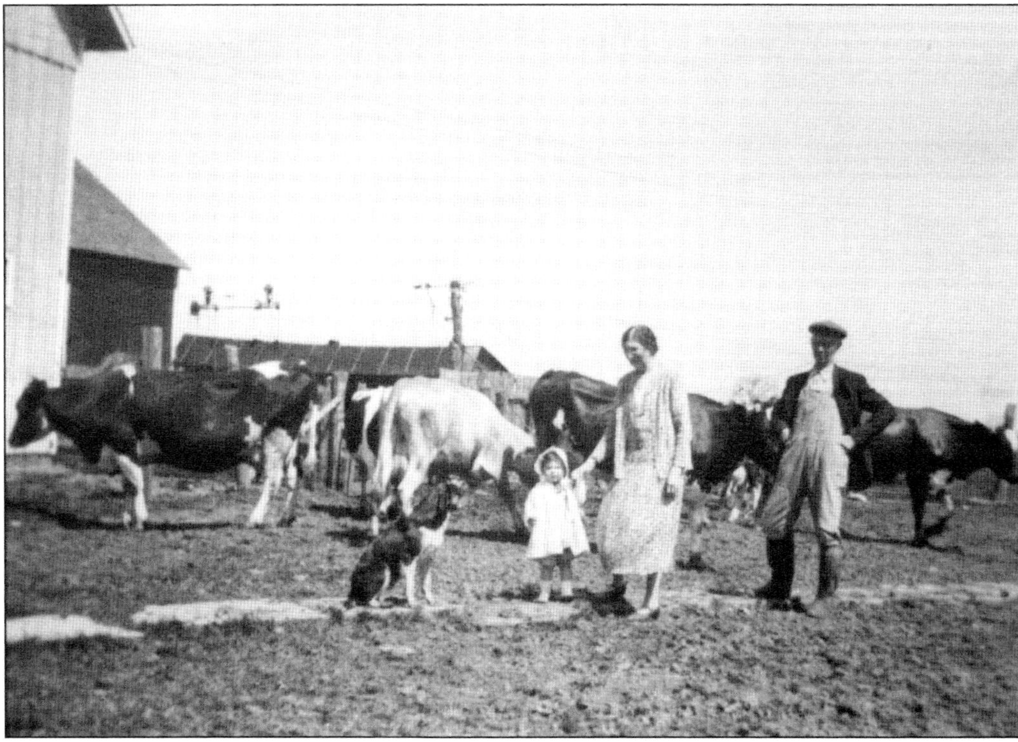

In 1921, Correl and Cora Wemett bought this property, which had become a dairy. They operated it with their five sons, Kenneth, Clifford, Elmer, Vernon, and Ray. Shown enjoying the many wonders of her grandparents' farm is three-year-old Sheila Wemett.

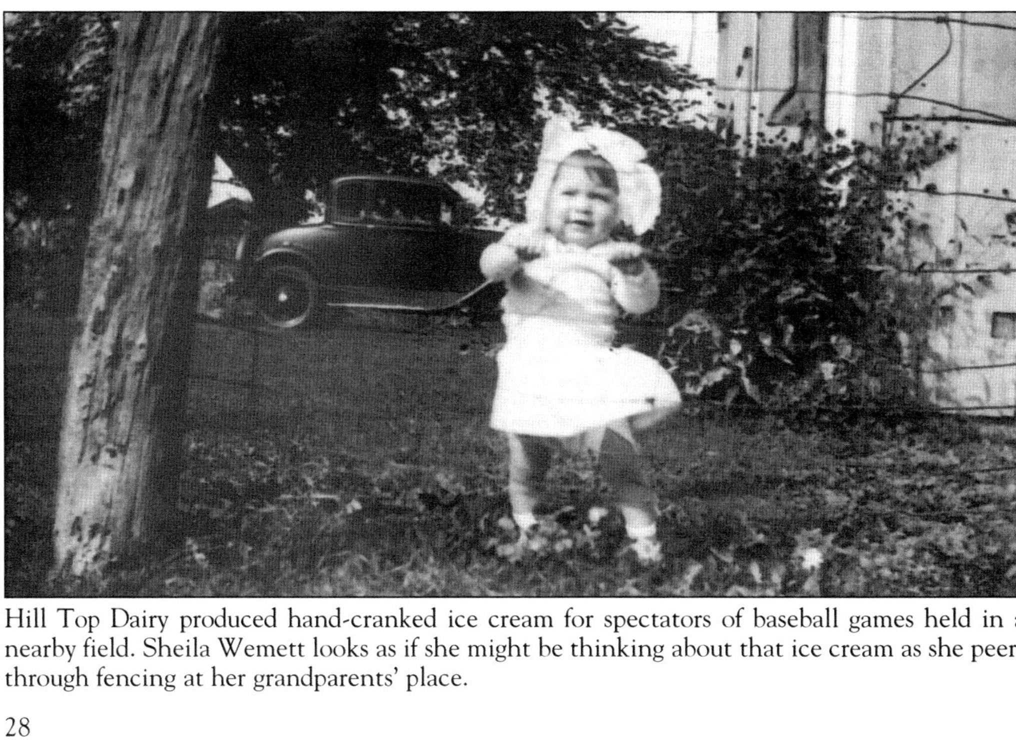

Hill Top Dairy produced hand-cranked ice cream for spectators of baseball games held in a nearby field. Sheila Wemett looks as if she might be thinking about that ice cream as she peers through fencing at her grandparents' place.

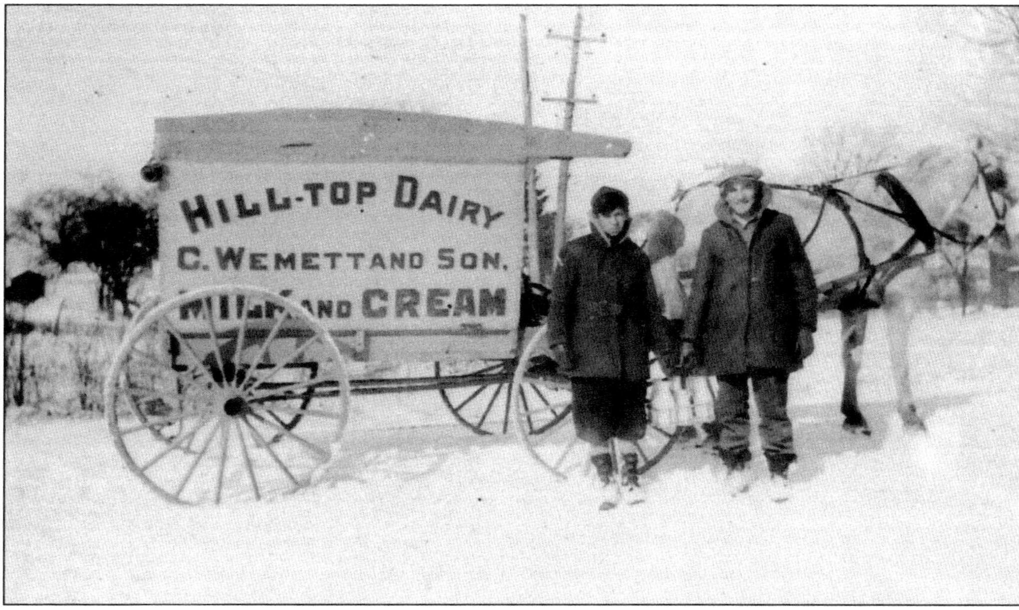

The Wemett's cart delivered milk to Lima and Honeoye Falls. The dairy had its own bottling system, and milk was sent to Rochester for bottling by distributors. Children on Lima dairies often heard a parent call in the early morning, "Better get that milk to the Lehigh depot before the train leaves for Rochester!"

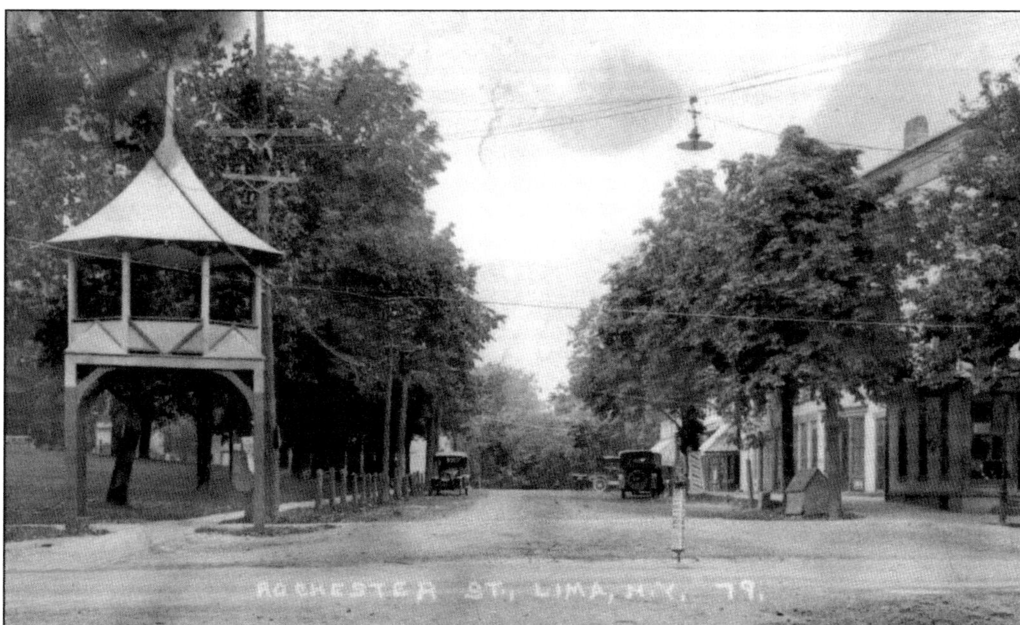

This 1919 postcard view is looking north on Rochester Street. The bandstand (left) was a popular gathering place at a time when concerts were regular events. Musicians had to climb a ladder to get into the bandstand. More than once, as listeners reclined on the lawn of the church, boys seized the ladder and ran off with it. That left the band stranded until the ladder could be located and put back in place.

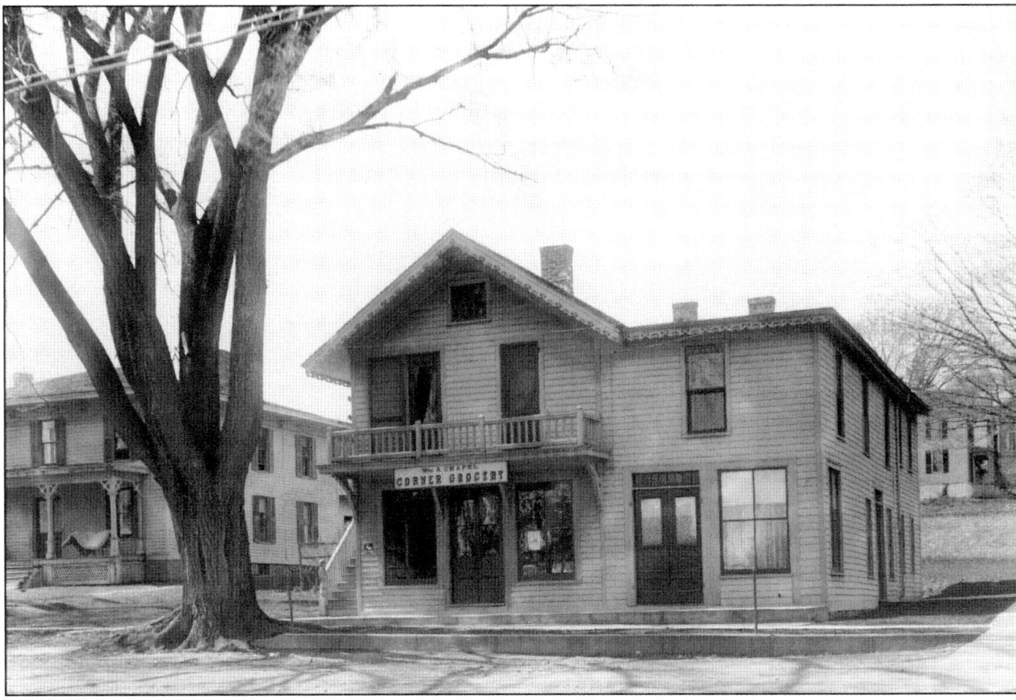

The Corner Grocery, located on the corners of Rochester and College Streets, kept the neighborhood well supplied. It later housed Lima Carpet and the Lima Antiques.

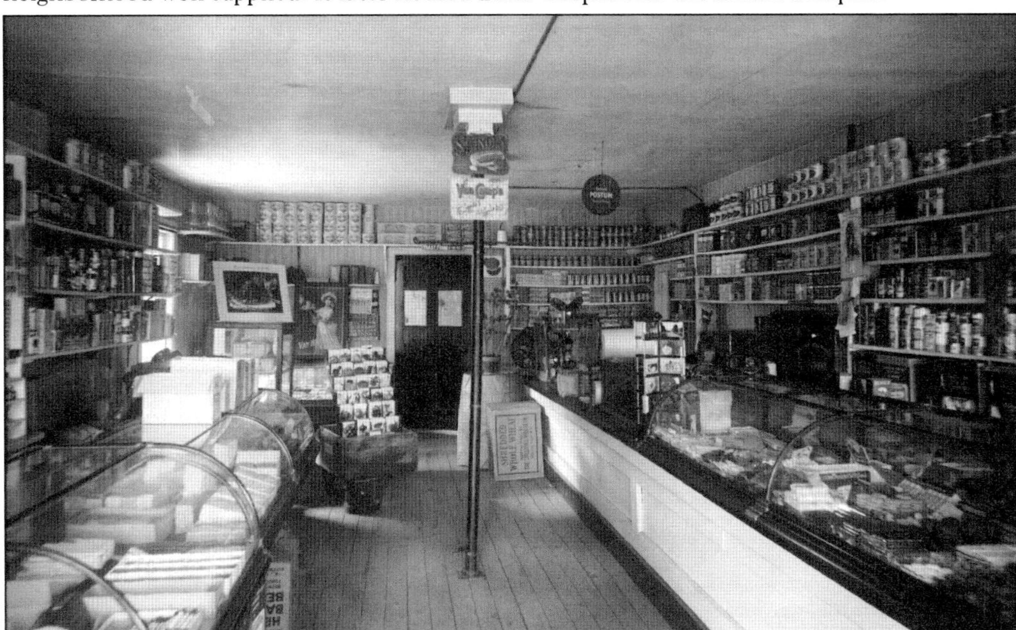

A tidy and complete inventory awaits shoppers at the Corner Grocery. Shelves sag under the weight of canned goods. Powdered milk, baking supplies, meats, and confections line the heavy cases. There are even seeds, likely the local Dibble brand. Students at the seminary kept business brisk. There was once a barrel of water with little ducklings up by the front window. What parents could resist their child's plea for a little pet that cost a mere 50 cents?

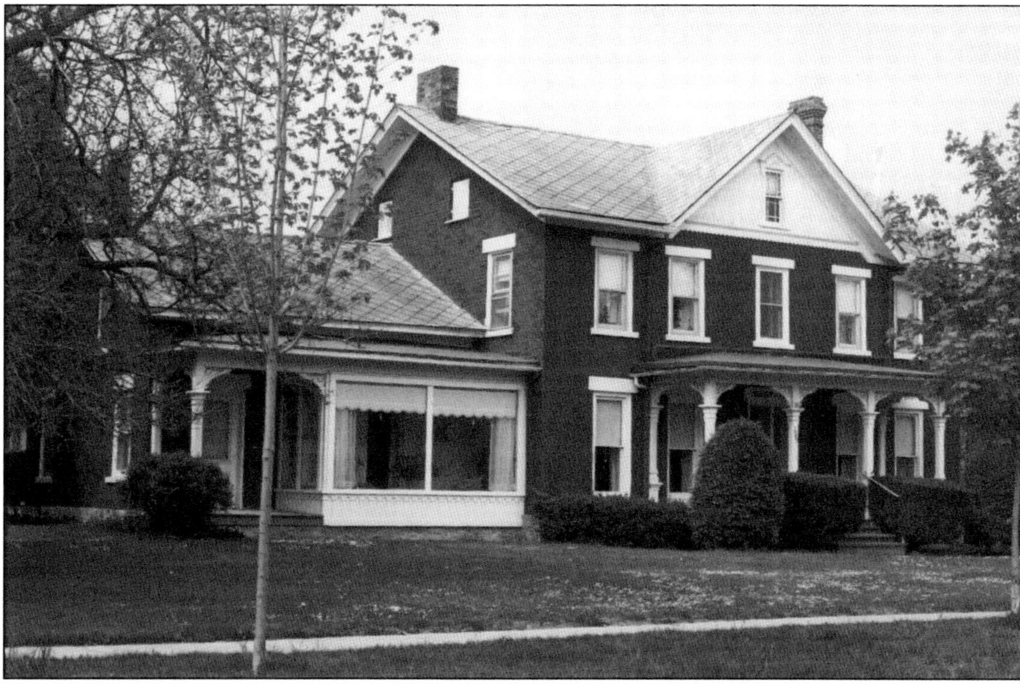

In 1806, Mathew Warner built this noted inn, using bricks from the Thayer brickyard. At a time when many pioneers either camped or, at best, scraped together enough to spend a night in a stall or some fleabag, Warner's must have seemed like a royal palace.

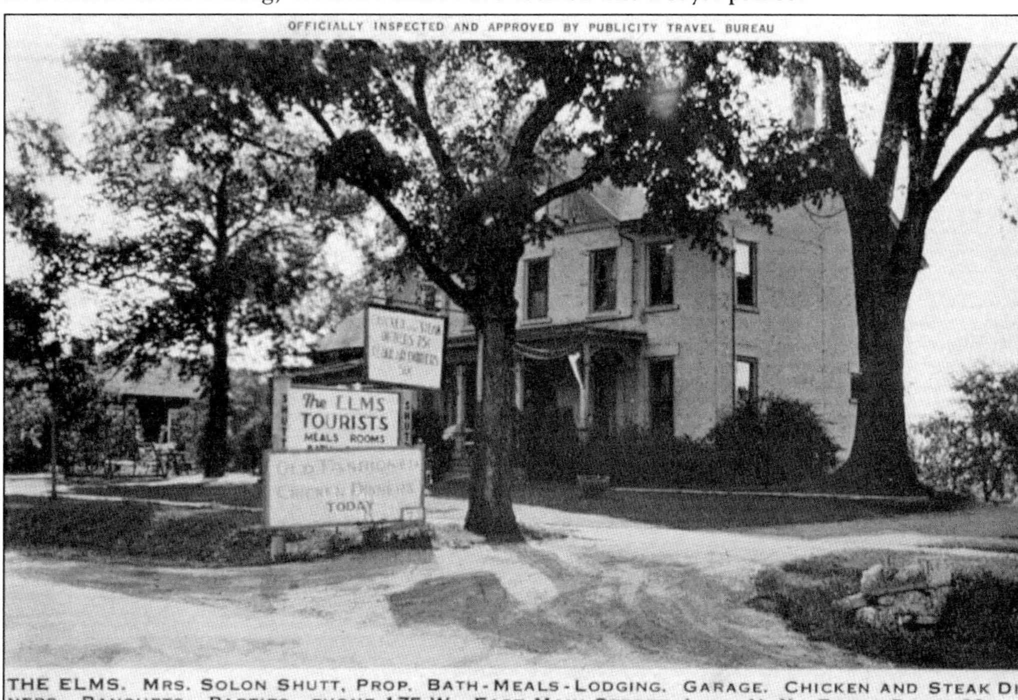

The Warner inn is shown in this 1930s postcard as the Elms tourist house. Today, it is known as the Hennessy house, named after Harold Hennessy, the much-loved local judge.

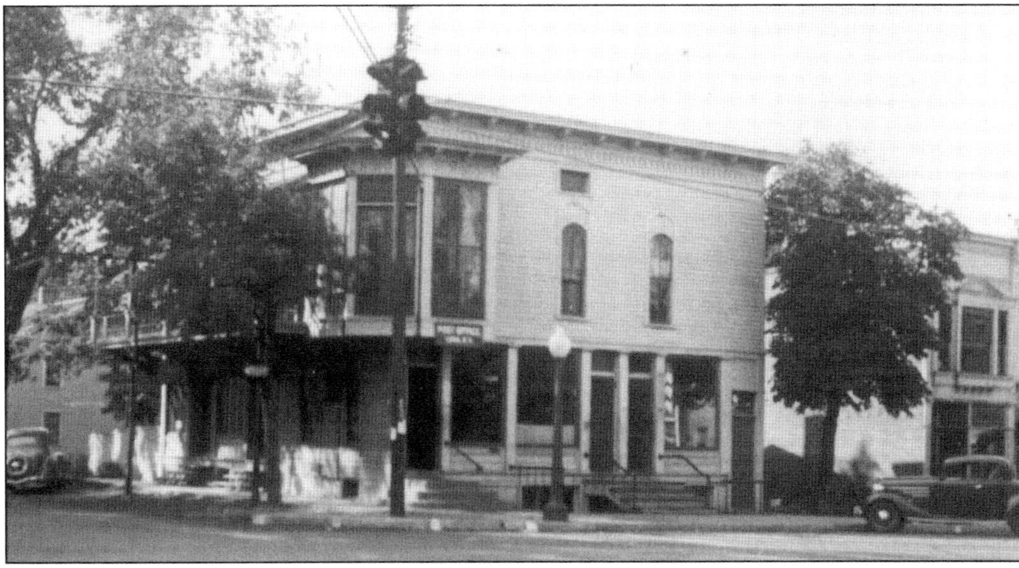

The Lima Post Office occupied this building in the Gordon Block for almost 60 years. A classic example of the small-town corner building, it was torn down in the late 1930s.

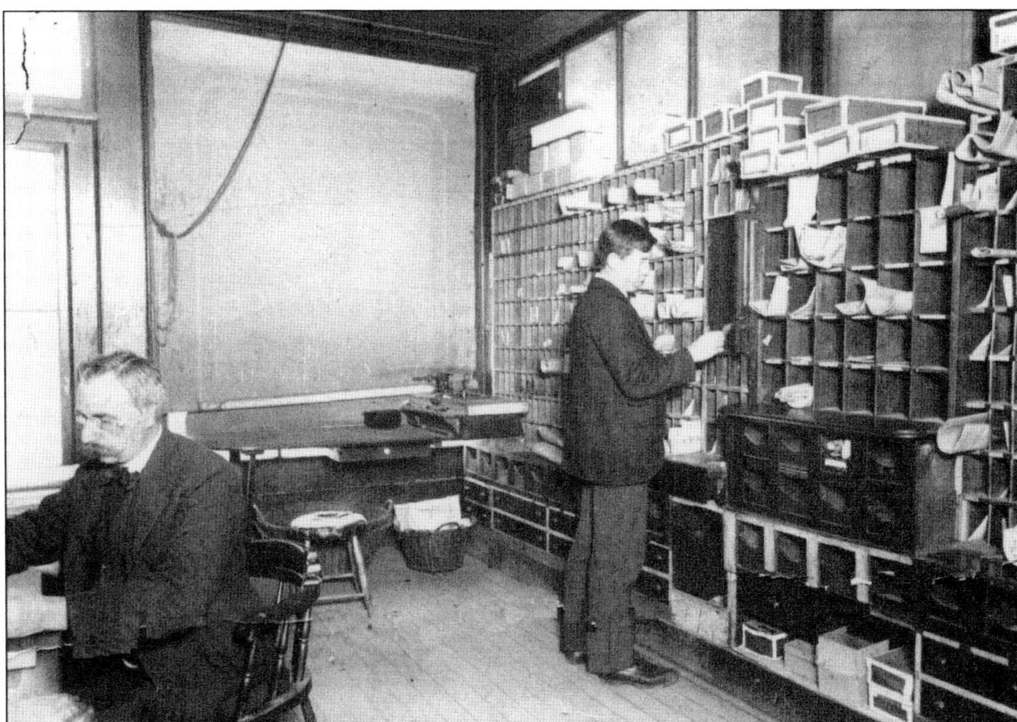

This is an interior view of the post office. In 1838, a U.S. mail coach line was established through Lima and Honeoye Falls into Rochester. In 1938, air mail came to Lima.

Rev. Isaiah McMahon of the Methodist church lived on Sun Set Hill, west of the Methodist cemetery. He owned a large polyglot Bible, printed in six or seven languages, ancient and modern verse, and he could read the Bible in all of the languages.

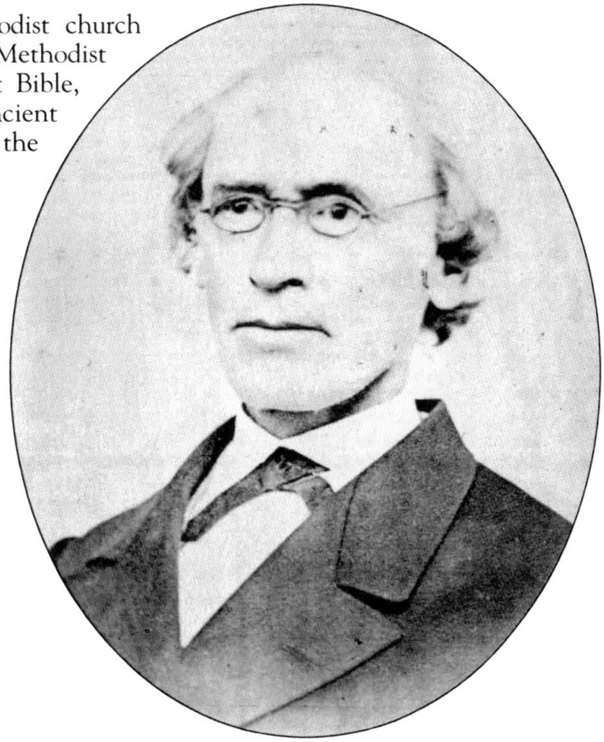

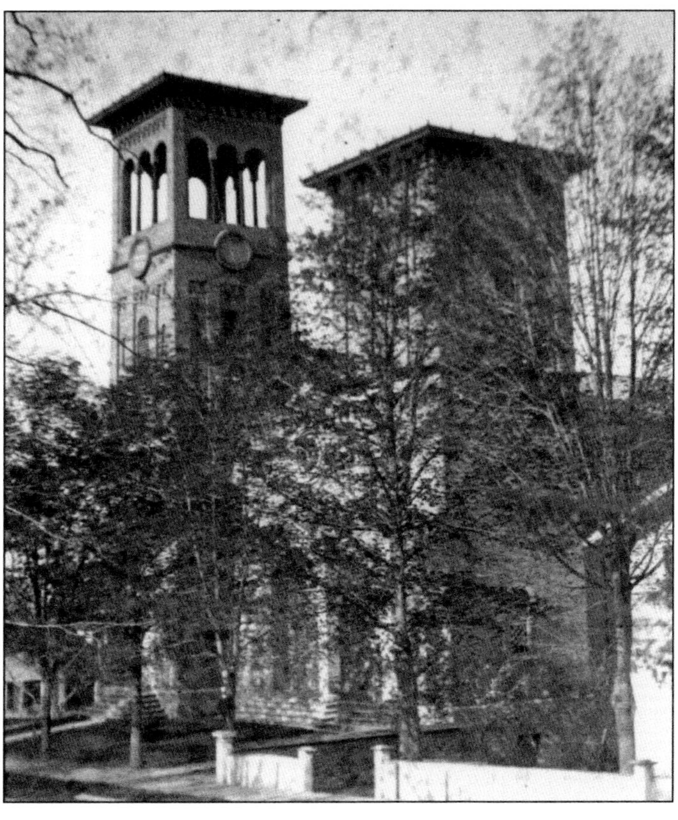

The Methodist church, shown in a stereo view, was built in 1858 on Rochester Street. It served the congregation for about 90 years. Storm damage required its demolition in the early 1960s. It was located across the street form the Lima Historical Society museum, and parts of it endure. The tower columns were removed and used on the front of the American Hotel in the early 1900s.

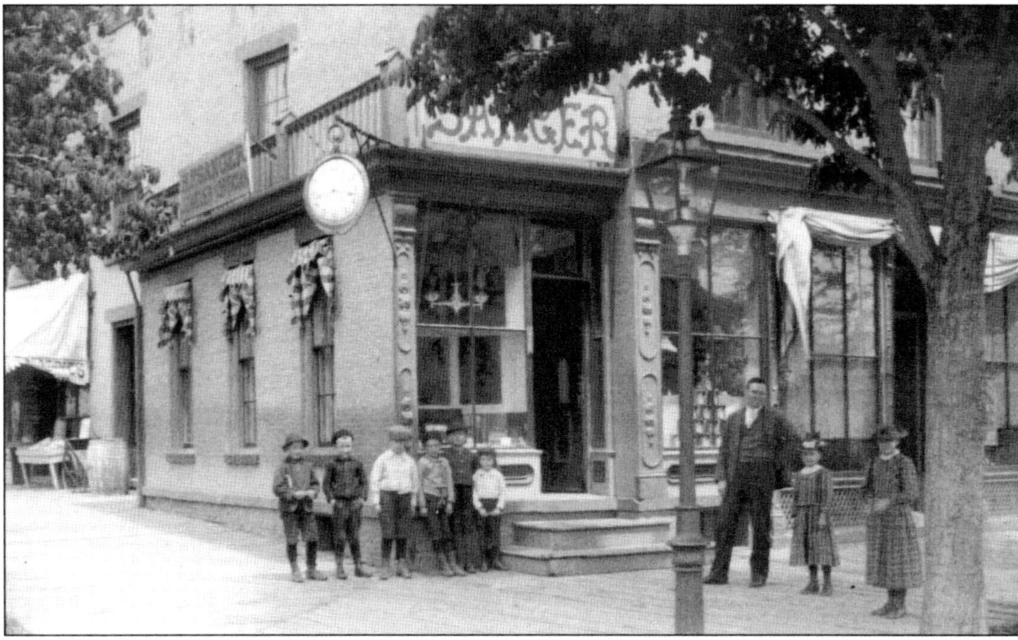

Harry Sanger (right) pauses in the shade of chestnut trees in front of his store. In this *c.* 1890s image, the boys look like the Lima version of Our Gang. This tiny store was packed with quality goods. As transportation improved, small-town dry goods stores like this one began to fail, but Sanger's managed to outlast many of them.

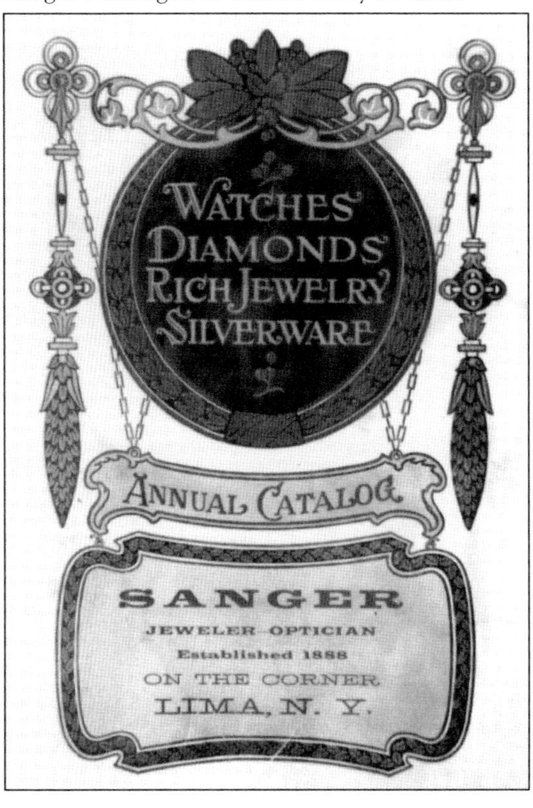

Sanger's produced a rather sophisticated catalog for such a small store. Its location on the main east–west highway provided a steady customer base. Sibley's of Rochester sent its salesmen to rural stores like this one to sell quality merchandise from its wholesale division.

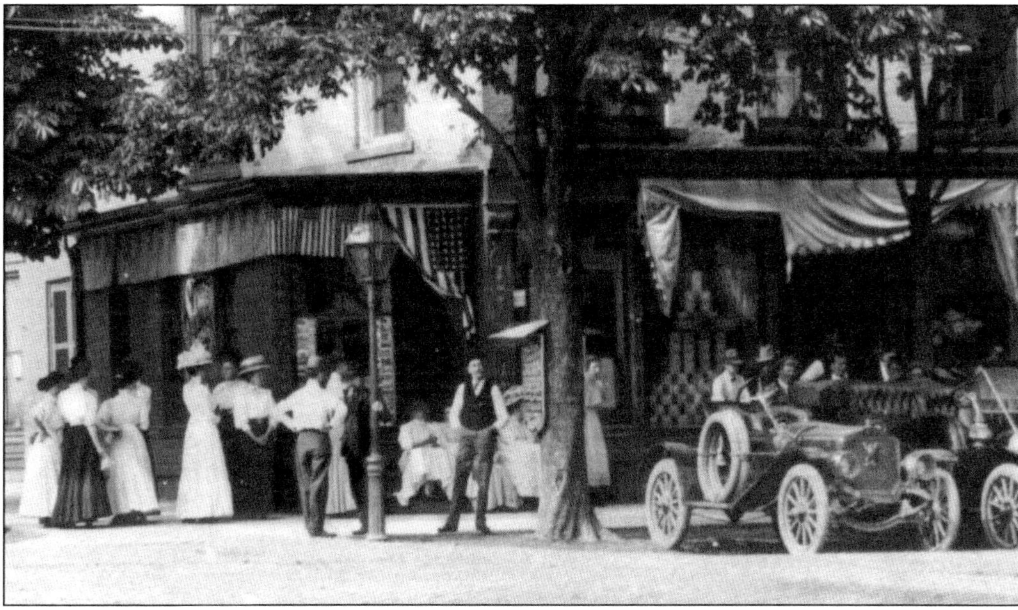

This corner has always been a popular gathering place. A profusion of flags suggests a parade may be coming. Beside the store some young women whisper, while the young men on the right seem interested mainly in their cars.

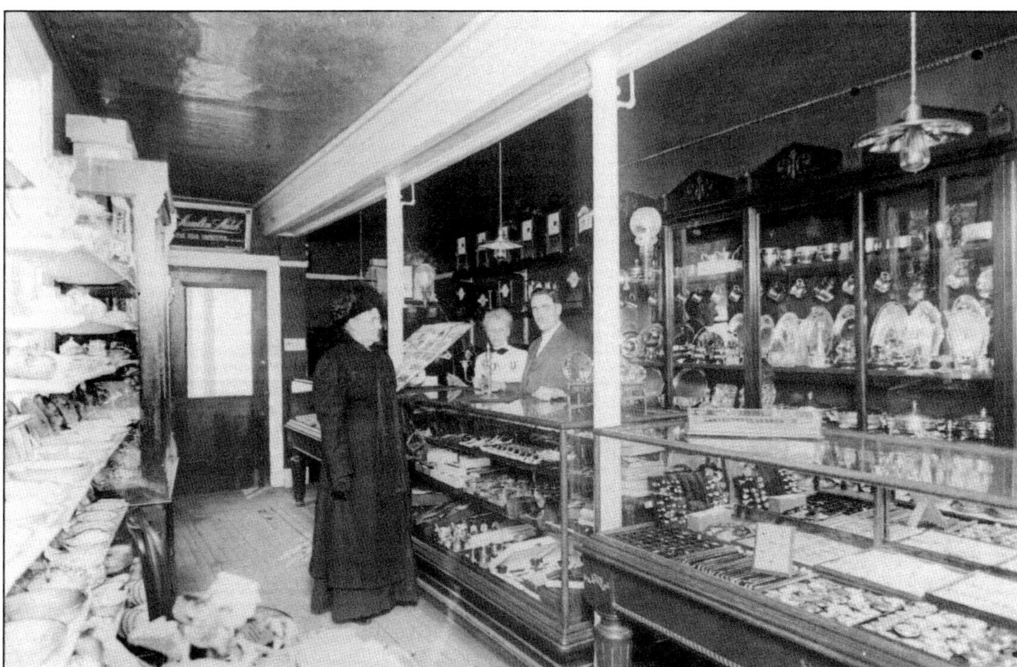

Clocks, watches, jeweled hairpins, and china are just some of the fine merchandise available at Sanger's. The man behind the counter is Harry Sanger.

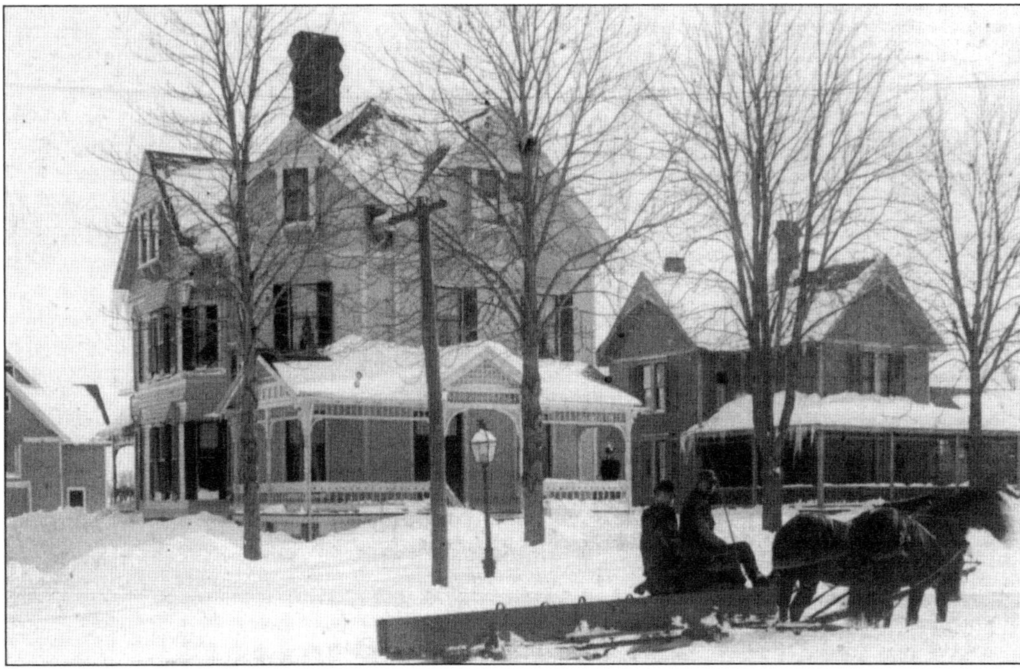

A team draws a coal sled up East Main Street on March 3, 1900. The Allen house looms beyond it. Note the quaint street lamp.

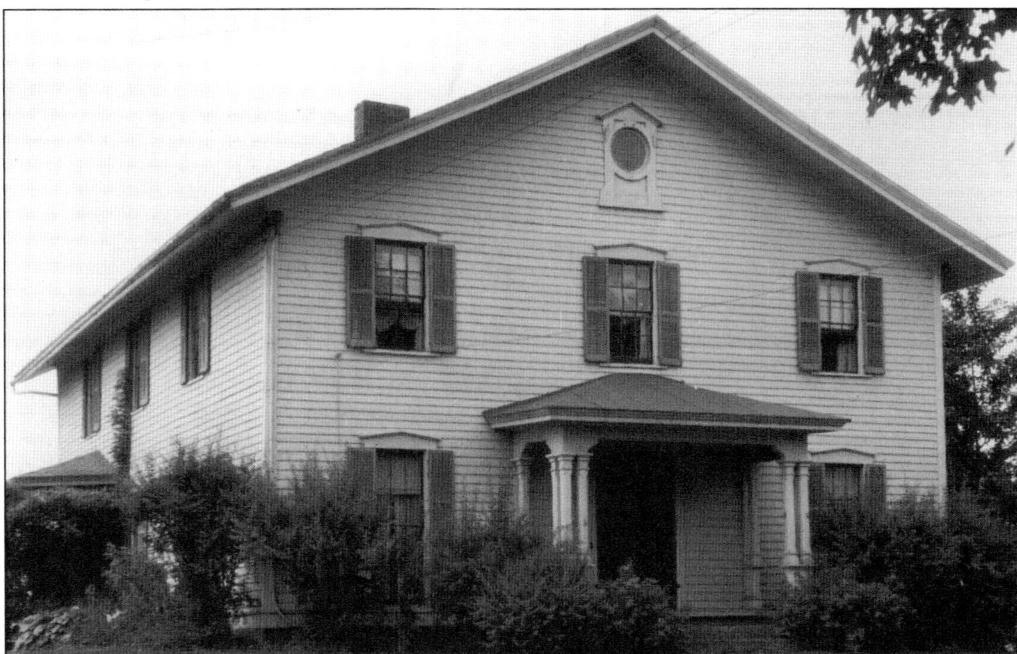

In 1810, Maj. Asahel Warner built this more-than-20-room place as one of the six inns along Main Street. To accommodate the westward tide of immigration, inns were built roughly a mile apart along the State Road between Canandaigua and the Genesee River. A sign in one tavern read, "No boots to be worn in bed and no more than five in one bed." The Warner inn also had the first Masonic lodge in Lima on its third floor.

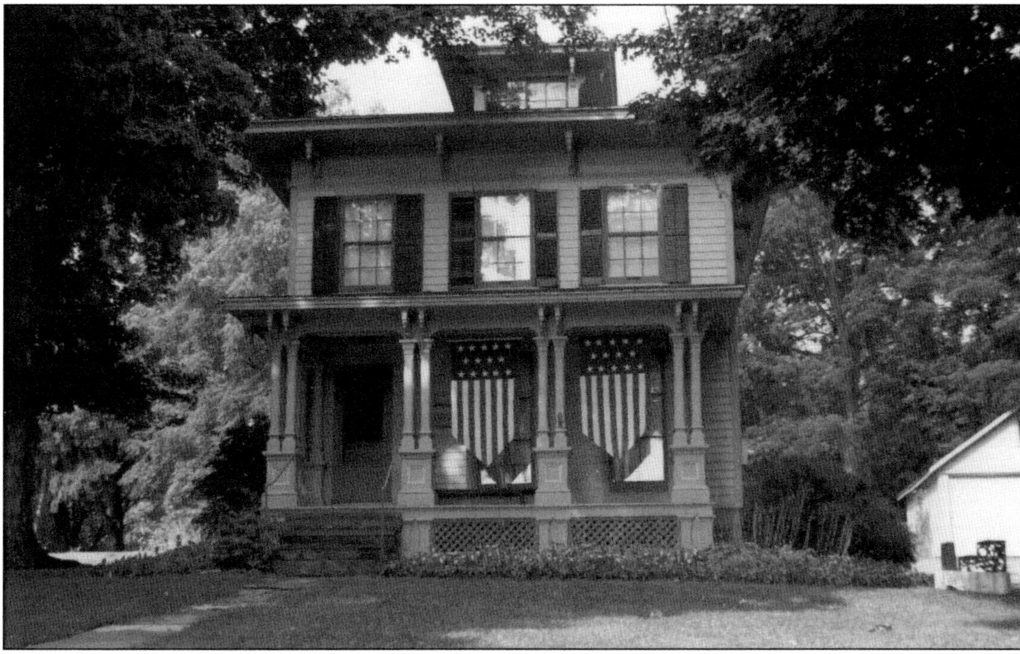

The Tennie-Burton Museum, at 1850 Rochester Street, was bequeathed to the Lima Historical Society by Belle Chapin Tenny. Built *c.* 1837, it was remodeled in 1863 by Samuel Ellis in the Italianate style that was the rage along Rochester Street. Since Memorial Day of 1978, the historical society has maintained its collections. (Author's collection.)

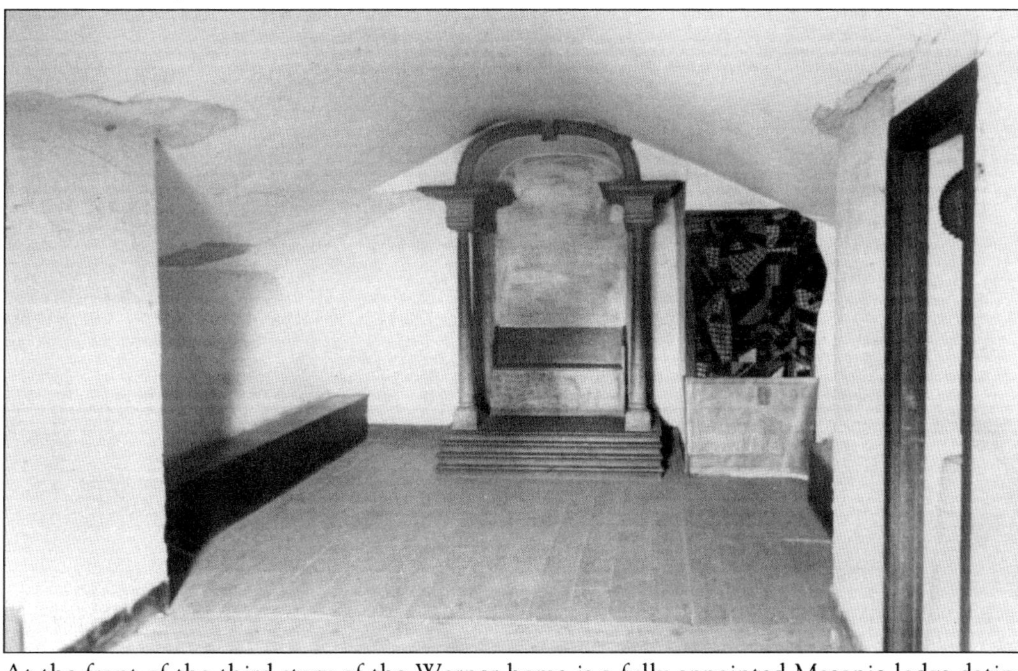

At the front of the third story of the Warner home is a fully appointed Masonic lodge dating back to the early 1800s. The fixtures, including this throne used by the master and a low bench that encircles the room, remain to this day. At the rear of the room is a large chimney where, it is believed, meats were smoked.

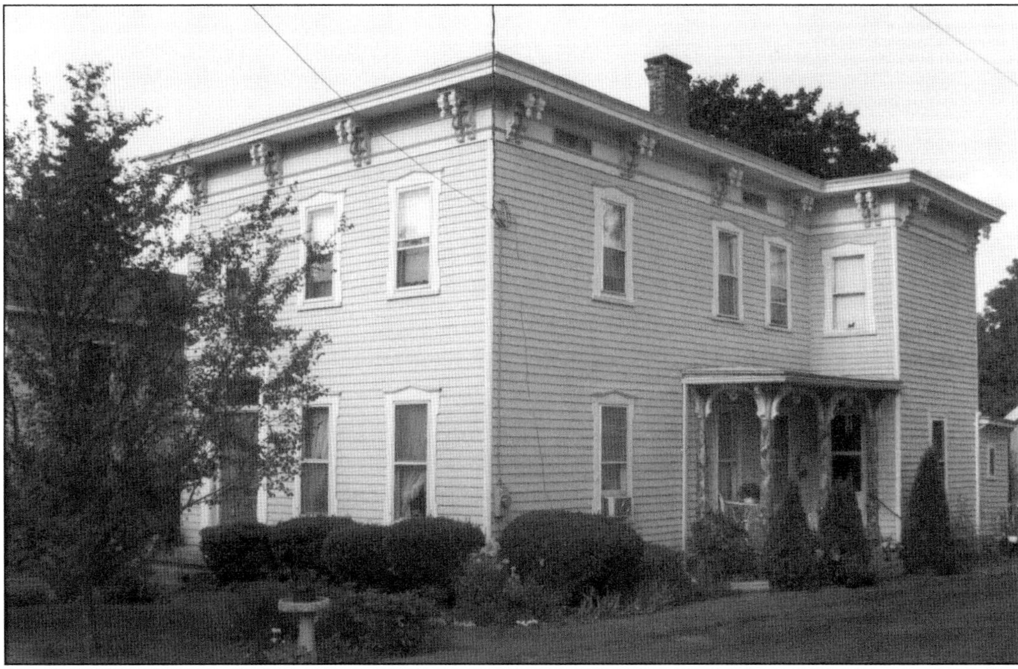

Joel Dailey built this Victorian Italianate in Rochester Street in 1870. Dailey was a retired stagecoach proprietor and Lima's first president (mayor). Tradition says that he kept his teams in big stables behind the town hall, at that time School District No. 5. He was civic minded and attempted to keep Genesee College from moving to Syracuse. (Author's collection.)

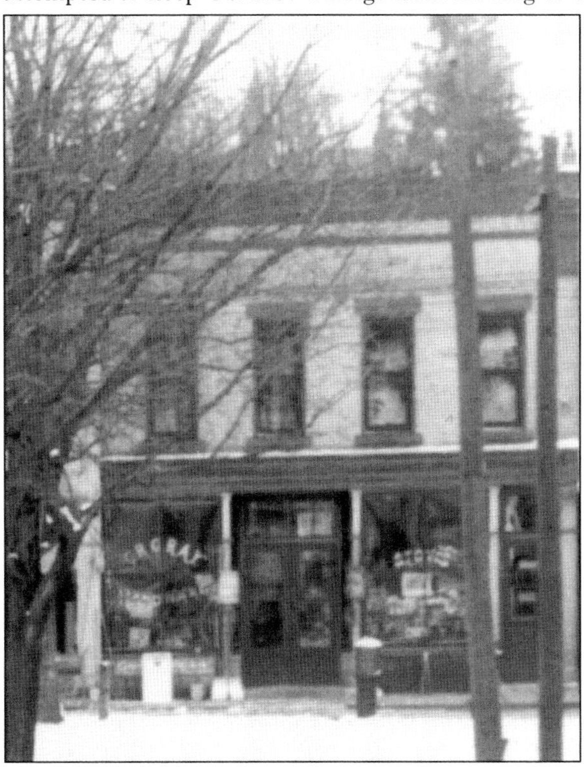

In 1908, Charles and Georgia Gray acquired the Dailey house. They ran this hardware store on West Main Street.

Julia Dailey was one of Joel Dailey's four children. She lived with her parents and remained in the Dailey house after they died. On the back of this portrait, it states, "Julia Dailey was an admirable woman;" from the look in her eye, it appears that she was. Students at the seminary often rented rooms in the big houses along Rochester Street, and scratched onto the windowpanes of the Dailey house are the initials of some who stayed there.

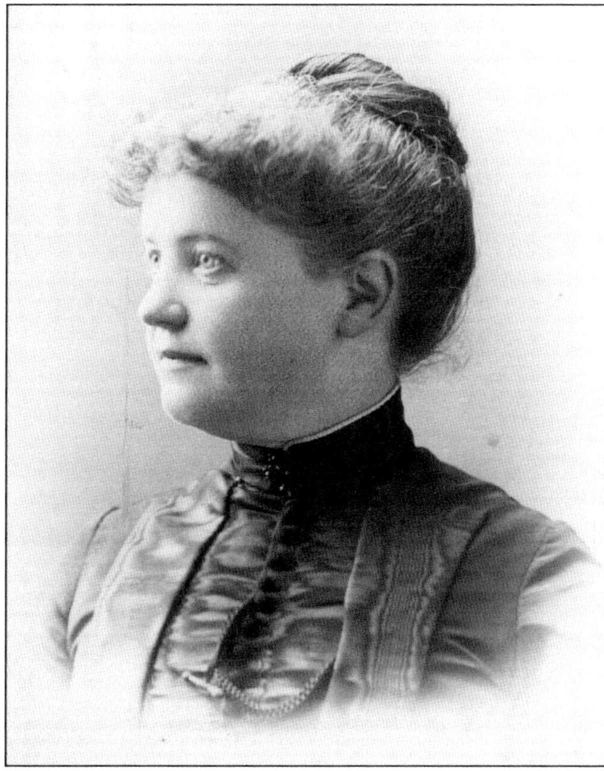

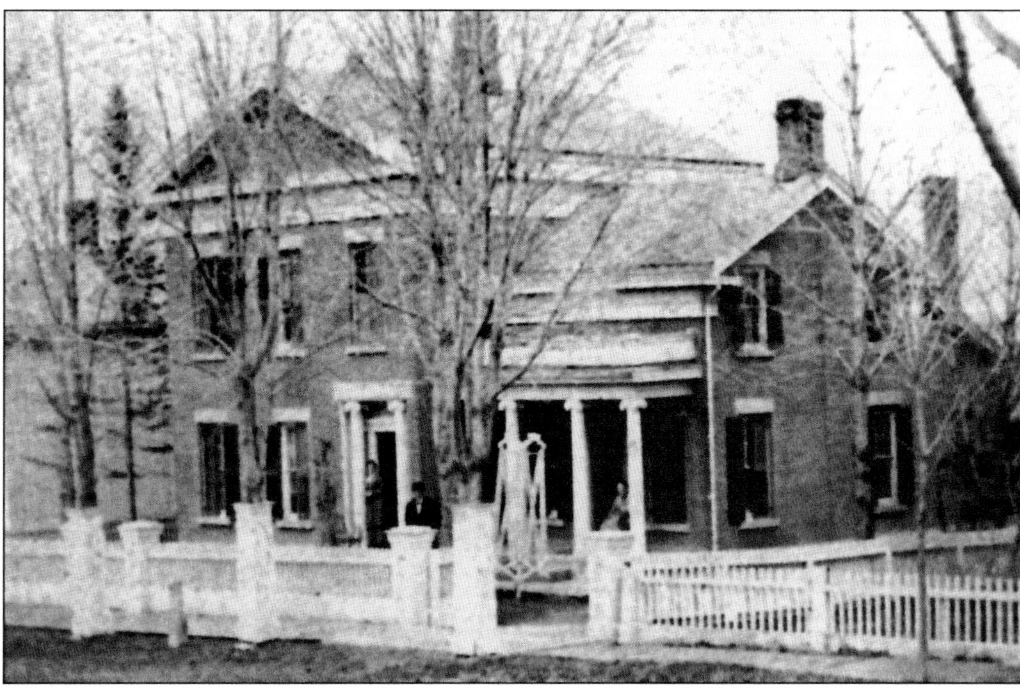

A stereo view of the c. 1852 Cargill House, at 1839 Rochester Street, shows a sophisticated little Greek revival, believed to have been designed by the same architect who designed College Hall.

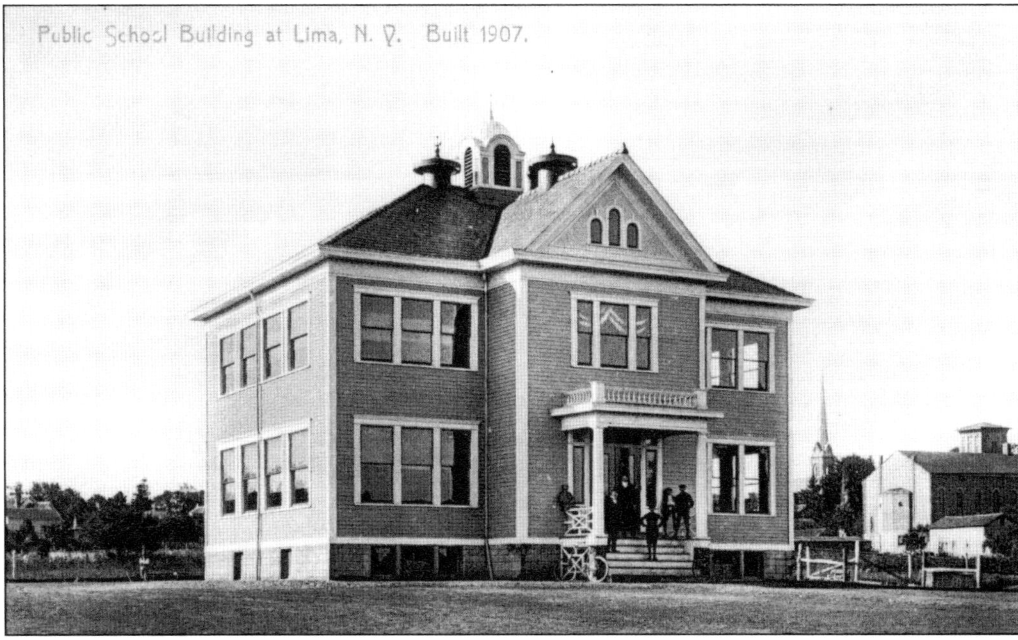

This is Lima Grade School, a stout four-room structure built with minimal embellishments. It projects the sense that students went there to learn and that horsing around was not to be tolerated. The back of the Methodist church is to the right, and the slender spire of the Presbyterian church is also visible. The school was demolished in 1937 to make way for a new high school.

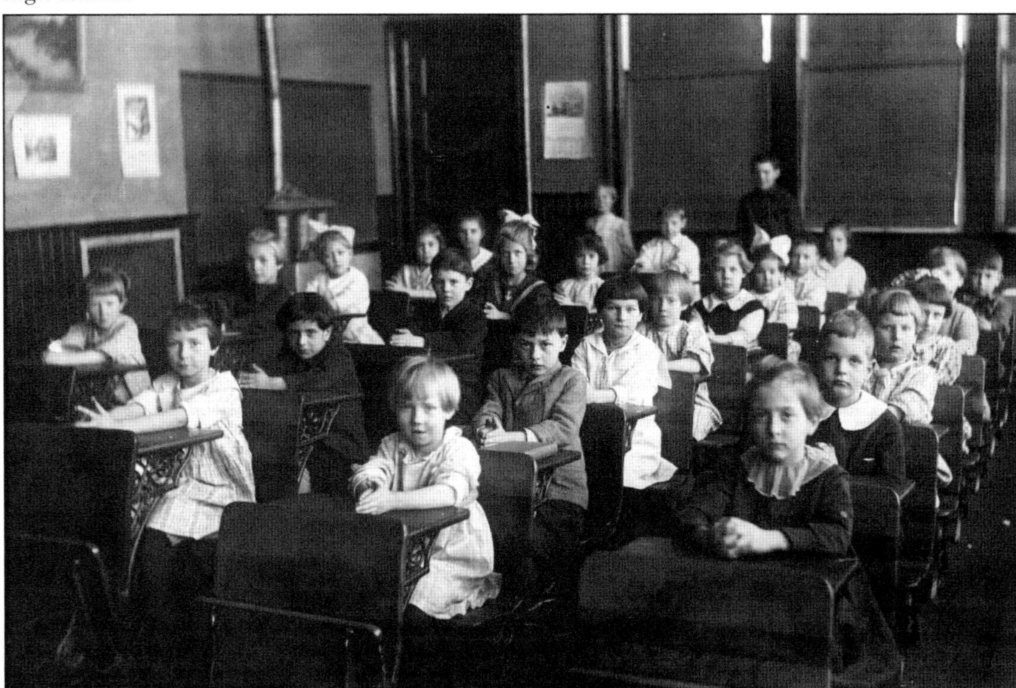

Hands are folded and backs are straight as students of teacher Blanche Coykendall prepare for a day of learning. This photograph was taken in the 1920s.

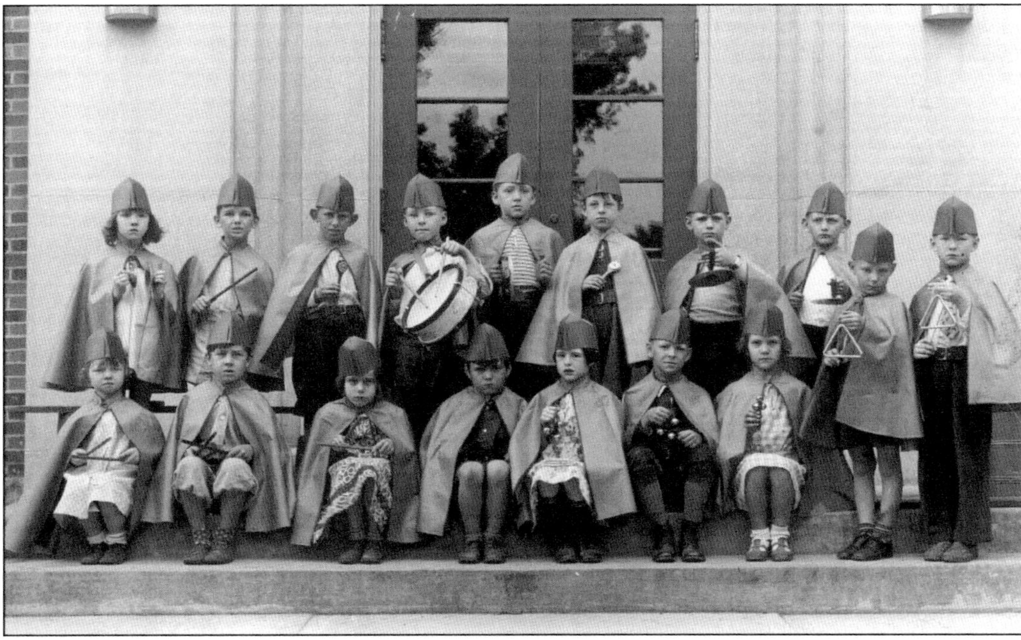

The first- and second-grade rhythm band is photographed in June 1939 on the school steps. Belle Chapin and Blanche Coykendall directed them in their musical renditions.

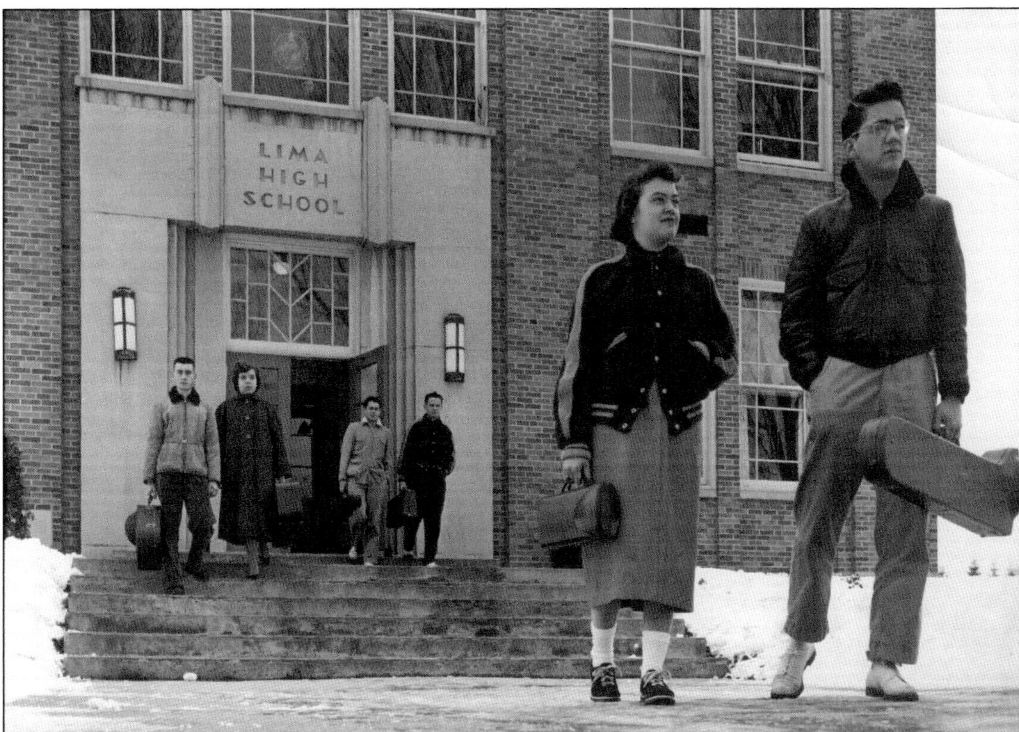

On a winter day, students leave Lima High School after band practice. The photograph is from the 1955 yearbook.

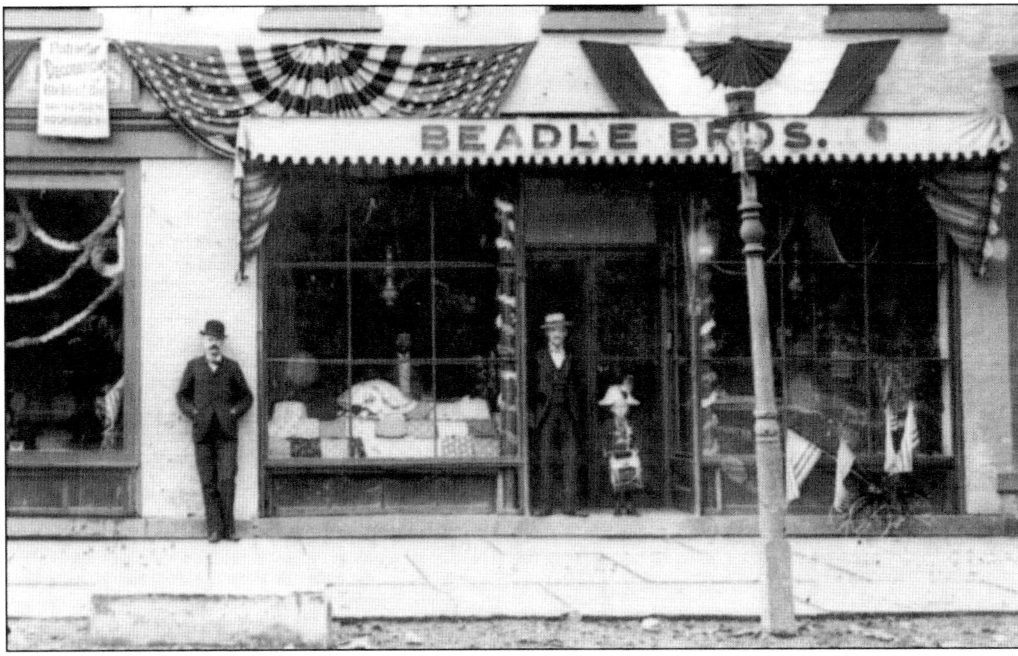

Thomas and Clifford Beadle operated Beadle Brothers dry goods store from the close of the Civil War until the 1920s. It was the biggest store in the area, employing as many as 12 clerks and occupying two floors and one room of the American Hotel. Note the simple oil lamppost and slate sidewalks.

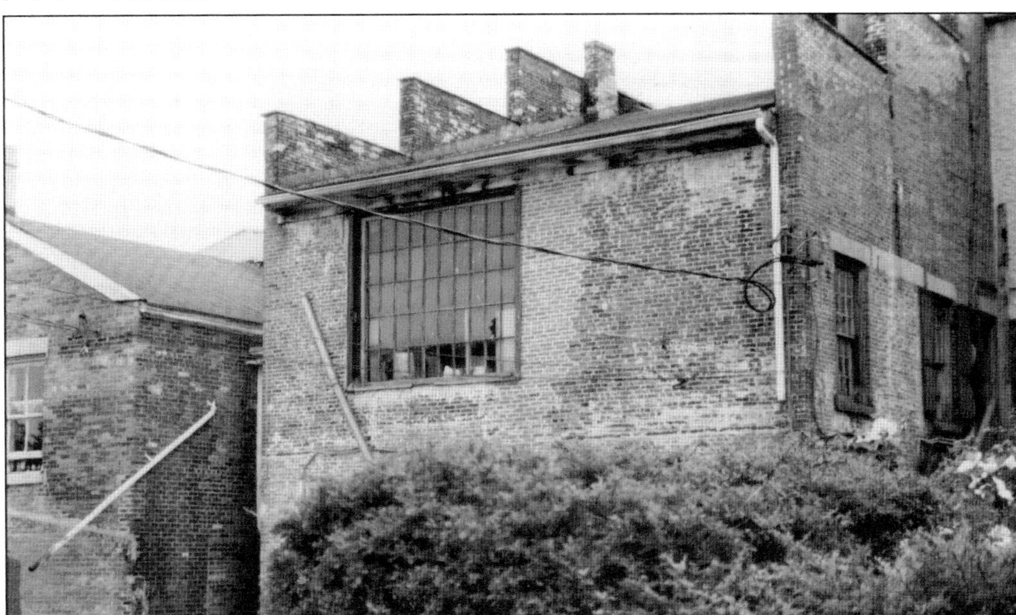

The large window belonged to a daguerreotype studio behind Stanley's Exchange. It provided the much desired northern light that photographers and artists find vital for quality work. Lima was fortunate to have many skilled photographers when other towns it size had none. Among the more accomplished were J.S. Galentine, H.F. Parker, L.A. Pierce, F.M. Bailey, and Bronson. They left an enduring record of small-town American life. (Author's collection.)

This little bank was remodeled in 1922. It stood on the north side of West Main Street beside the Presbyterian churchyard. In 1955, when this photograph was taken, it housed the Lima office of the Genesee Valley Trust Company of Rochester.

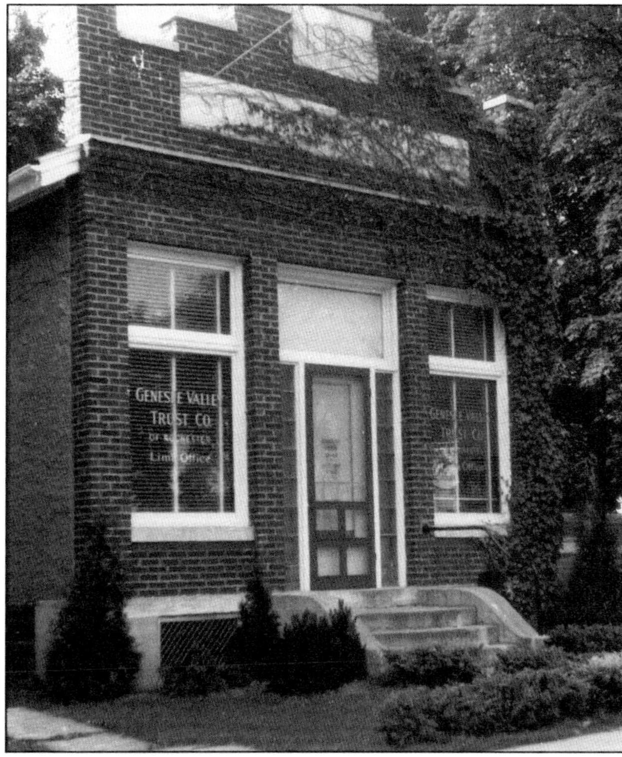

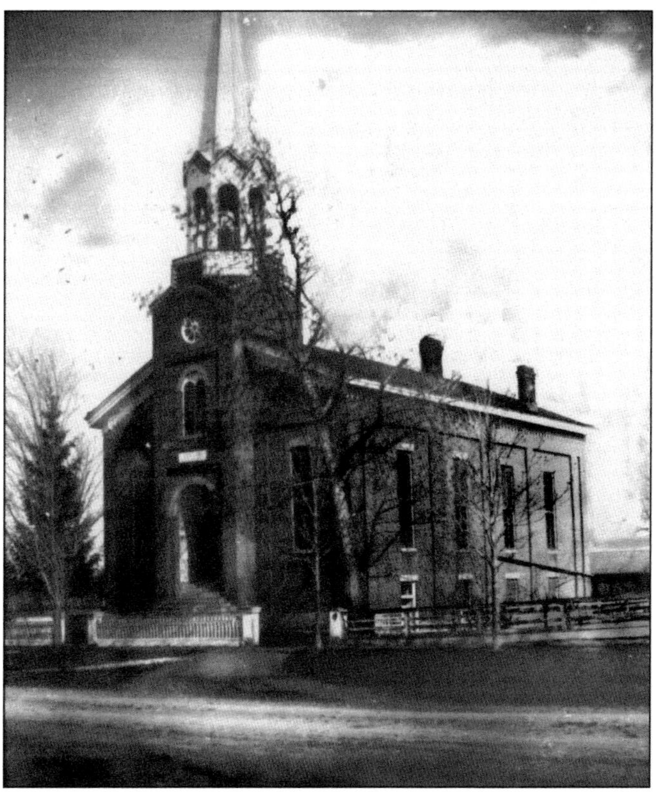

This early image of the Lima Baptist Church is from a glass negative originally used for a stereo view. The church was built on the south side of Main Street in the village in 1855. In the early 1900s, the white spire was removed and replaced with a less appealing battlement affair. The church serves as an antiques mall today.

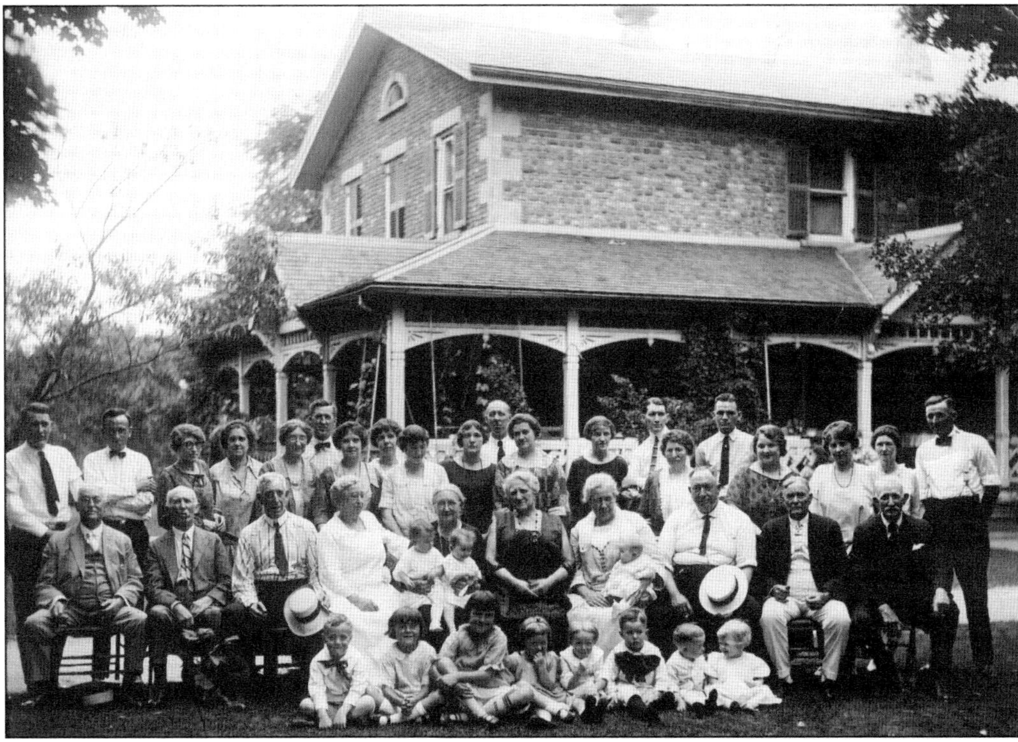

Members of the Gillette family have gathered for a reunion portrait. Behind them is one of the area's most admired cobblestone houses.

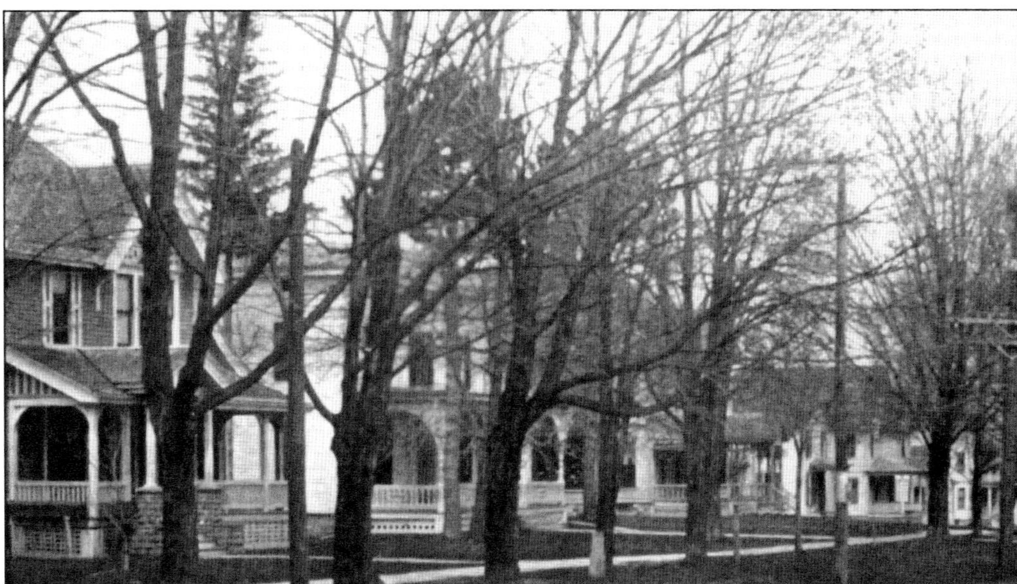

Inviting porches are visible between the elms in this *c.* 1907 postcard view of East Main Street. On warm evenings homeowners would sit and converse with passing neighbors. They might hear music spilling from the American Hotel or the Exchange dance hall. A steam engine might rumble down at the Lehigh depot. The Lima-Honeoye Falls Railroad engines would have made their last run, and Pinco's kilns probably would have left the night air sooty.

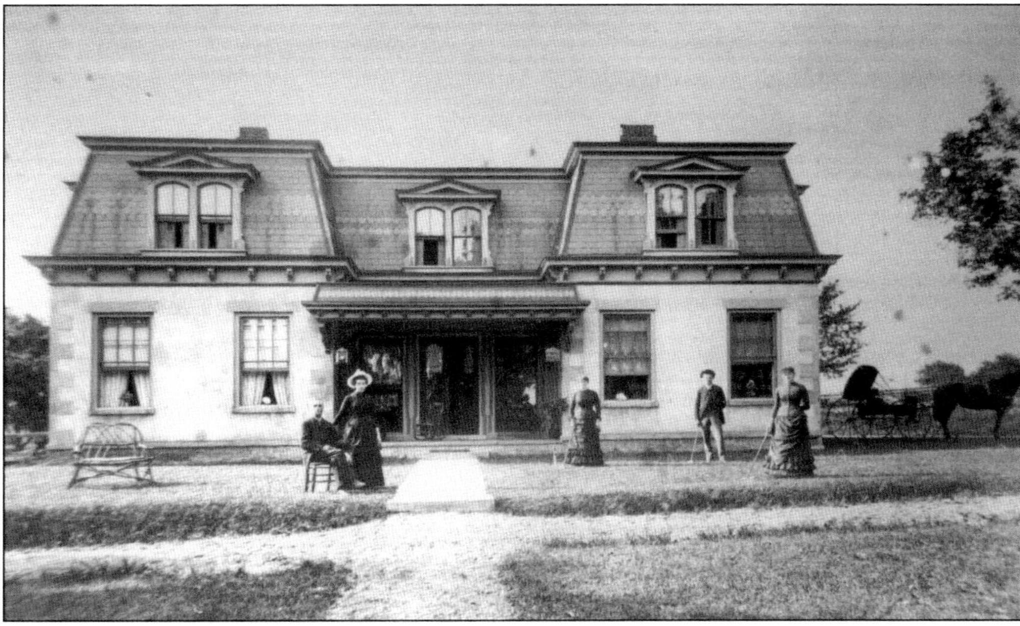

Members of the Crouse family gather on the lawn of their West Main Street home. The house was demolished, but most of the foundation was preserved for a new structure.

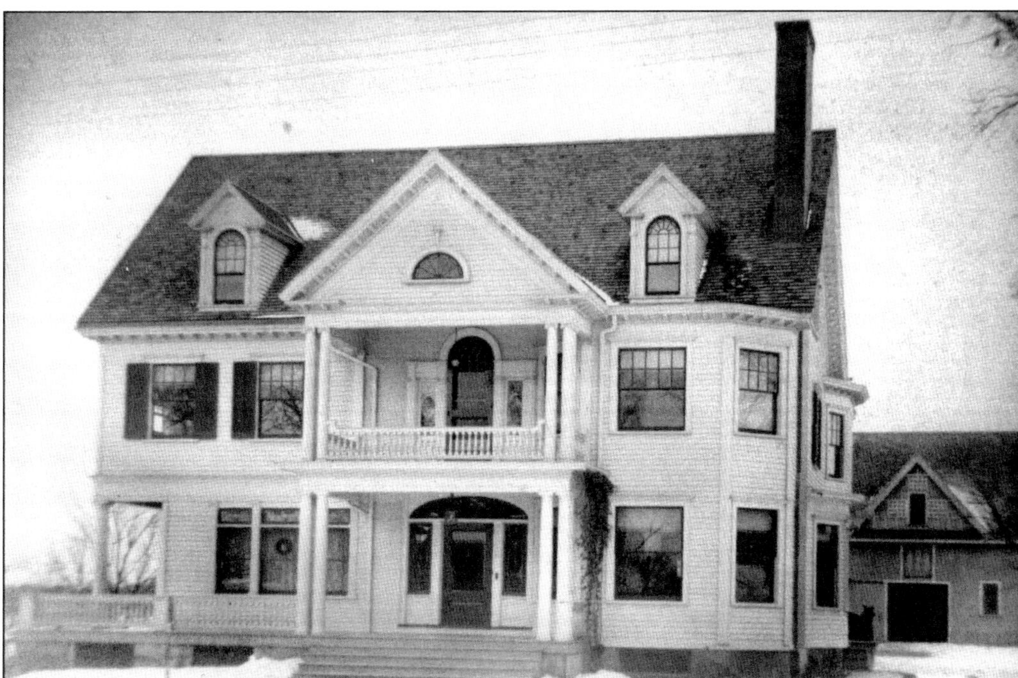

A new Crouse home sits grandly upon its old foundation. Remnants of an impressive stone fence around the property still exist.

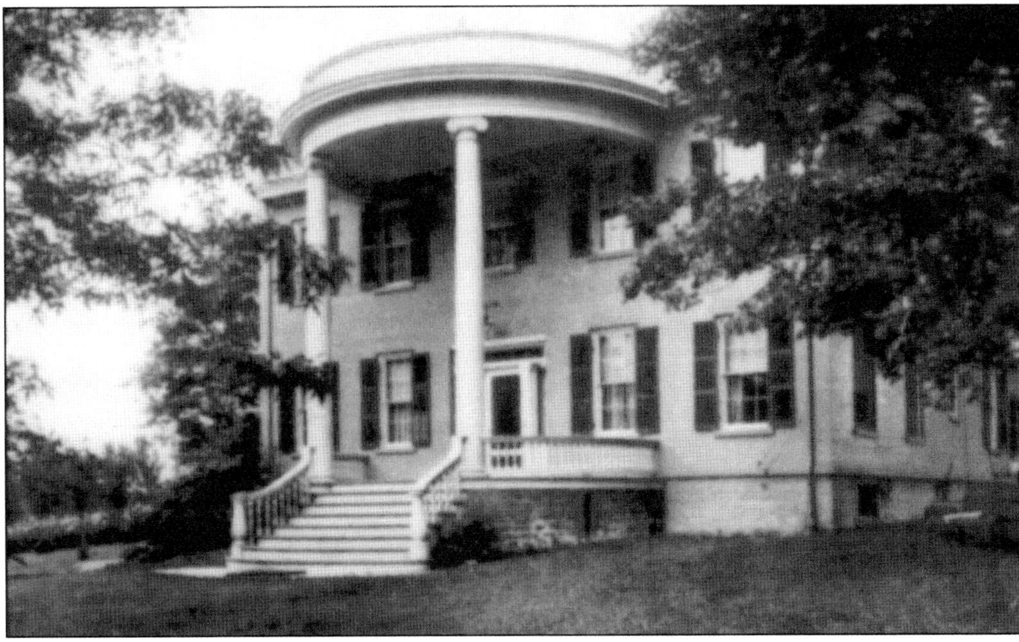

Hillcrest, built in 1838 by Erastus Clark, remains one of the most noted local landmarks. Situated atop a hill in the village, it affords a commanding view of the region. The house sits fully within a 17th-century Seneca village, where longhouses descended gracefully down the slopes. Jim and Judi Cooper oversaw the extensive restoration of the property.

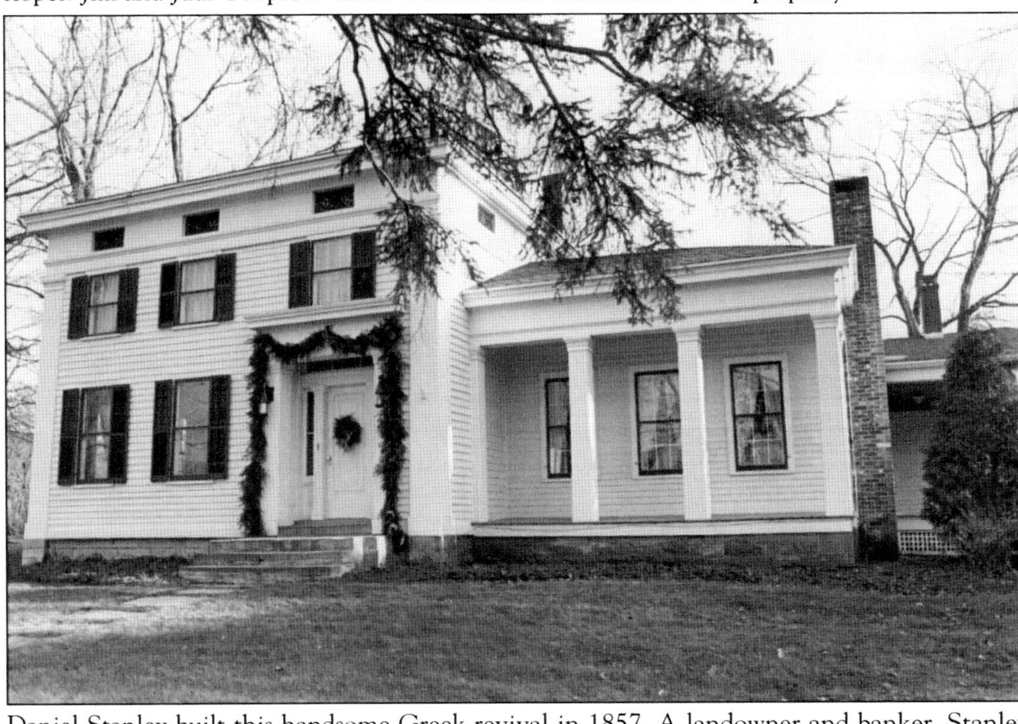

Daniel Stanley built this handsome Greek revival in 1857. A landowner and banker, Stanley founded Stanley's Exchange. The house is on the south side of East Main Street. George and Fran Gotcsik have restored it to its original glory. (Photograph by Fran Gotscik.)

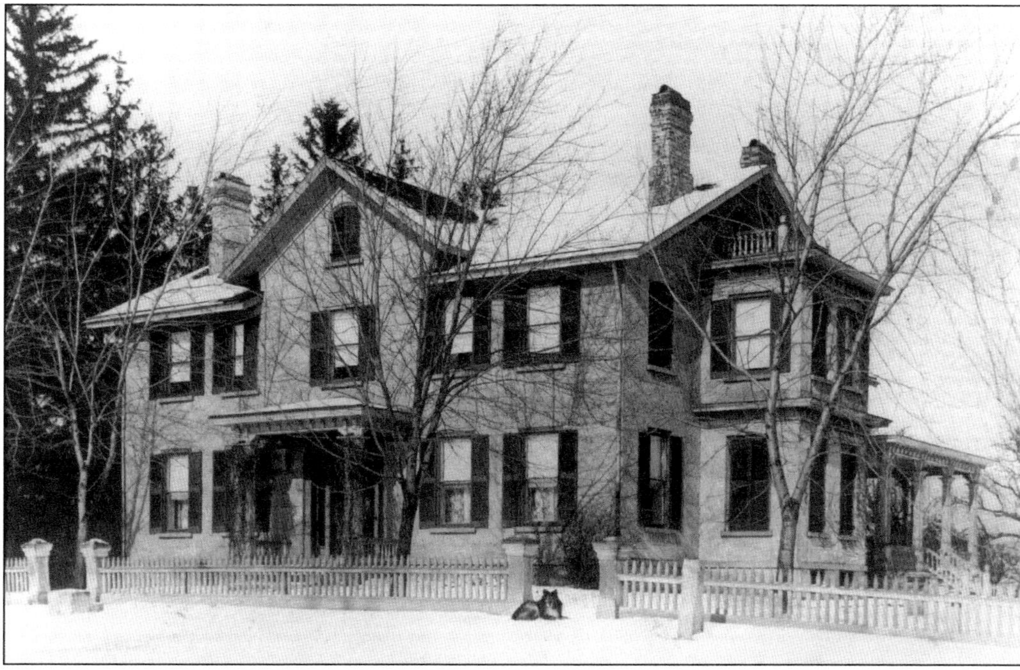

This impressive stone house at 7955 East Main Street is what John Ruskin must have had in mind when he wrote, "When we build, let us think that we build forever. Let it not be for present delight nor for present use alone. Let it be such work as our descendants will thank us for; and let us think, as we lay stone on stone, that a time is to come when those stones will be held sacred because our hands have touched them, and that men will say, as they look upon the labor and wrought substance of them, 'See! This our father did for us.'"

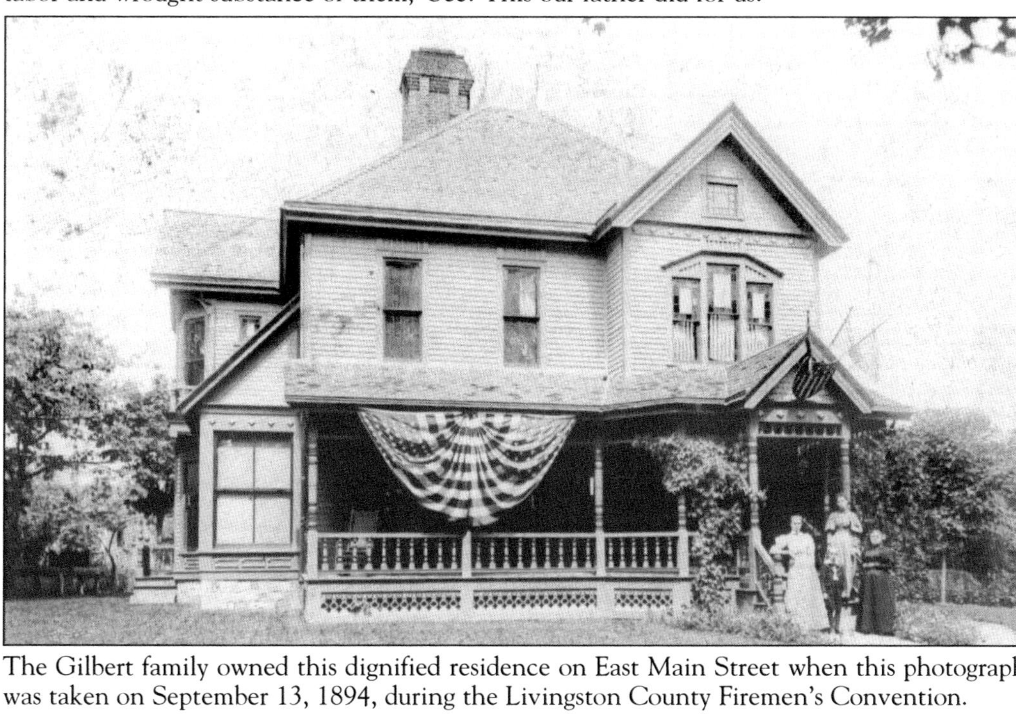

The Gilbert family owned this dignified residence on East Main Street when this photograph was taken on September 13, 1894, during the Livingston County Firemen's Convention.

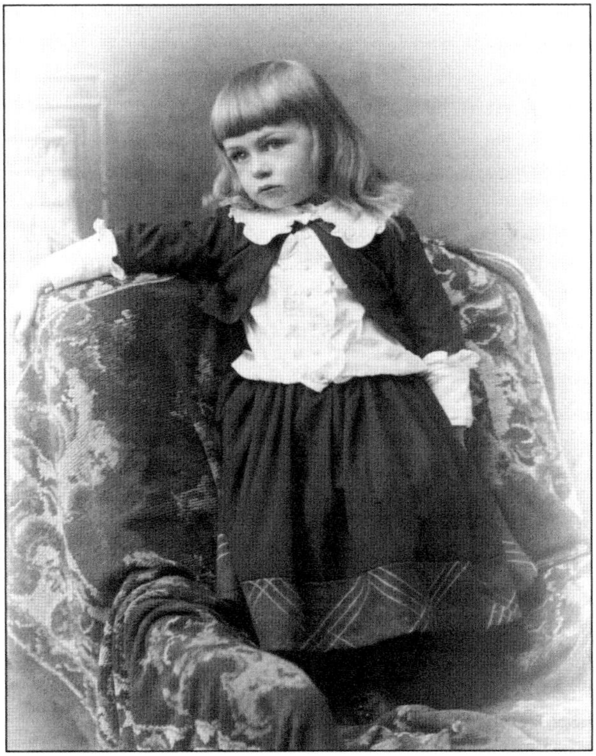

This is Wayne G. Vary at age three years and ten months. The son of Samuel and Ruth Vary, he was born in Lima on February 4, 1889, and he died here on November 8, 1945.

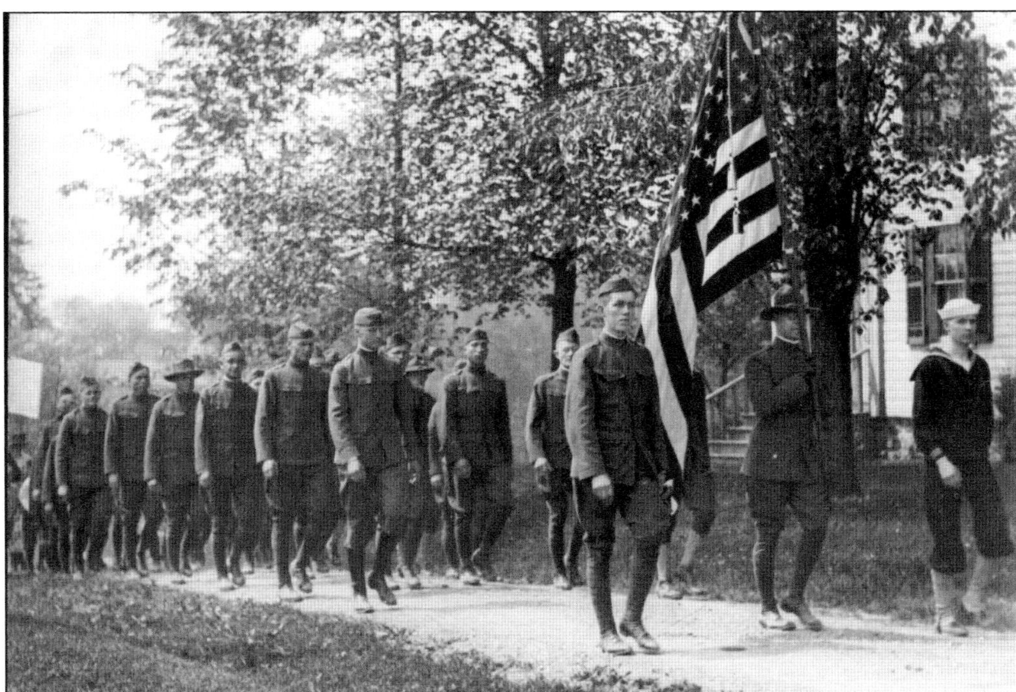

Wayne Vary marches in the 1919 Decoration Day parade. He is in the forth row back, on the left, looking toward the camera.

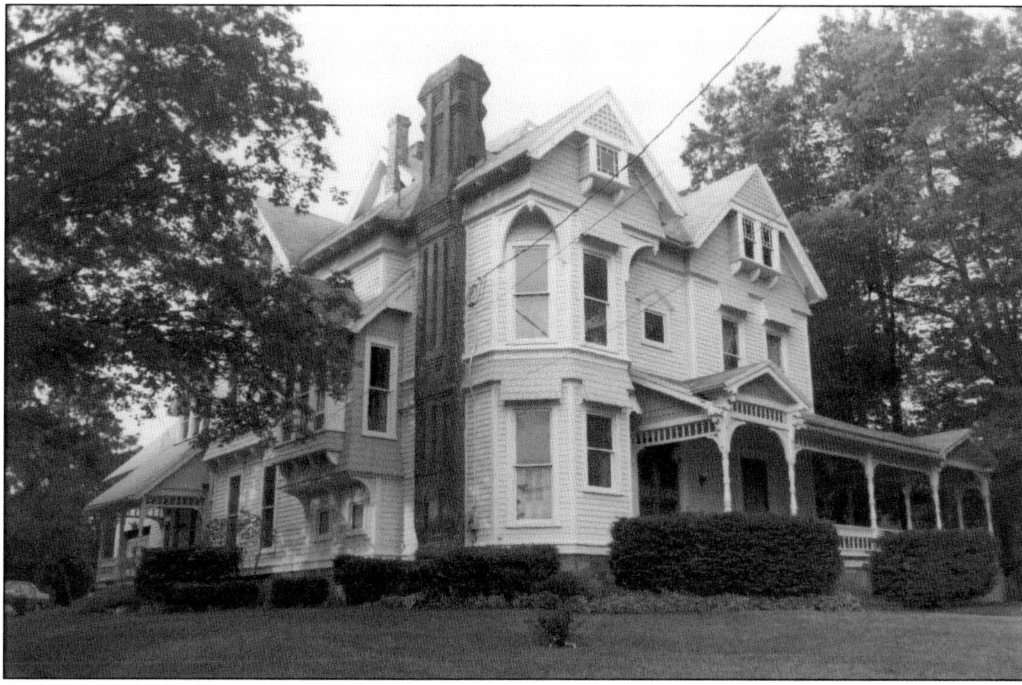

William Vary built this impressive home east of his mother's house in 1885 when he was 25 years old. Located at 7378 East Main Street, it is an Eastlake-stick-Queen Anne, said to have cost $8,000. It embodies the sophistication of the architectural heritage of Lima, which has more than 50 properties on the National Register of Historic Places.

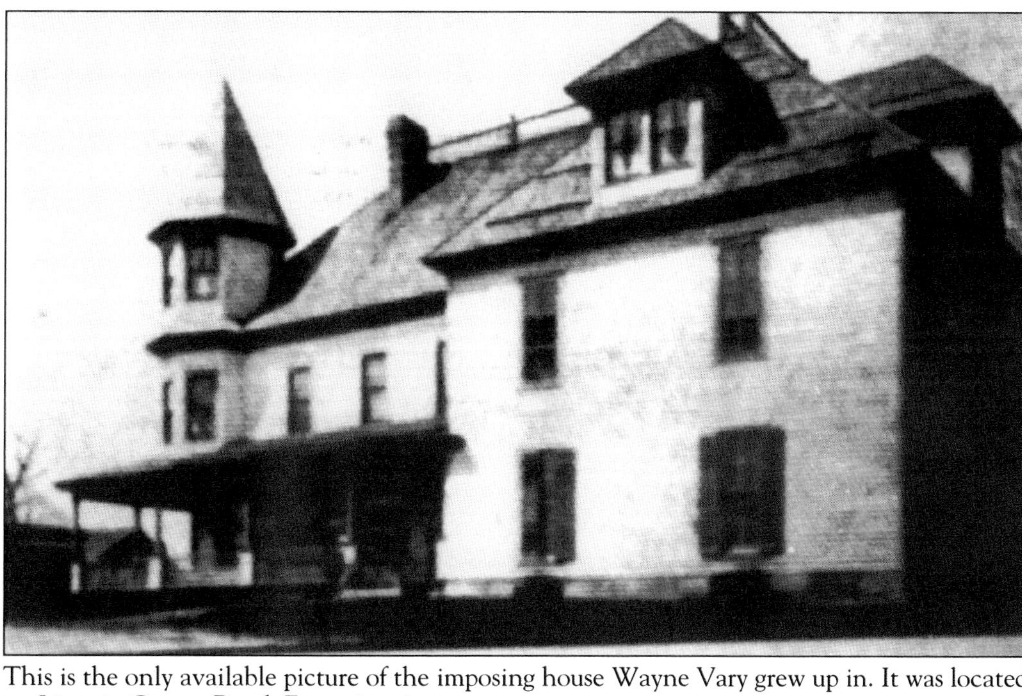

This is the only available picture of the imposing house Wayne Vary grew up in. It was located on Livonia Center Road. For a time it was a tearoom.

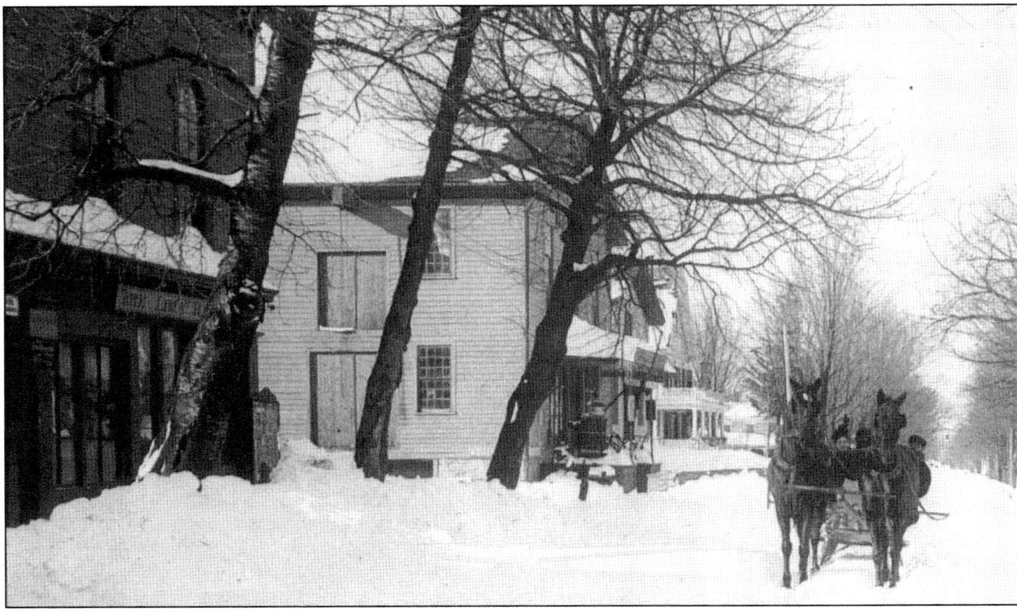

On May 11, 1907, a ferocious spring storm hit the area. These riders, however, hardly seem dispirited as they bring their sleigh up Rochester Street. On the left is the Lima Recorder print office.

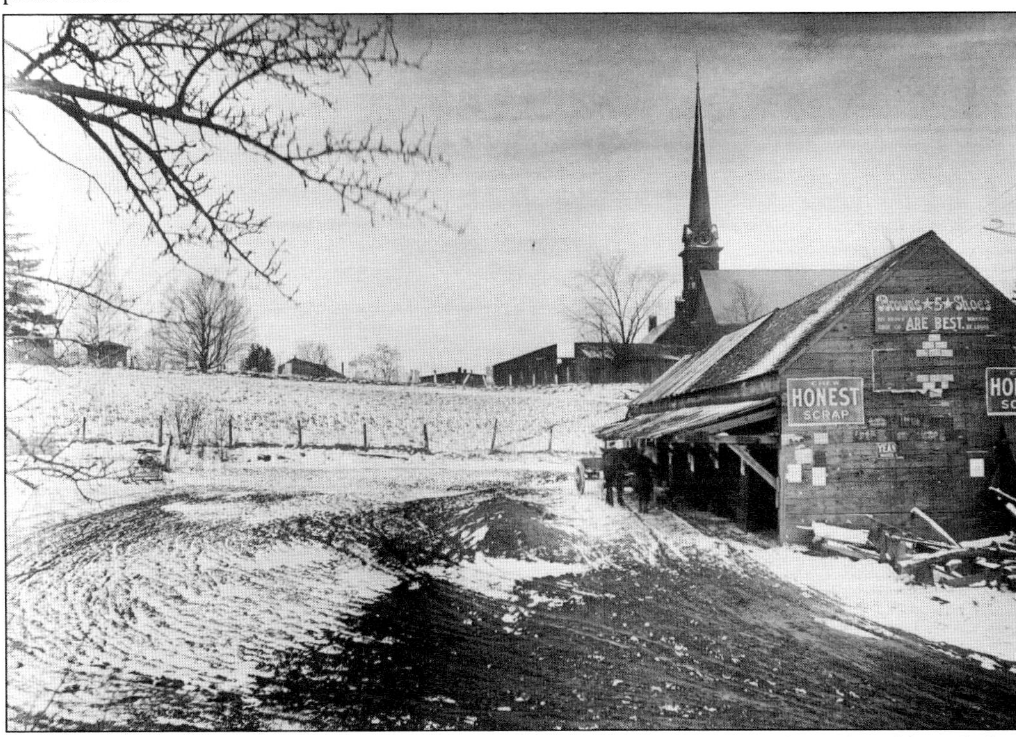

The tower of the Presbyterian church stands starkly against a winter sky. The old coal shed for the Lima-Honeoye Falls Railroad stands wretched with its placards for Chew Honest Scrap and Brown's No. 5 Shoes. The photograph was taken on February 5, 1915, at the time of the robbery of the Lima Bank.

The Murphy furniture and undertaker block stood in the vicinity of the present Lima Diner. This handsome building is decorated for the Livingston County Firemen's Convention. On the left is a blacksmith shop; on the right, an old house.

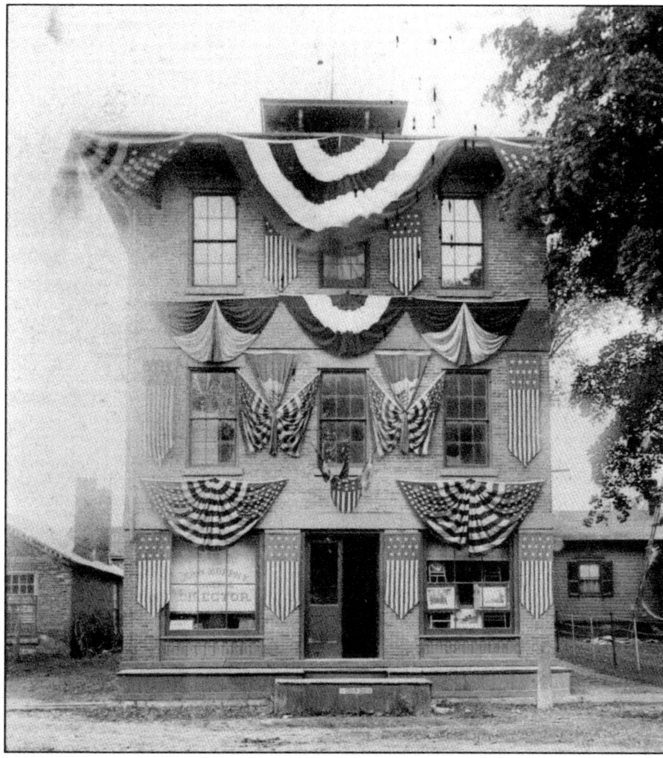

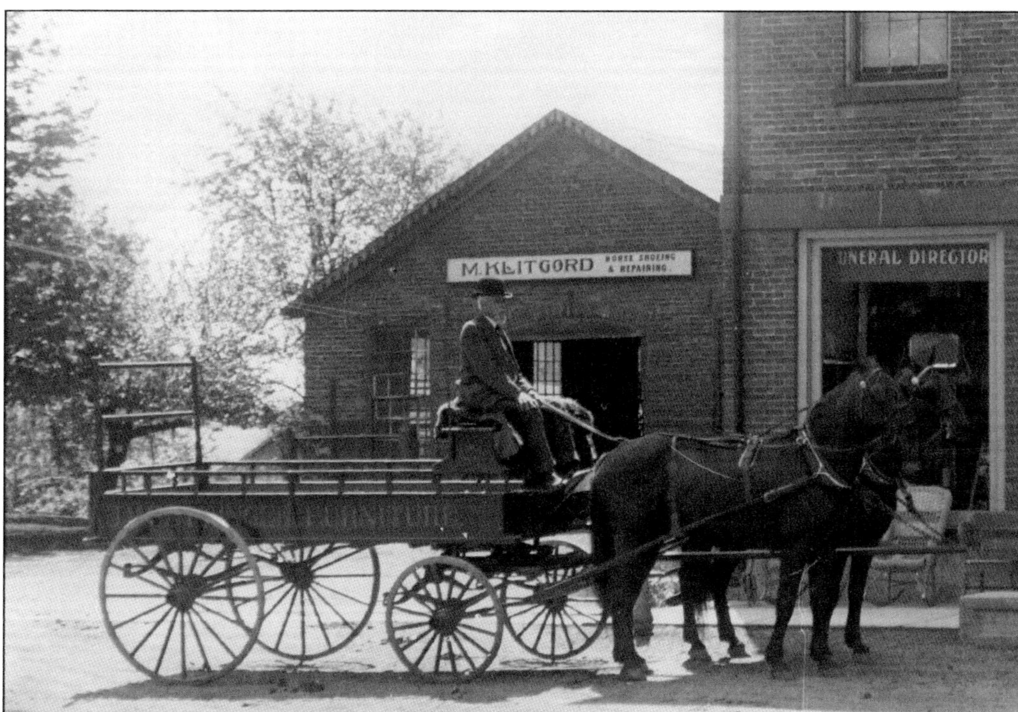

Mr. Bettinger, owner of the furniture and funeral business located in the Murphy building, stops briefly to have his picture taken. The Klitgord blacksmith shop is visible just beyond him.

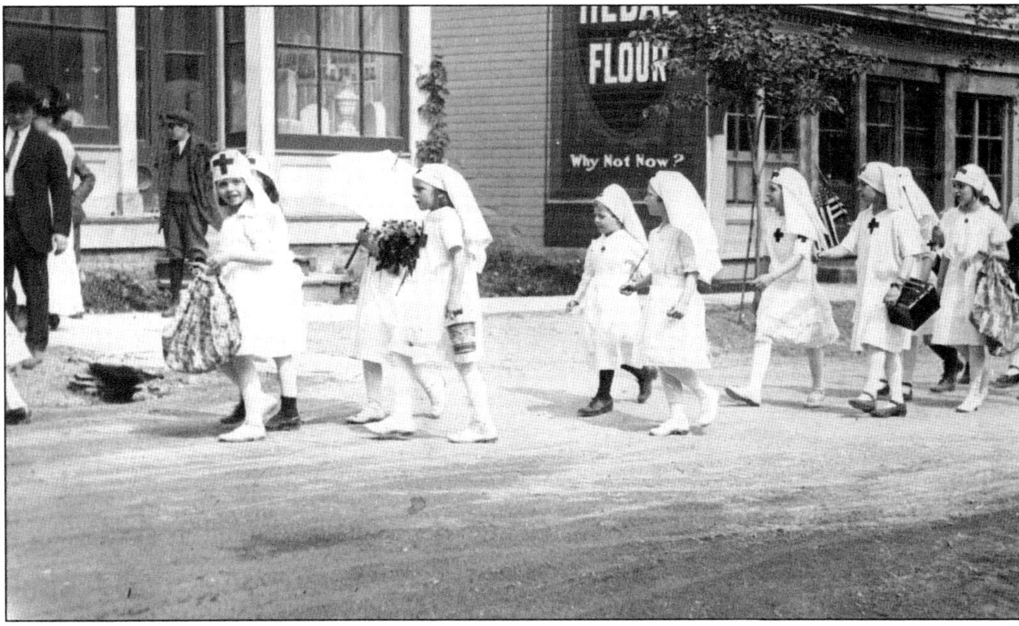

Little girls march in the 1919 Memorial Day parade as it travels south on Rochester Street. The white building beyond them is Ben Ollerenshaw's marble shop; beside that is Van Gelder's print shop, where the *Lima Recorder* was published.

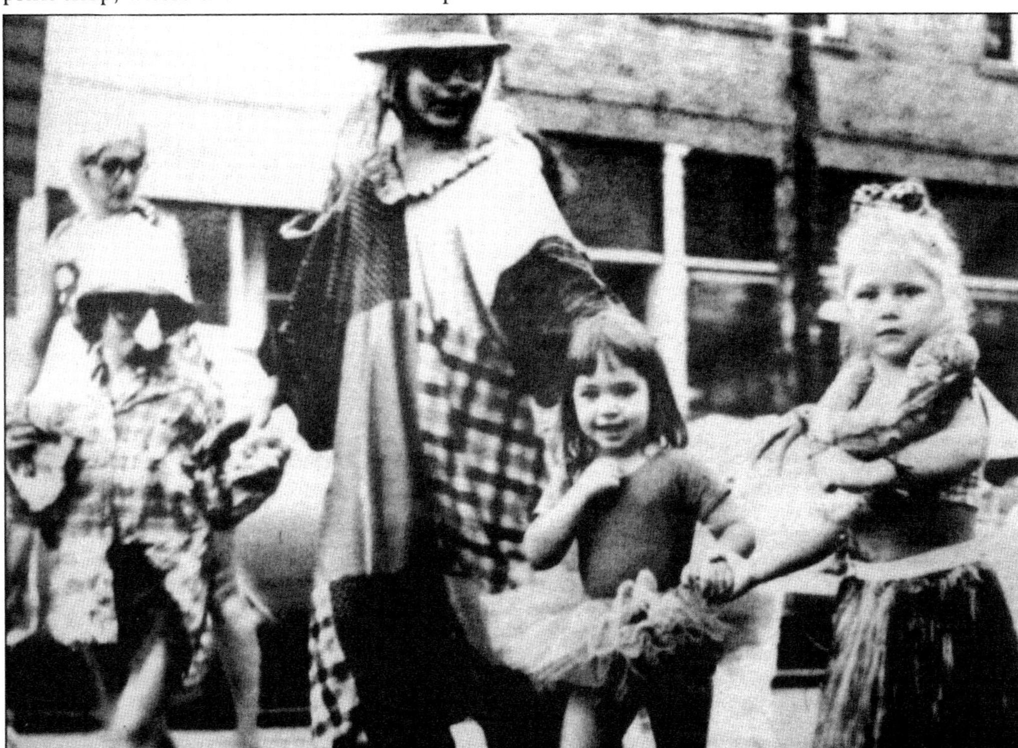
It is Thursday, August 27, 1970, and the Firemen's Carnival is in town. These youngsters are participating in the opening Kiddies Parade down Main Street. (Lima Recorder photograph.)

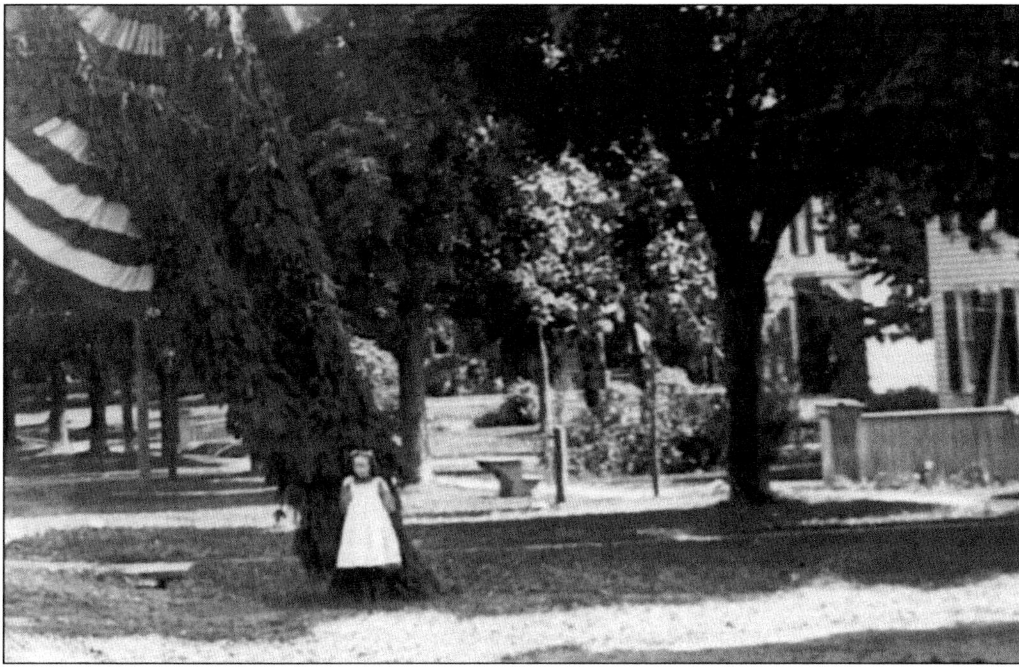

The 1894 Livingston County Firemen's Convention was a grand affair for Lima. This view is looking east on East Main Street. A little girl poses beneath a towering display of spruce bows and bunting, as morning sunlight begins to wash the front yards of tidy houses. Note the wooden carriage steps in the center.

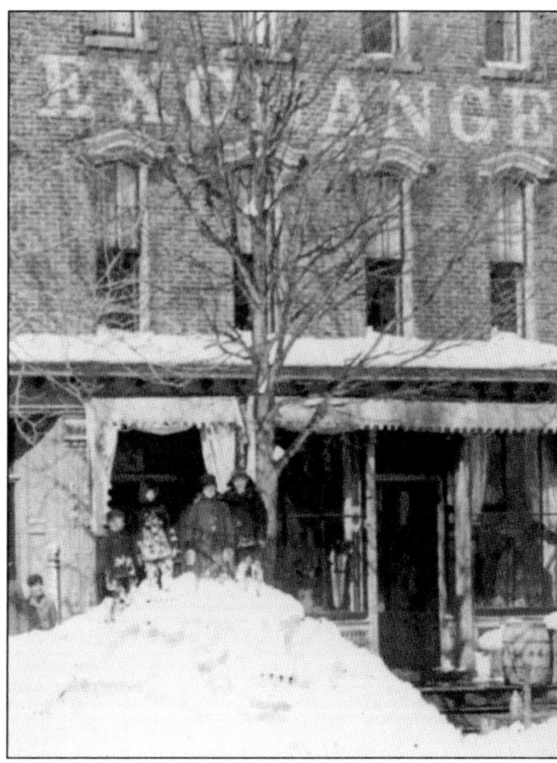

Snow hills are as irresistible today as they were to children *c.* 1900, when this photograph was taken in front of the Stanley Exchange.

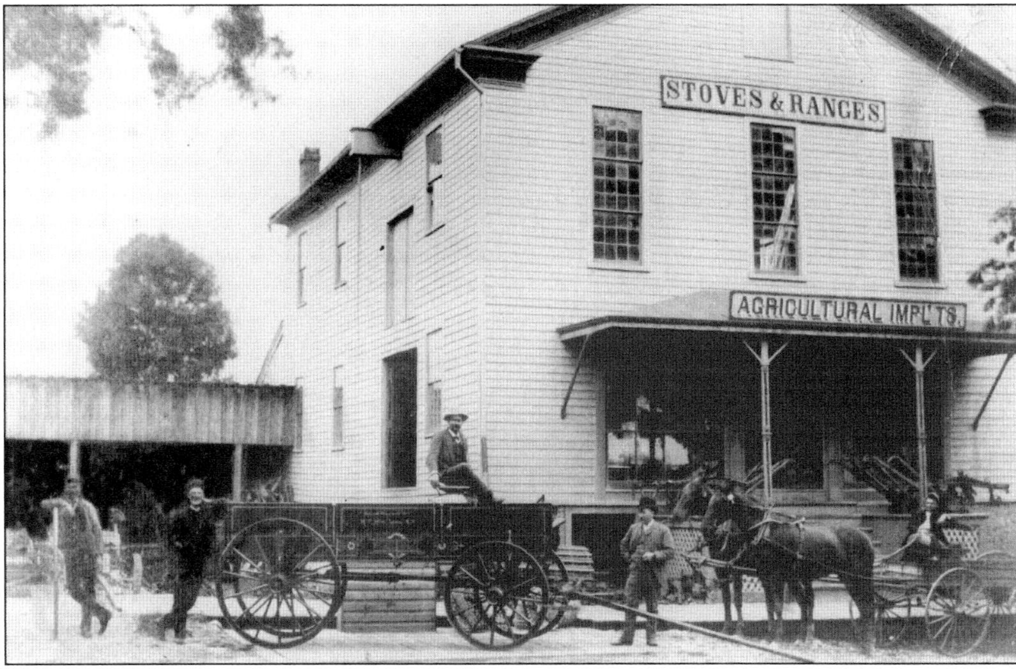

Here is a building with a story. Built in 1828 as a small house of worship on West Main Street, the building was moved in 1843 to the east side of Rochester Street and then was uprooted again and moved in 1857 to the west side of the street. It served for a time as an Episcopalian church and later as a Methodist church. When this picture was taken in the 1880s, it was the M.P. Allen Hardware Store.

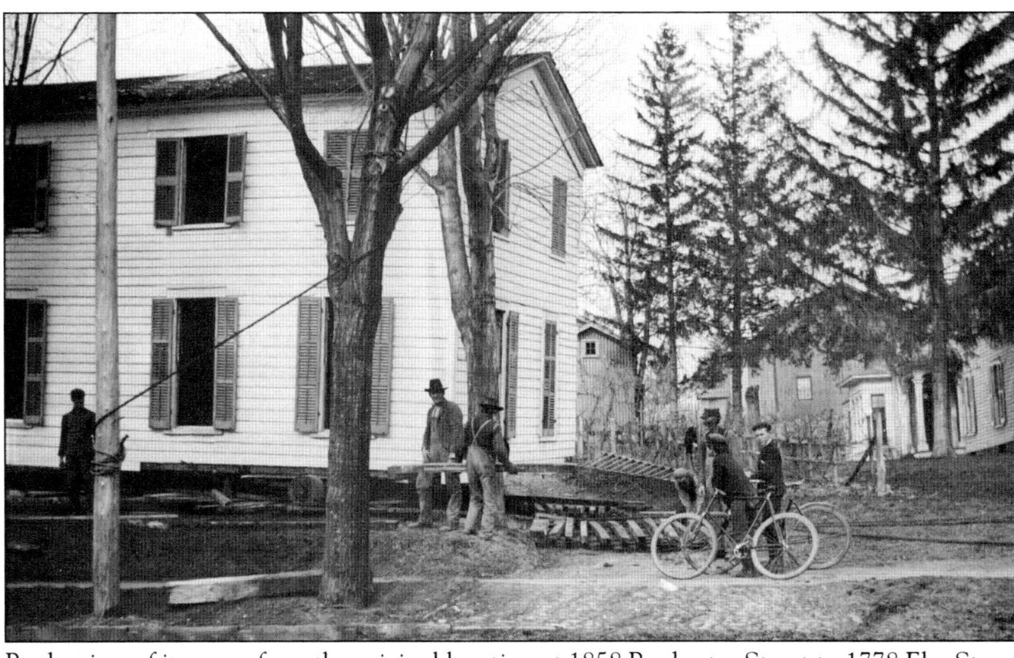

By the time of its move from the original location at 1858 Rochester Street to 1778 Elm Street, this house had already had three owners. The three were Dr. J.A. Mackenzie, Petro Nataline, and Raymond O'Brien.

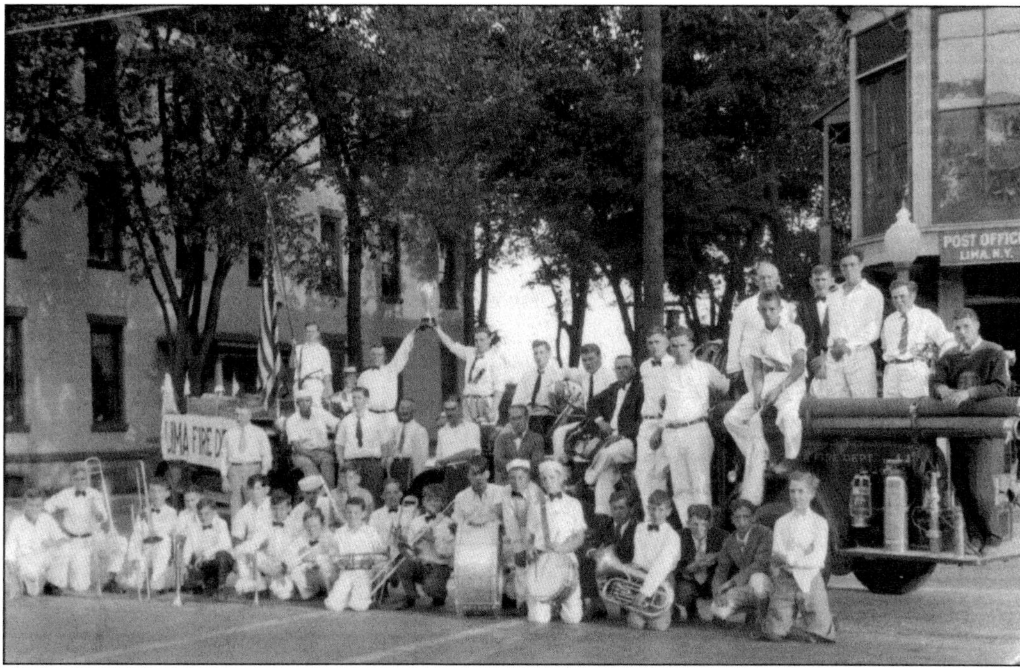

The Lima Fire Department Band has just won a competition held at the Livingston County Firemen's Convention in Avon. The cup is proudly displayed at the crossroads. The youngsters in the front row show that, in those days, civic participation began early.

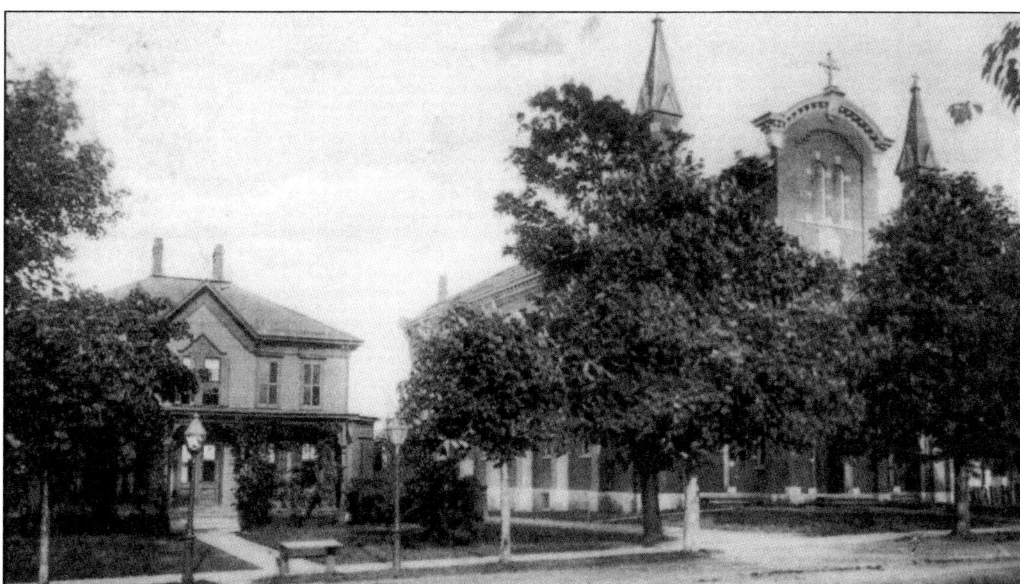

A sense of order is captured in this John Coventry postcard view of St. Rose Church and rectory. Note the small wooden carriage step flanked by two simple lampposts. Lima had up to four publishers of postcards, providing over 200 images of the community.

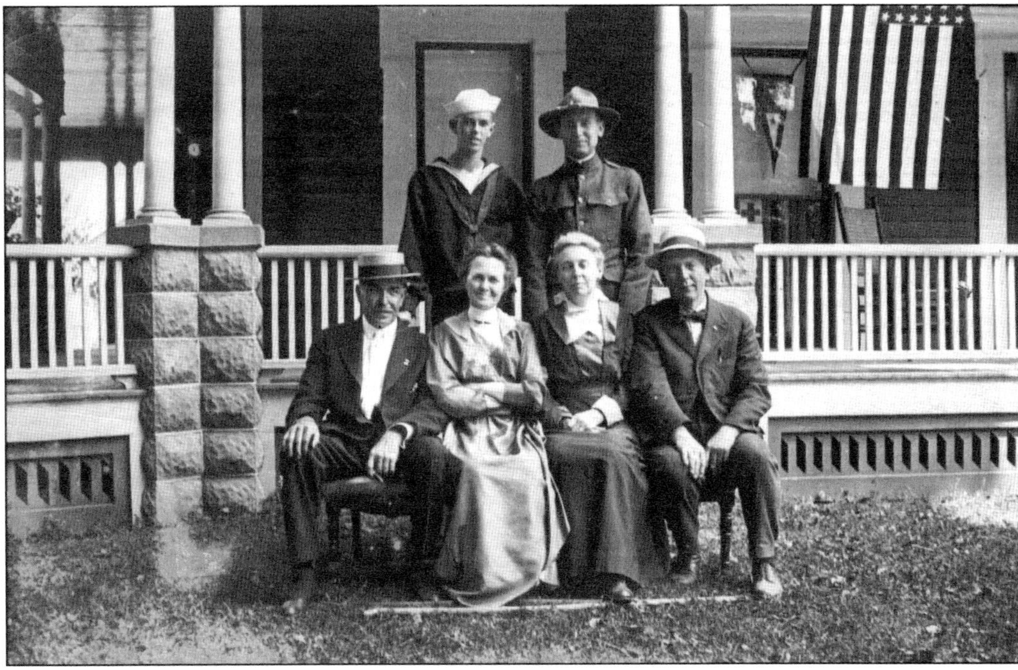

The Harvey house, on the corner of West Main and Genesee Streets, is the setting for this patriotic portrait. On the left are Mr. and Mrs. Kinear. The young sailor behind them is their son Alec Kinear. Beside them are Mr. and Mrs. Harvey, with their son Bill Harvey in back.

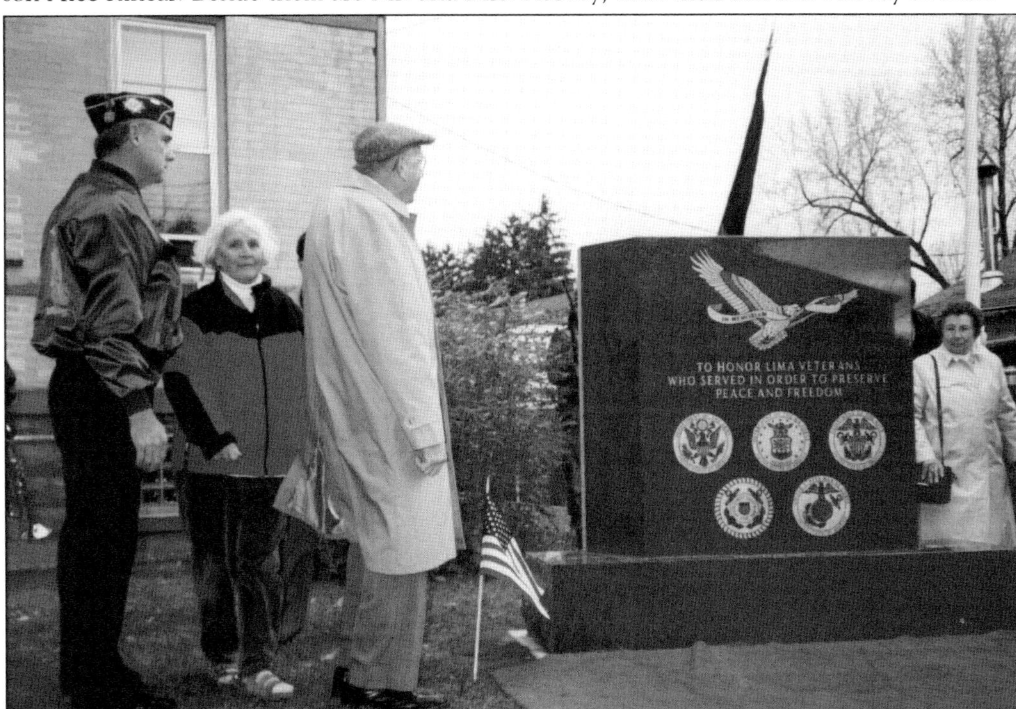

The 1998 dedication of Lima's new war memorial is being observed by, from left to right, Mike Hayes, Joyce Rapp, Richard Rapp, and Ellen Gillette.

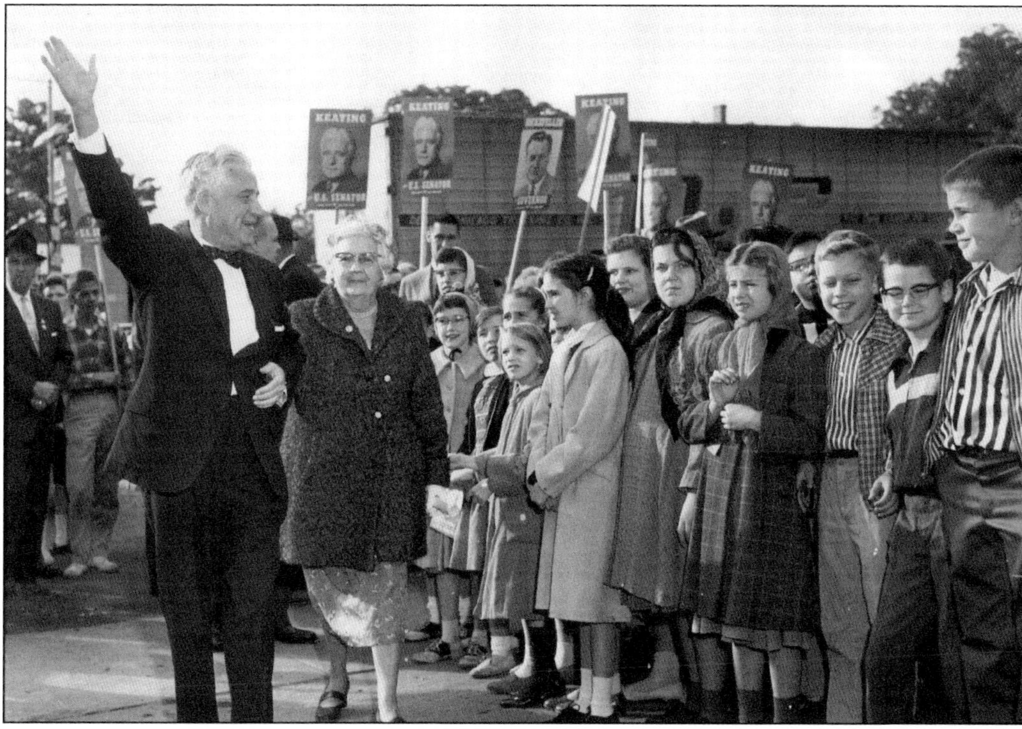

With a grand wave, Sen. and Mrs. Kenneth B. Keating greet Lima students during the senator's campaign for reelection.

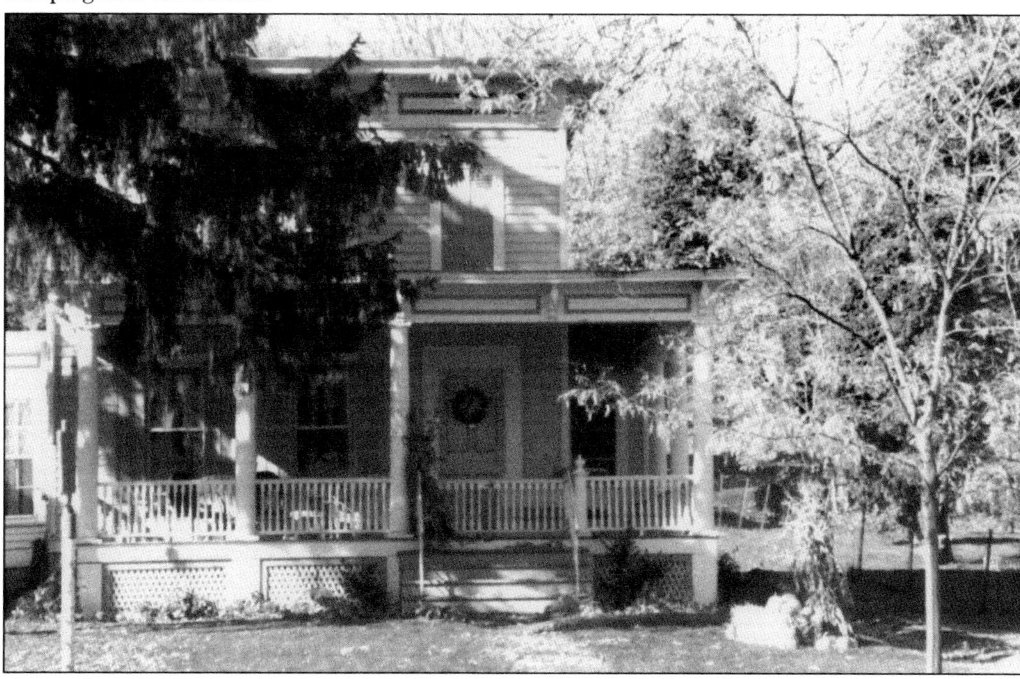

Kenneth Keating was raised in this house at 1818 Rochester Street. Built in 1836 by the Bennett family, it was remodeled in 1873 in the popular Italianate style. In 1984, the Kruk family purchased the home and undertook an extensive renovation of it. (Author's collection.)

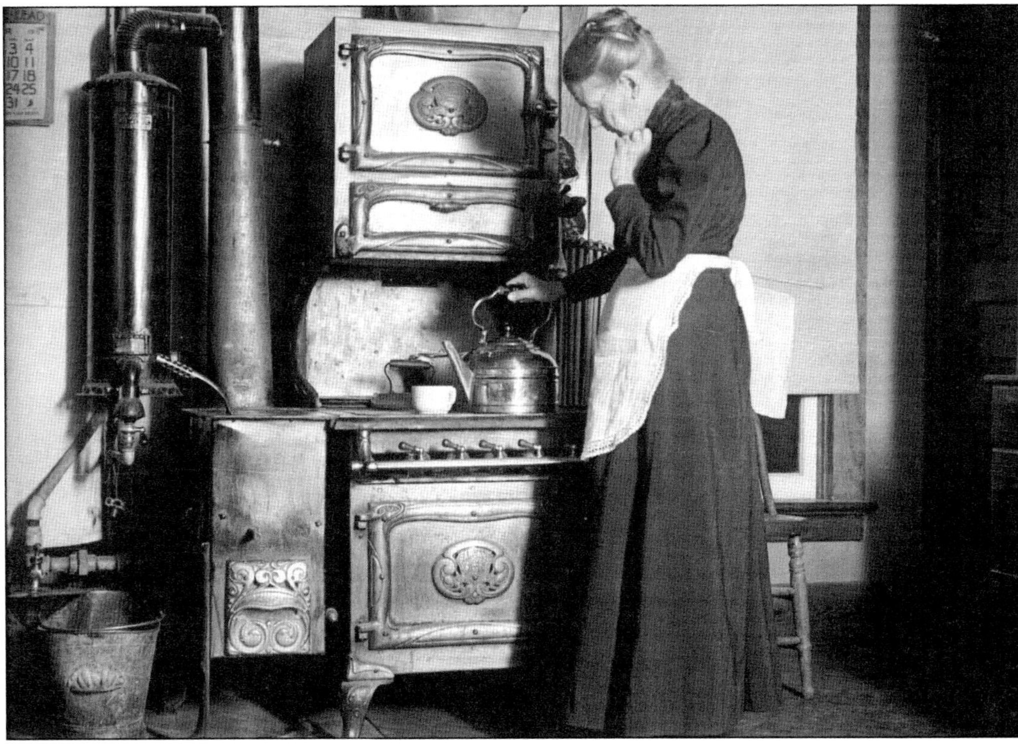

Ellen Mulhill Works pours tea in her then highly efficient kitchen. The stove is both coal and gas fired. To the left is a smaller coal stove to heat water for the house. There are hookups to power a gas iron and a gas lamp. At the far left is an asbestos-wrapped holding tank that contains the water used to heat the radiators.

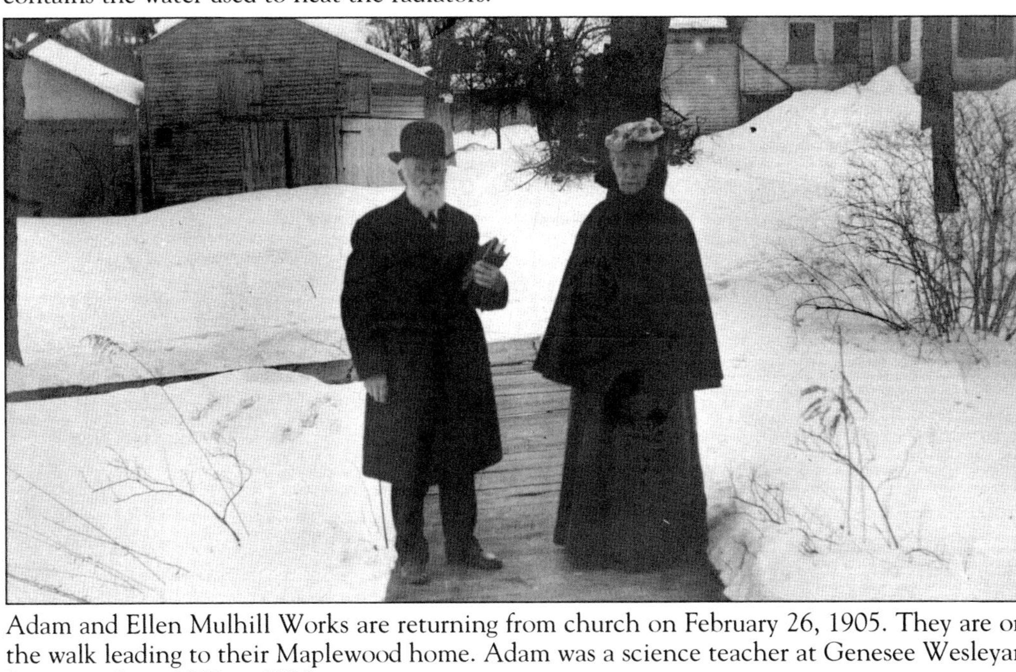

Adam and Ellen Mulhill Works are returning from church on February 26, 1905. They are on the walk leading to their Maplewood home. Adam was a science teacher at Genesee Wesleyan Seminary from 1872 to 1908.

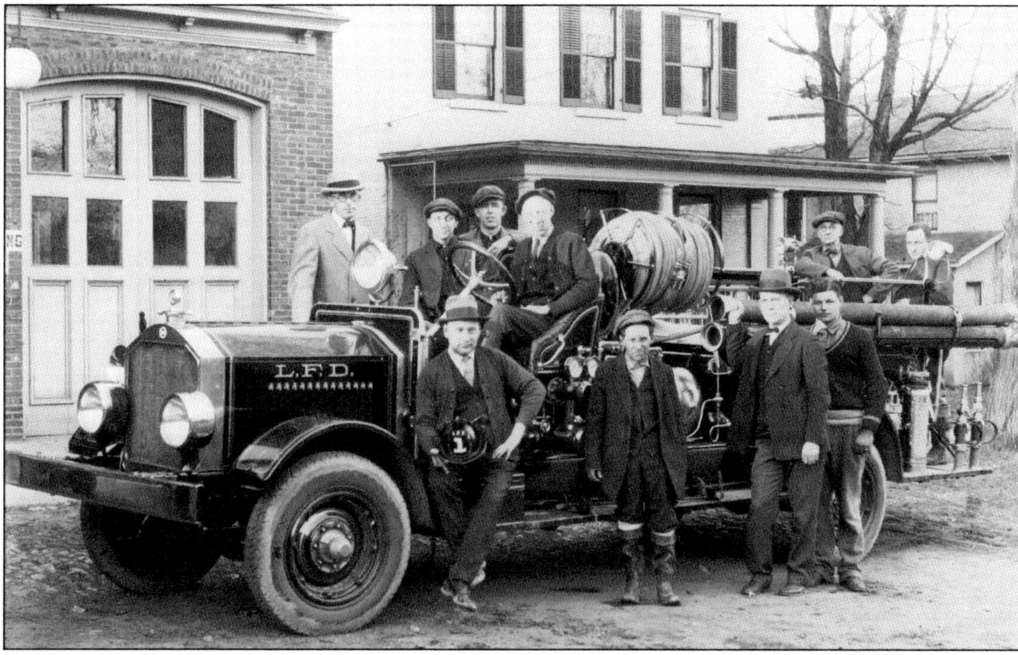

A 1920s view of the Lima Fire Department shows a crew ready for business. Pictured, from left to right, are the following: (front row) Frank McDonald, Roy Coykendall, Martin Hendrick, and Willard McDonald; (back row) John McSweeney, Lee McComber, Harold Relyea, Erson Gillette, Sam Vary, and Howard Allen.

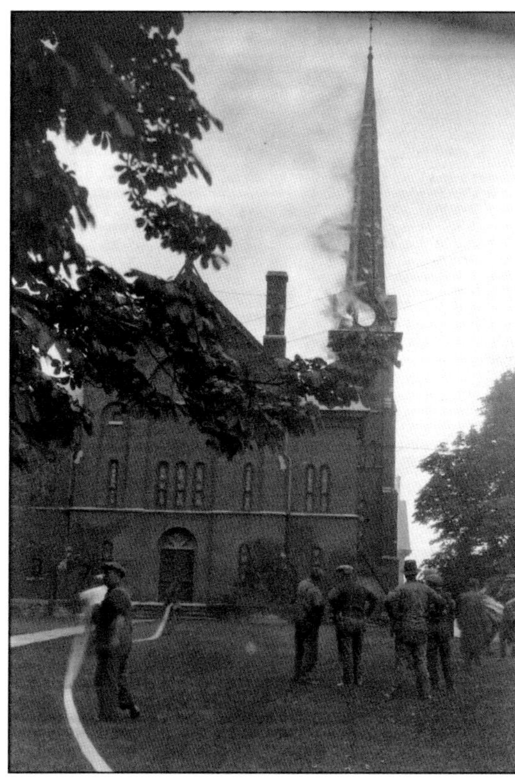

At around 2:00 p.m. on Monday June 14, 1926, the spire of the Presbyterian church was set afire by a lightning strike. The Lima Fire Department succeeded in keeping the flames from spreading to the main building.

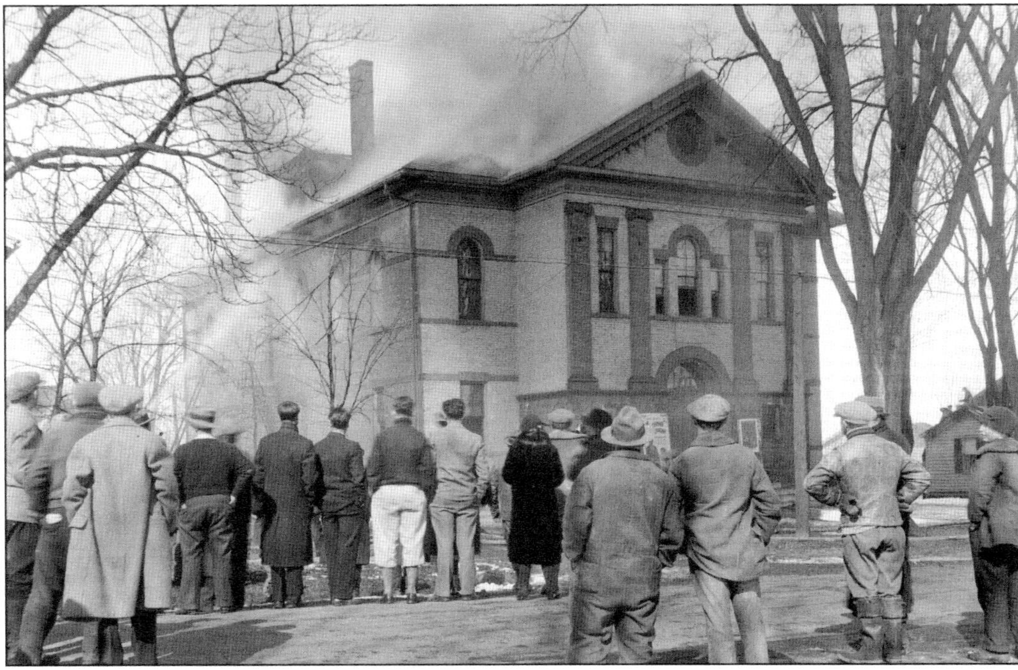

Onlookers watch firefighters battle a blaze at the town hall in March 1927.

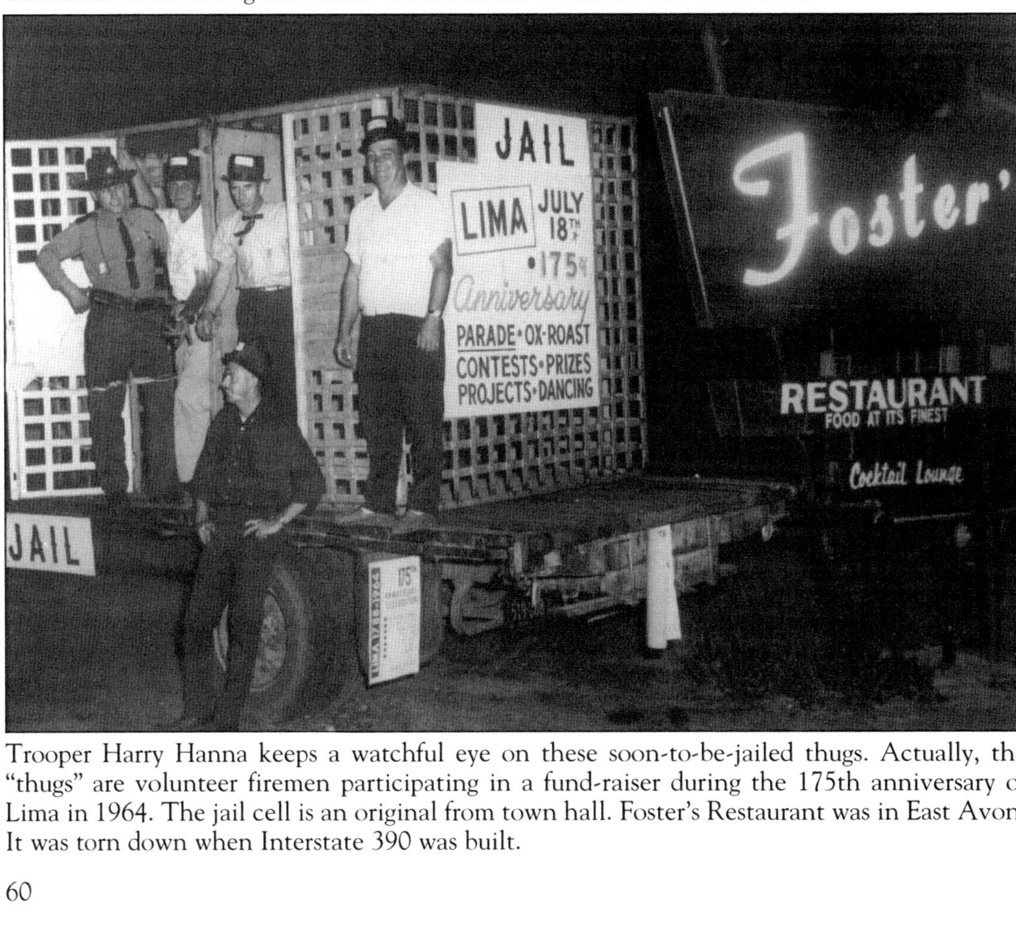

Trooper Harry Hanna keeps a watchful eye on these soon-to-be-jailed thugs. Actually, the "thugs" are volunteer firemen participating in a fund-raiser during the 175th anniversary of Lima in 1964. The jail cell is an original from town hall. Foster's Restaurant was in East Avon. It was torn down when Interstate 390 was built.

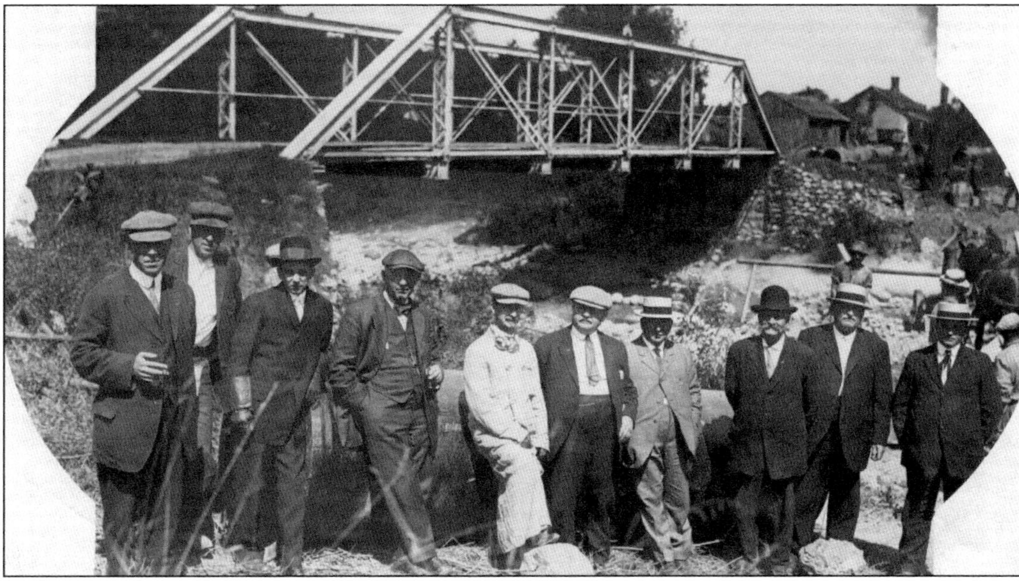

The Lima Town Board, having just inspected the Factory Hollow Bridge, poses at the site in 1910. The extent of waterpower for Lima resided at Honeoye Creek between Lima and West Bloomfield. The length of the creek from here to North Bloomfield was made lively by gristmills, sawmills, a machine shop, a cooper shop, a wool-carding and fulling mill, a six-story flour mill, a flax mill, a cider mill, a tile factory, a distillery, a blacksmith shop, a potash factory, and several other water-powered industries. The flow of the creek was diminished when Rochester took over the water rights to Hemlock Lake, from which Honeoye Creek originates.

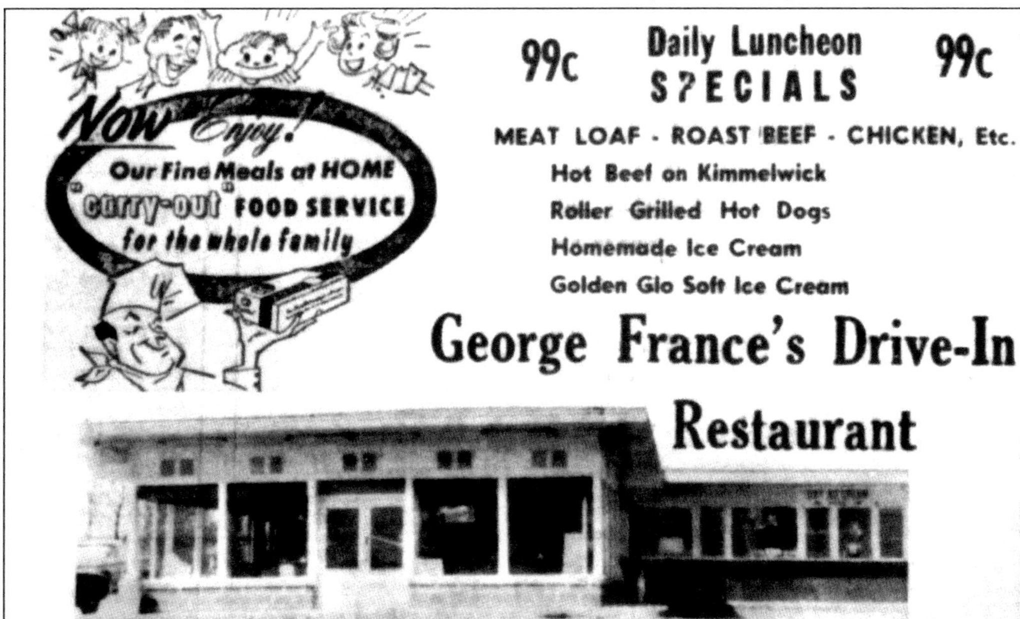

Landmarks come in all sizes and shapes. George France's Drive-In attracted people from the city out for a day's drive to the Finger Lakes. This advertisement was in a 1970s edition of the *Lima Recorder*. The restaurant is under new management today, and the tradition of fine food in a chatty and friendly environment continues.

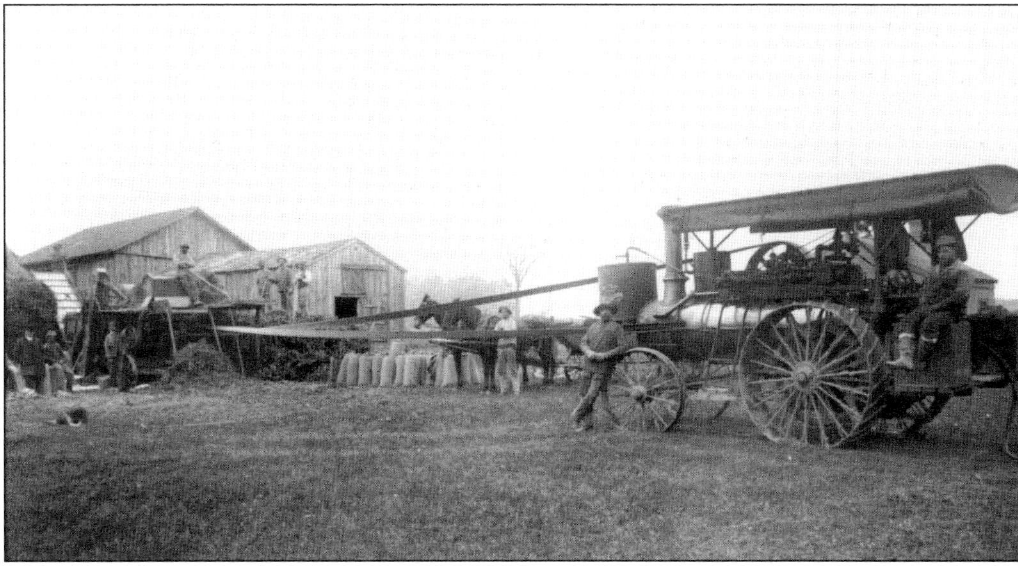

A long-wavering belt has been stretched between a drive wheel on the steam tractor to a threshing machine, as thrashing, or "threshing," gets under way at the Moss homestead *c.* 1900.

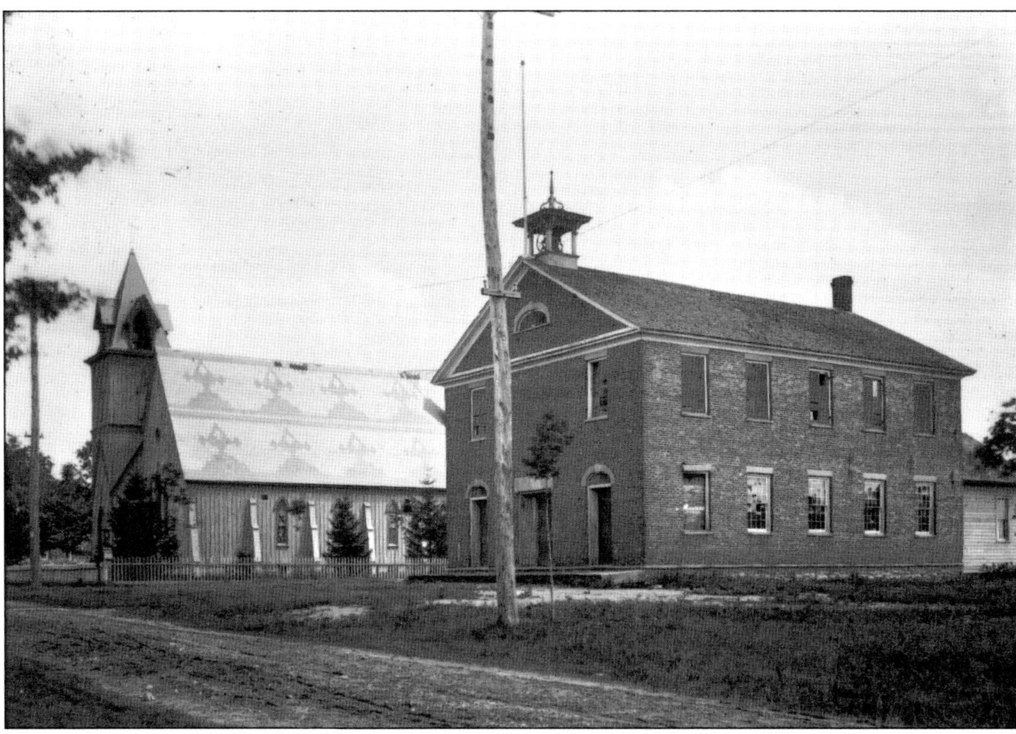

The Lima Universalist Church (left) was built in 1825 and was actually in North Bloomfield. The brick structure is the District No. 5 schoolhouse. Both buildings were near the corner of Bragg Street and Martin Road. The church is gone, but the schoolhouse remains, serving as a residence today.

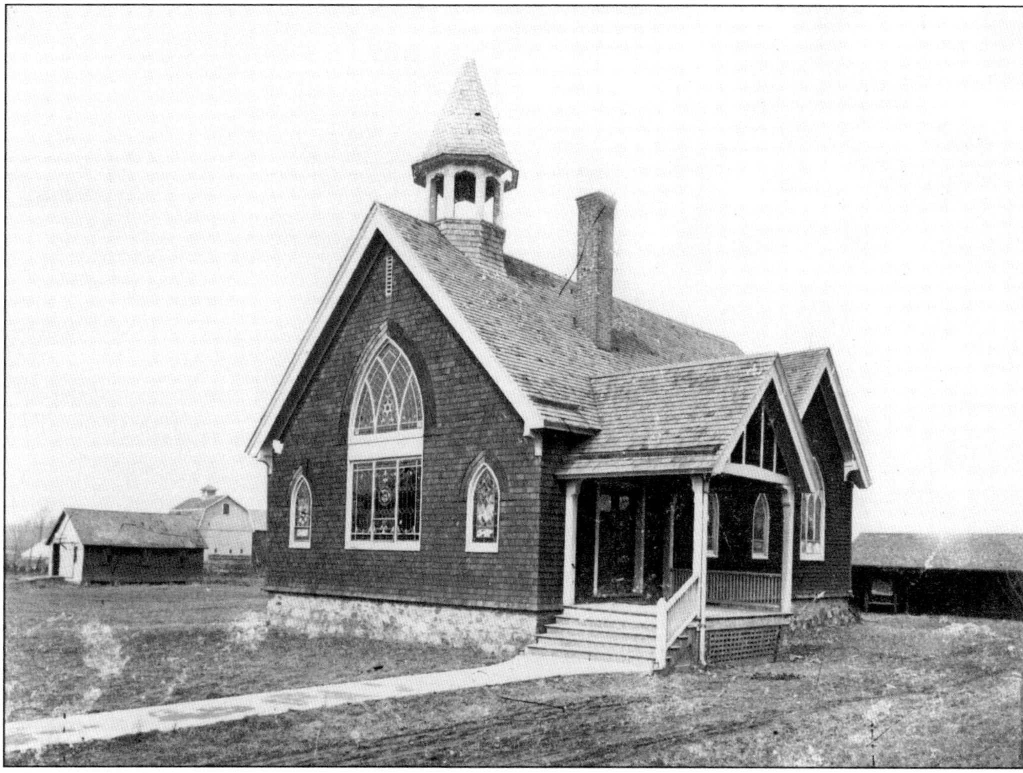

This small church in South Lima is now a residence. When the Erie Railroad brought its line through in 1853, the telegraph operator designated the place as "G.I." for Goose Island. This may have been because of the enormous migratory flocks of geese that descended on the extremely rich acres after they were turned in the fall.

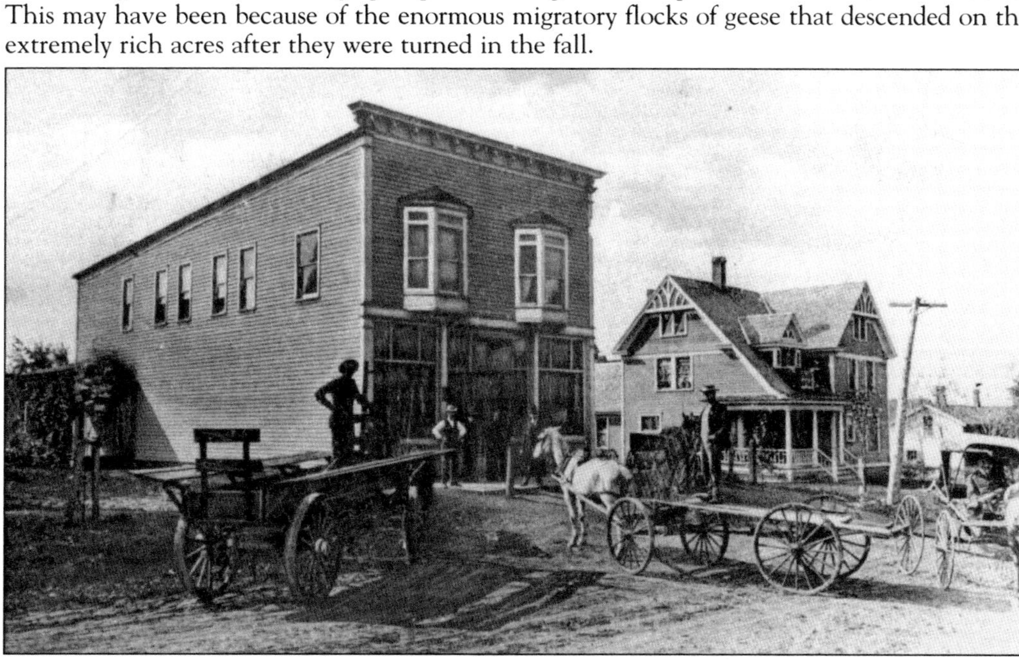

The view of South Lima shows the general store of J.M. Brennan and the Brennan residence just beyond it. (Courtesy Shirley Ruth.)

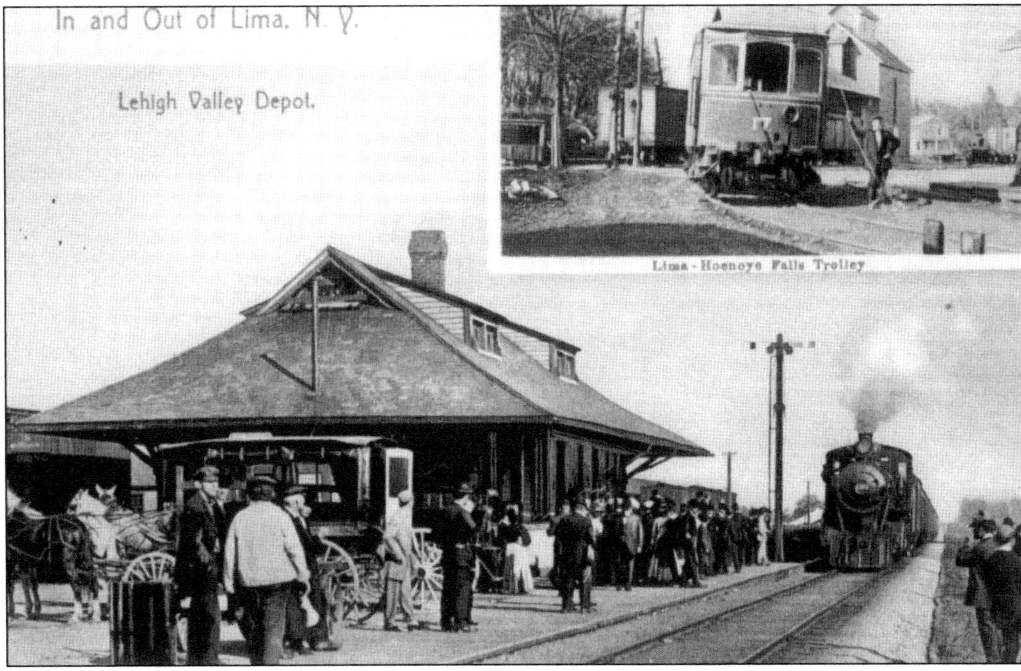

This postcard shows the extent of Lima's railroad options. The small inset depicts the Lima-Honeoye Falls Electric Light and Railroad Company. The large view is the Lehigh Valley depot. The Lehigh put in a branch from Rochester Junction to Hemlock Lake in the 1890s. Originally used at Rochester Junction, this depot was dismantled *c.* 1895 and brought to Lima.

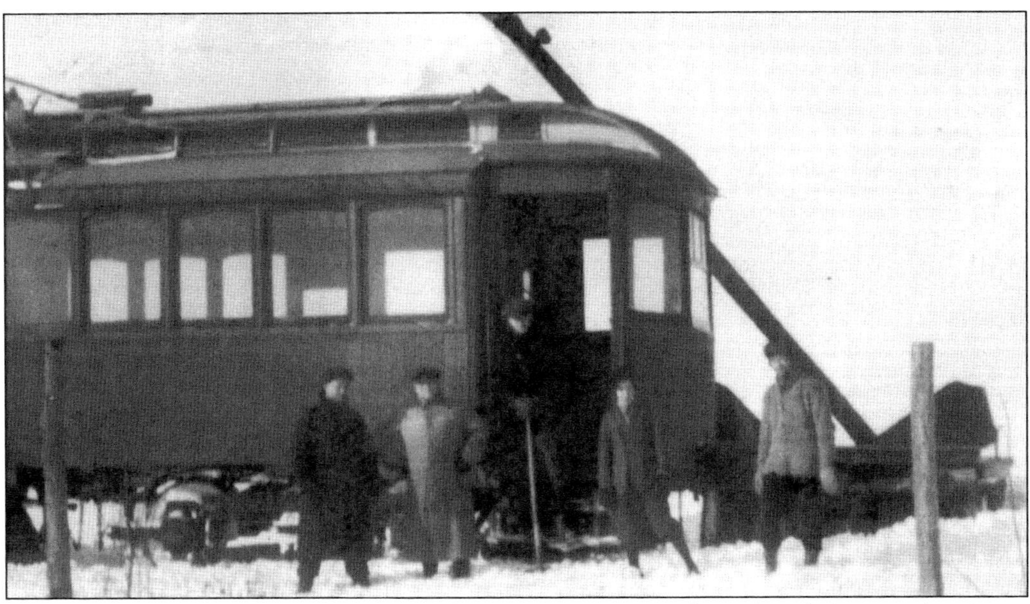

A 1914 postcard reveals an accident on the Lima-Honeoye Falls Railroad. A snowplow being pushed by the trolley has derailed and snapped a trolley pole. Members of the work crew, from left to right, are Bert "Duff" Warner, Ruben "Butsee" Ollerenshaw, Wayne "Pop" Vary, Francis "Monk" O'Dea, and Faye "Dutch" Beecher. The derailed plow is visible behind O'Dea.

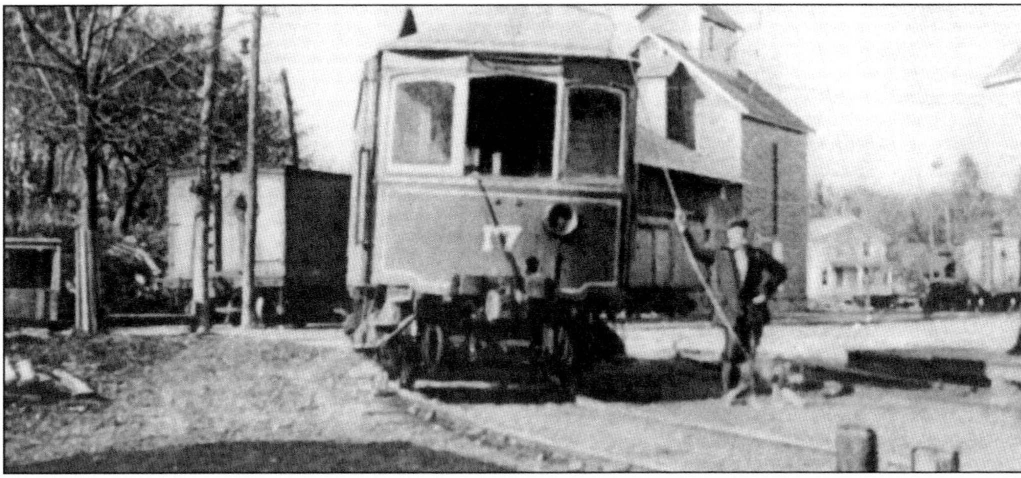

Car No. 17 enters the Lima terminus. The mill in the background is where the library stands today. The hapless little Lima railroad, the adventure of local capitalists desperate for their own link to the outside world, was a financial and maintenance headache from day one. When Lima was chosen as the site for Genesee Wesleyan Seminary, it was because it had no railroad. When the college decided to move to Syracuse, it was, ironically, for that same reason.

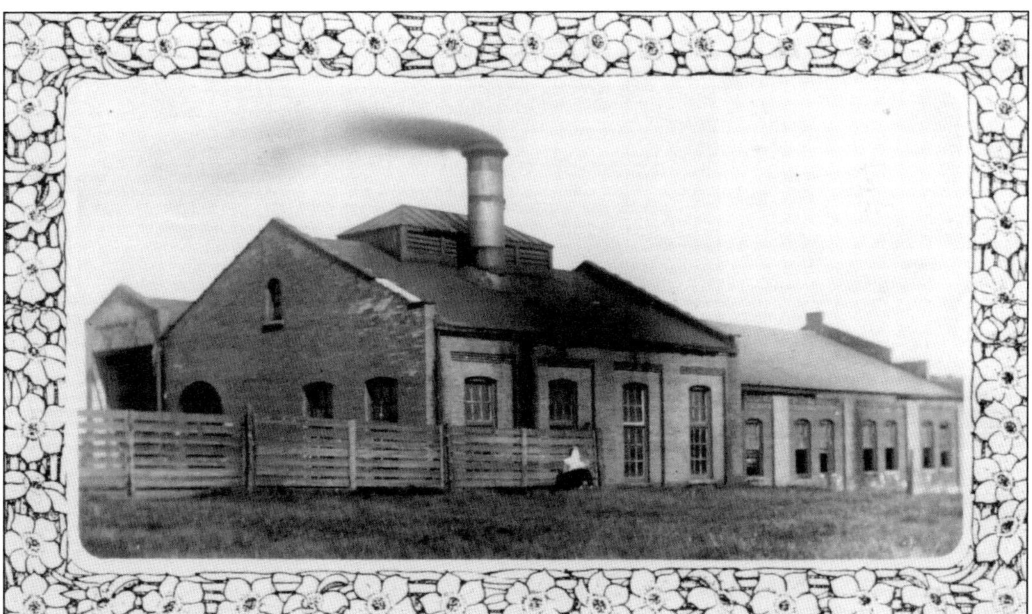

When the railroad converted from steam engines to trolleys, this boiler house was built. The Lima-Honeoye Falls Electric Light and Railroad not only carried passengers over its four miles but also generated electric power to light each village. Students at the seminary gained from the railroad. It connected them to larger lines to get home and took them to dances in Honeoye Falls. Flop that it was, the little line remains a fascinating historical subject.

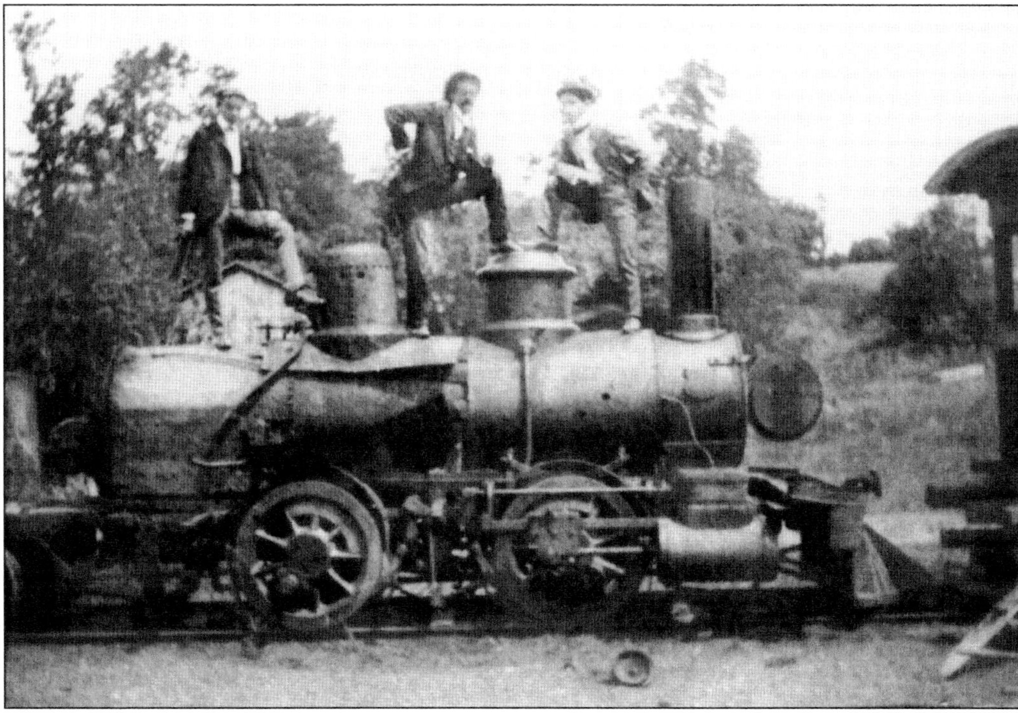

It is the end of line for "Old Jake" of the Lima-Honeoye Falls Railroad. Few traces of the railroad remain today. Paul S. Worboy's book A *Railroad for Lima* offers history and railroad buffs an intriguing account of the little short line. (Jim Laemlein collection.)

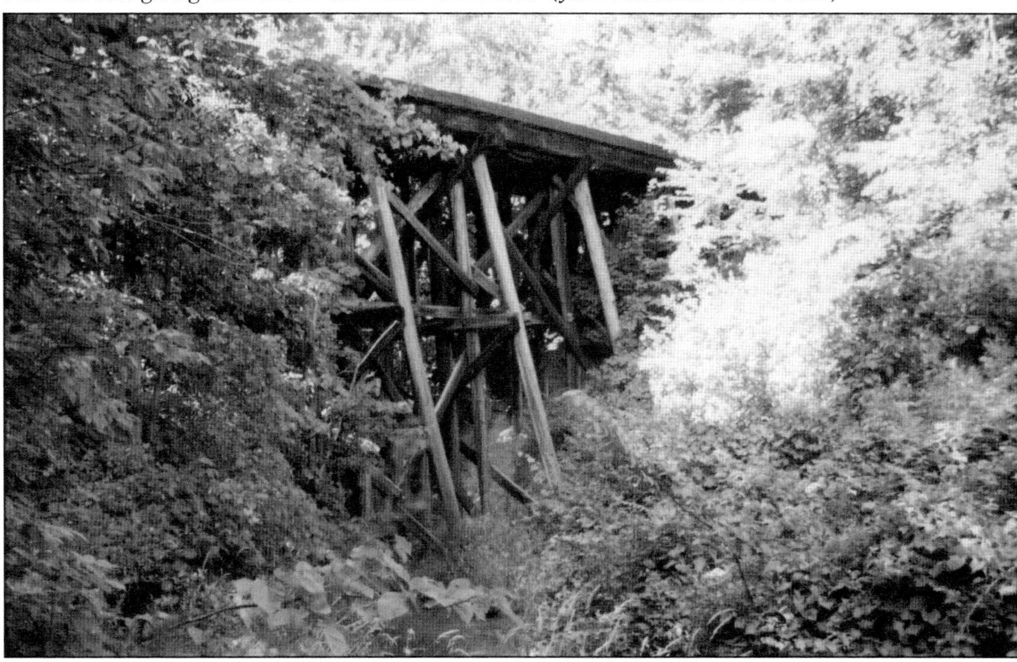

Hidden in farm country south of the village is this abandoned Lehigh Valley trestle. It was here that the line made its turn to Lima. A spur brought clay and carried products from Pinco. The same spur brought employees to Hemlock Lake for joyous annual picnics. (Author's collection.)

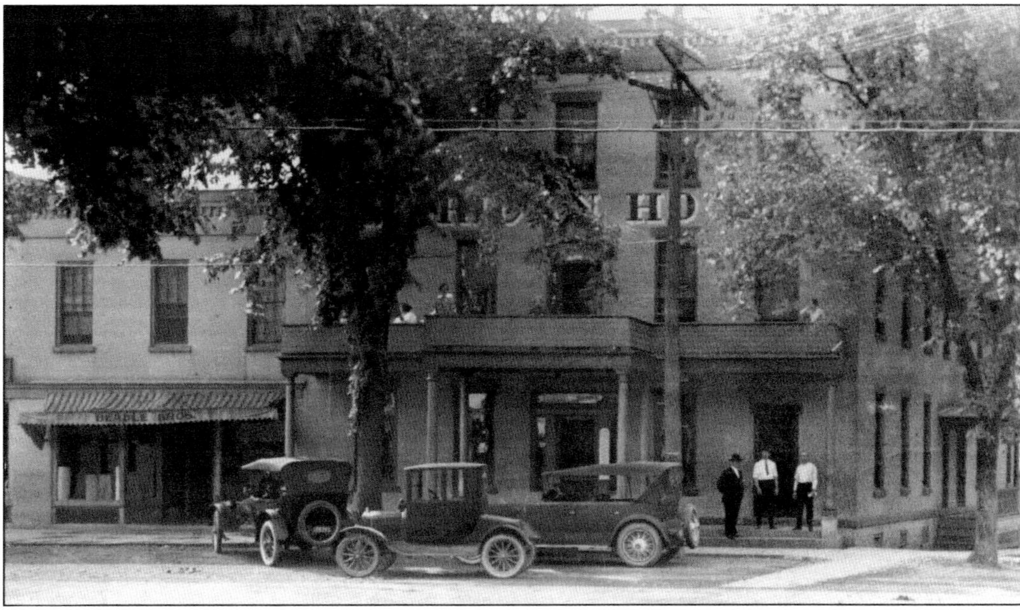

A 1920s postcard view of the American Hotel shows it with its original lower windows. The columns came from the Methodist church towers. There has been an American Hotel on this corner since the 1790s. The hotel has been owned and operated by the Reynolds family since 1920.

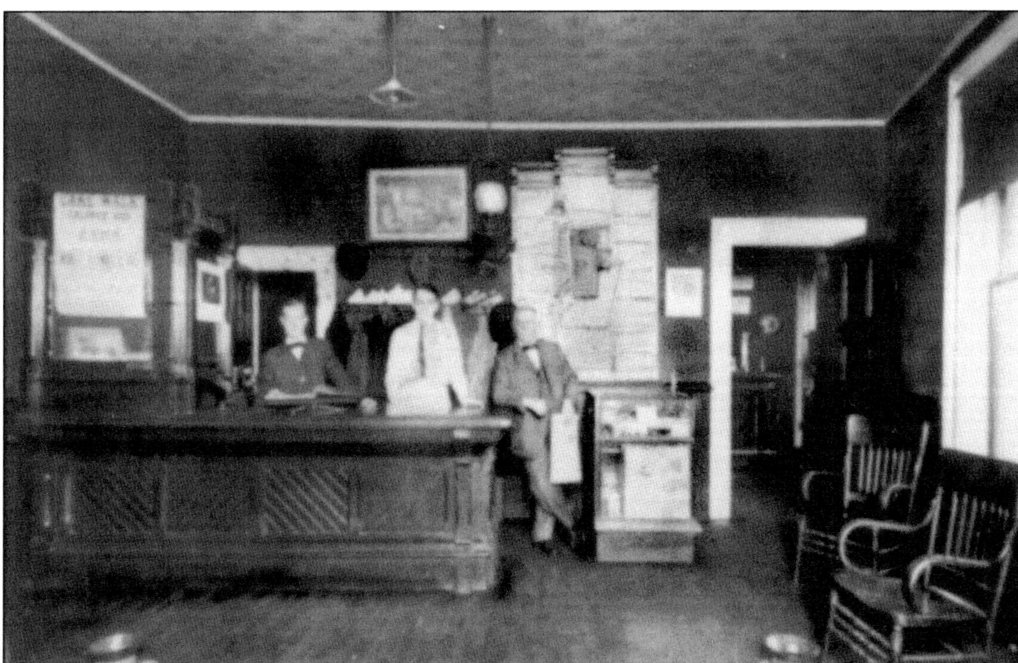

A rare interior image of the American Hotel shows the check-in desk. In this room men could purchase and smoke cigars. Note the spittoons with towels under them.

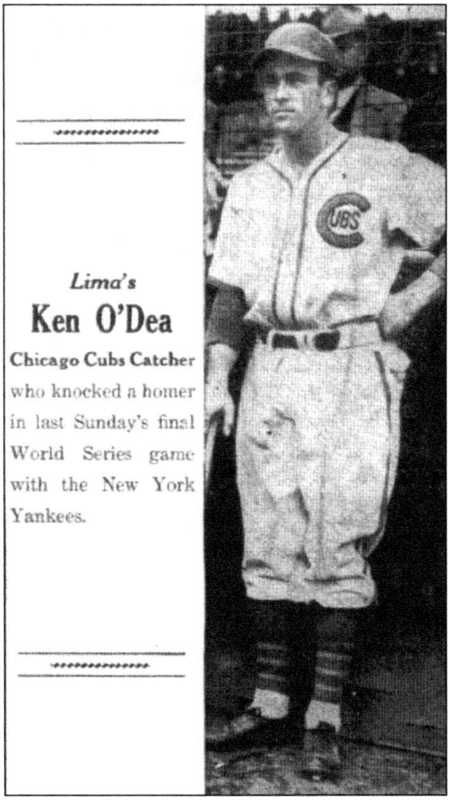

Ken O'Dea of Lima liked to tell hotel patrons about his home run in the last game of the 1938 World Series against the Yankees. He was a Chicago Cubs catcher when he hit a four-ply smash into the right-field stands. Another story he told was how he sometimes kept cool during hot summer games: he would put a few large moist cabbage leaves under his cap. He said it worked.

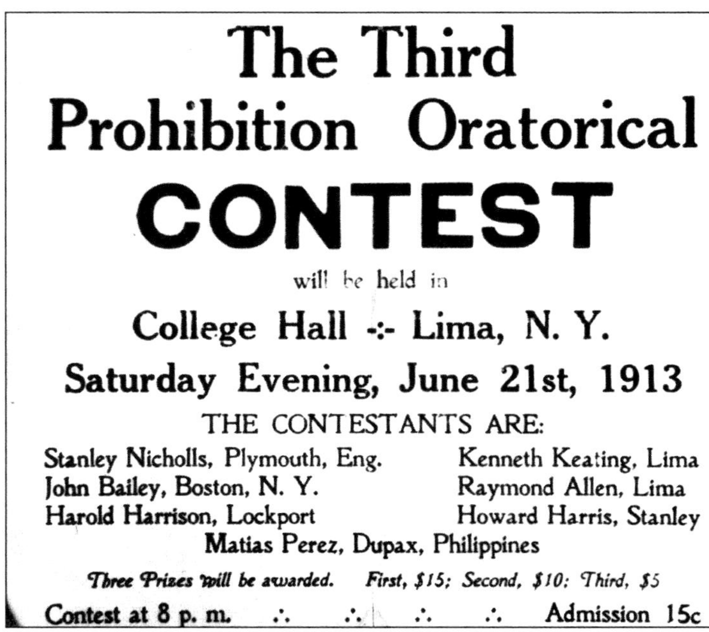

The Third
Prohibition Oratorical
CONTEST
will be held in
College Hall -:- Lima, N. Y.
Saturday Evening, June 21st, 1913
THE CONTESTANTS ARE:

Stanley Nicholls, Plymouth, Eng.	Kenneth Keating, Lima
John Bailey, Boston, N. Y.	Raymond Allen, Lima
Harold Harrison, Lockport	Howard Harris, Stanley

Matias Perez, Dupax, Philippines
Three Prizes will be awarded. First, $15; Second, $10; Third, $5
Contest at 8 p. m. ∴ ∴ ∴ ∴ Admission 15c

For 15 cents you could attend this 1913 oratorical contest on the pros and cons of prohibition. Kenneth Keating spoke, along with guests from around the country and one from the Philippines. The American Hotel weathered the "noble experiment" by converting the bar into a soda fountain. The hotel also served full-menu breakfast, lunch, and dinner to travelers along Routes 5 & 20.

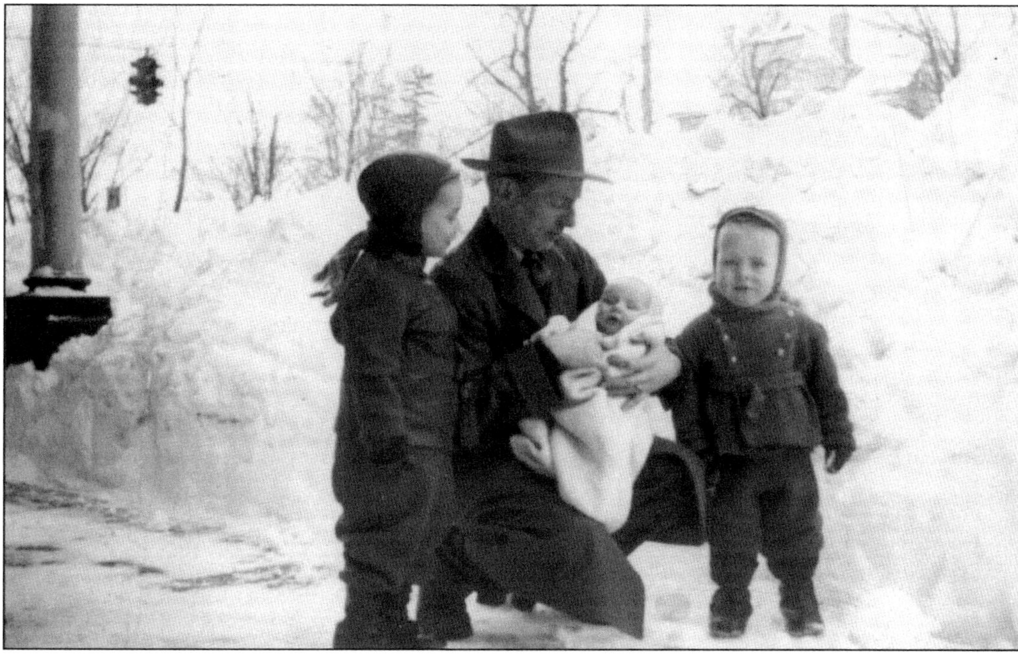

John Reynolds holds his infant son Paul Reynolds beneath the entrance of the American Hotel on a snowy morning. Looking on delightedly are sons Tom Reynolds (left) and Frank Reynolds (right). (Courtesy Pat Reynolds.)

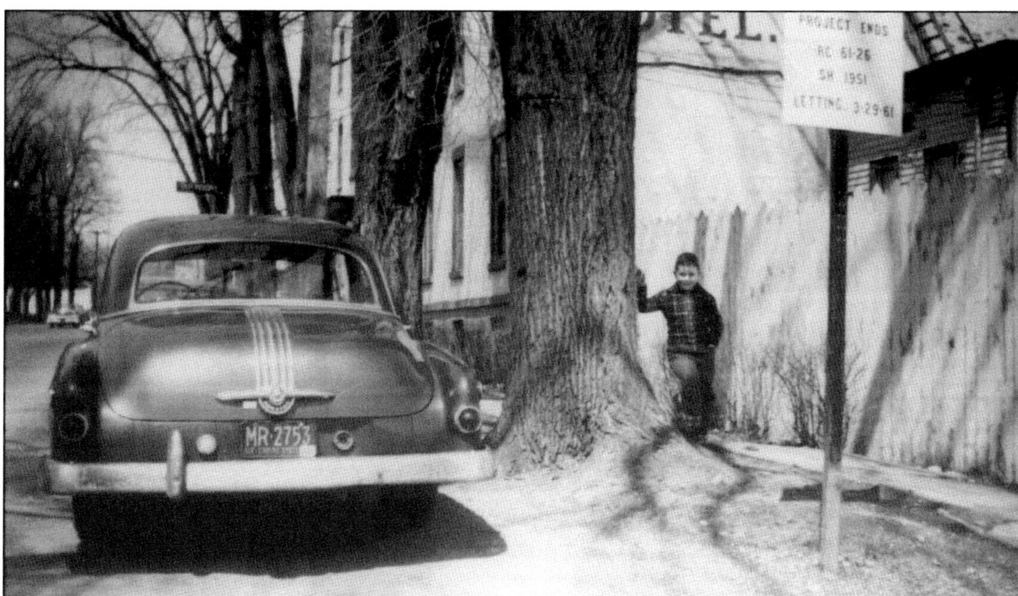

With their family occupying the third floor of the American Hotel, the Reynolds children found downtown Lima to be a suitable playground. In this 1961 photograph, Terry Reynolds stands beside one of the giant elms that shade his hotel. Today, Pat Reynolds carries on the family's tradition of hospitality in partnership with his sister Rose, who has developed a menu of more than 60 soups.

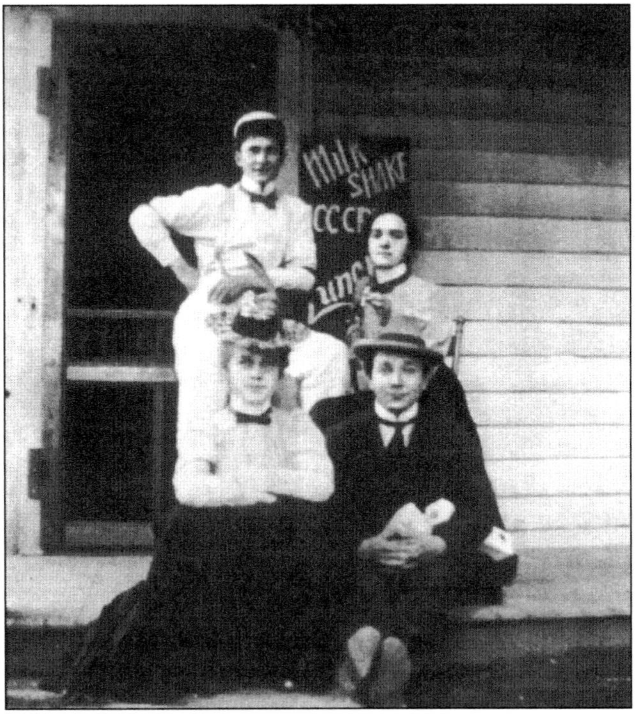

At the time this picture was taken, the store at the corner of Main and Michigan Streets in East Bloomfield offered milk shakes and candy. Relaxing on the steps of that store, these folks seem satisfied. (Courtesy Historical Society of the Town of East Bloomfield.)

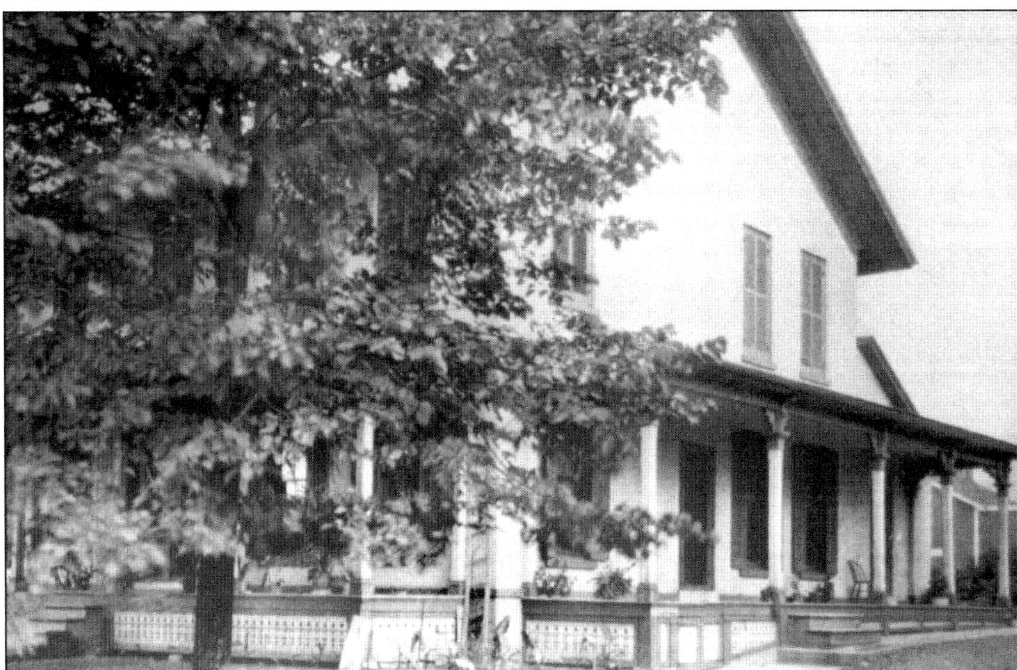

Col. Nathaniel Rochester owned this farm from 1815 to 1818. Bloomfield was founded in 1789, a year after the Phelps-Gorham purchase of nearly three million acres between Lake Ontario and Pennsylvania from the Commonwealth of Massachusetts was sealed. The colonel came from Maryland in the time of land agents and homesteading. In 1833, Bloomfield was divided into East Bloomfield and West Bloomfield.

Three

The Road to Bloomfield

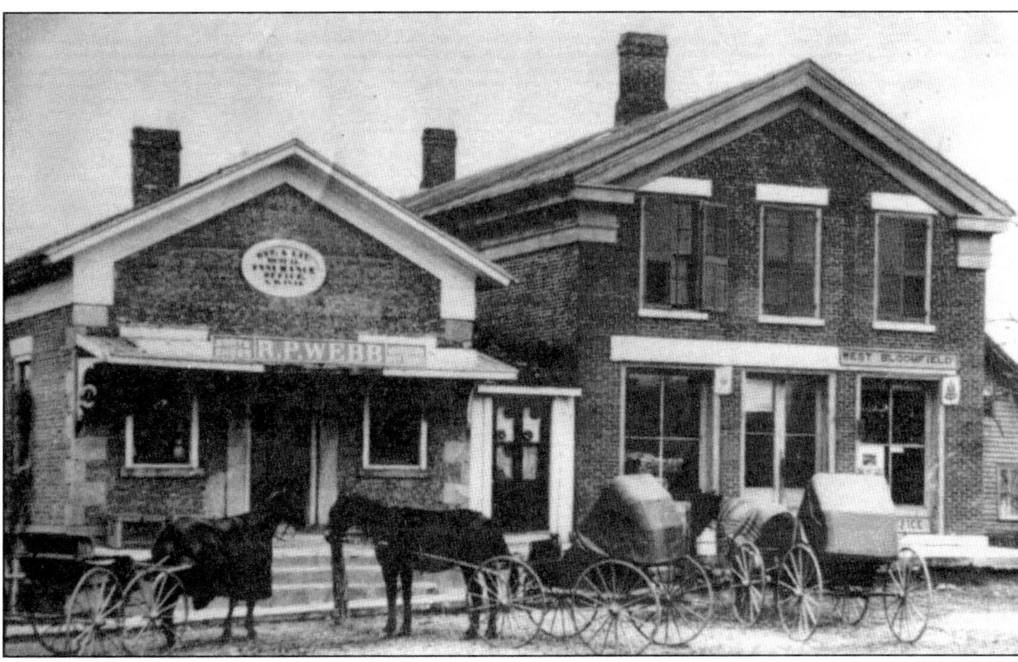

The cobblestone structure (left) was built in 1841 as an insurance company. The brick building (right) was a general store and post office. The store undoubtedly was well stocked with general merchandise, crockery, and domestic goods. This 1910 view of West Bloomfield looks north from the State Road.

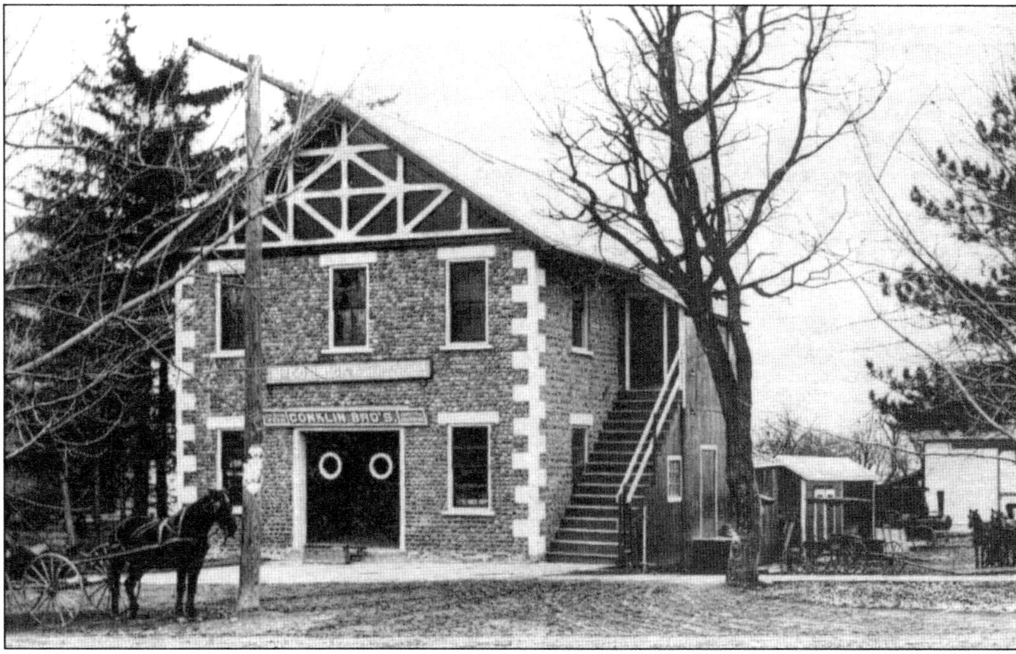

This interesting cobblestone building was constructed prior to 1850 in West Bloomfield. The 1910 view shows it during the period in which it was owned by Conklin Brothers, dealers in farm implements and operators of a feed mill.

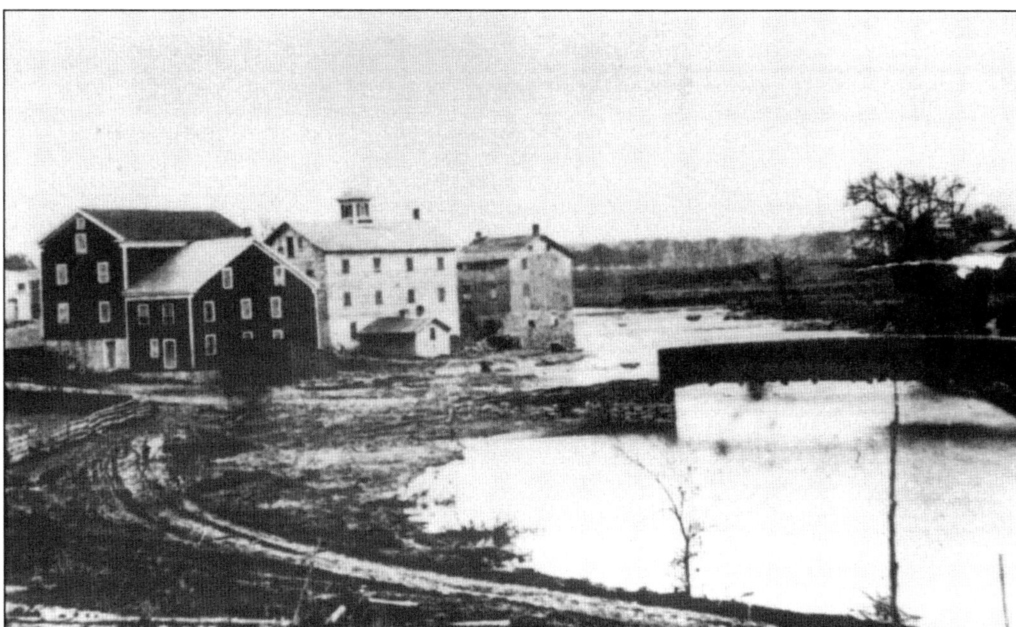

Muddy and trampled and virtually plantless, this mill complex across from Bean Road in North Bloomfield conveys the drudgery and grind that early citizens faced. Not far from this site, Frs. Joseph Charienot and Fremen, on behalf of France, evangelized to Senecas in a small chapel while trying to swindle them out of their lands. (Courtesy West Bloomfield Historical Society.)

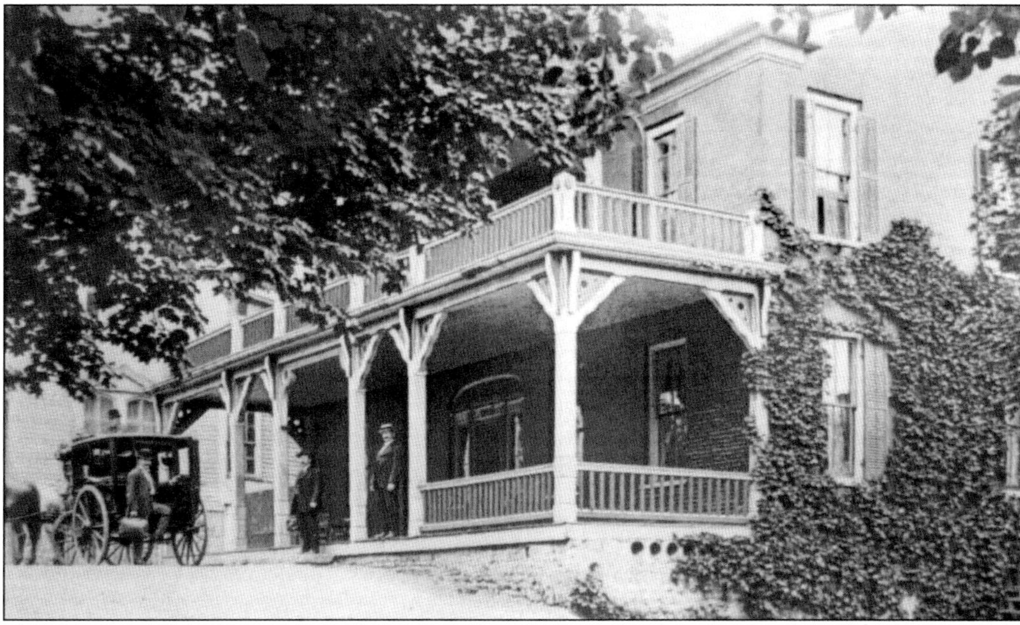

As Bloomfield prospered, rustic gave way to elegant. The East Bloomfield House, built in 1812 by Jared Boughton, has an important aspect to it. The owners prided themselves on the accommodations they offered stagecoach travelers. Unlike canal travel, which was quiet and smooth, stagecoach travel was miserable. Passengers were cramped, jostled, and deprived of sleep. (Courtesy Historical Society of the Town of East Bloomfield.)

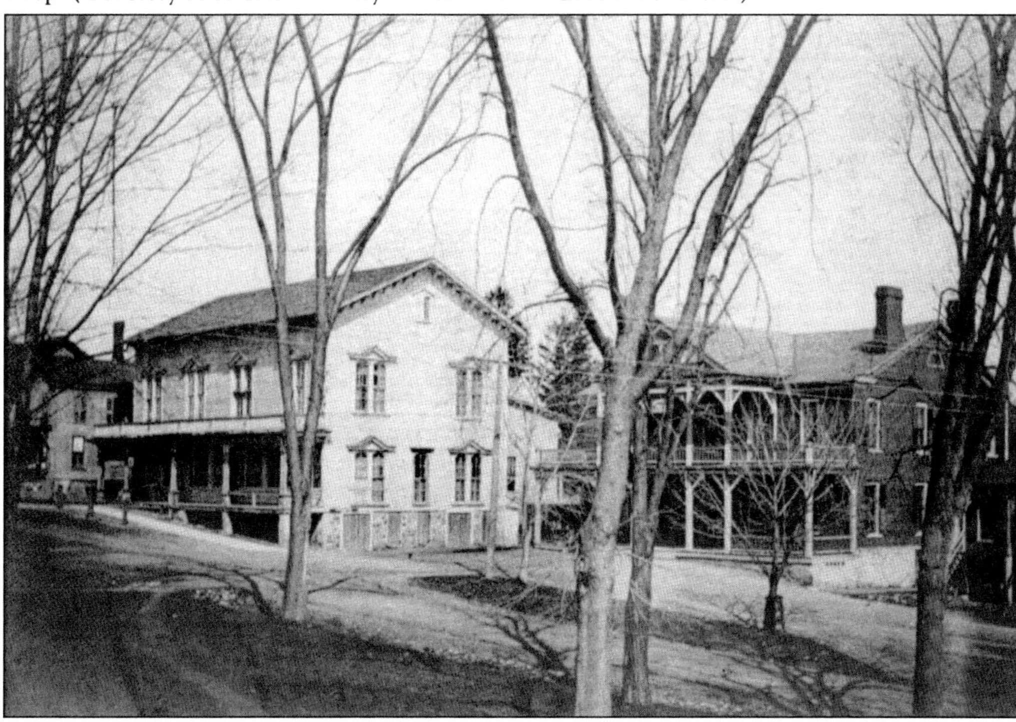

The building on the left is Bradley Hall, site of Victorian era social events. Behind it is the East Bloomfield House. (Courtesy Historical Society of the Town of East Bloomfield.)

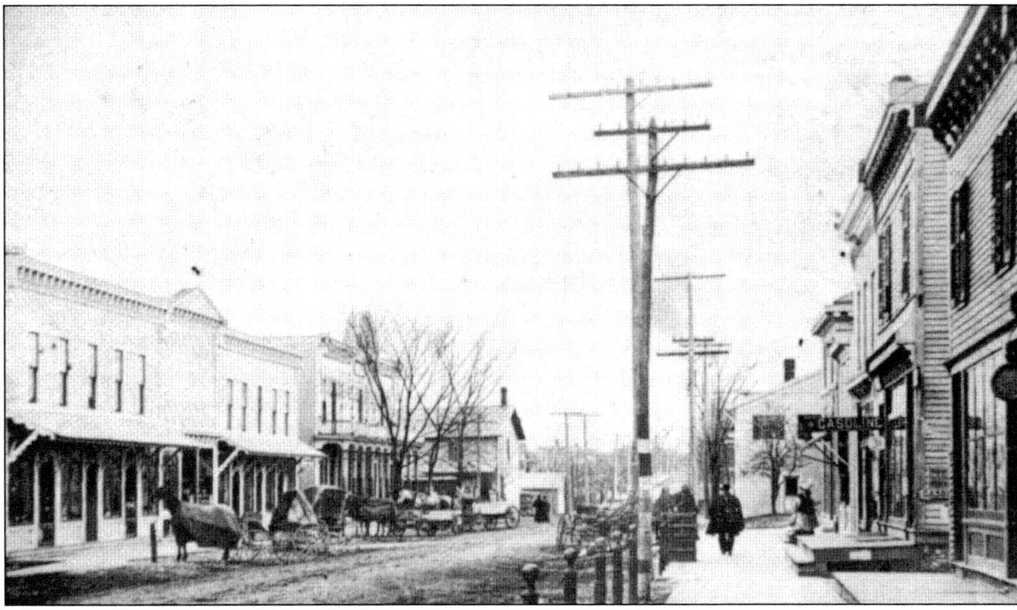

This c. 1910 view shows Main Street in Holcomb (East Bloomfield). Most of the buildings on the right are still standing today. (Courtesy Historical Society of the Town of East Bloomfield.)

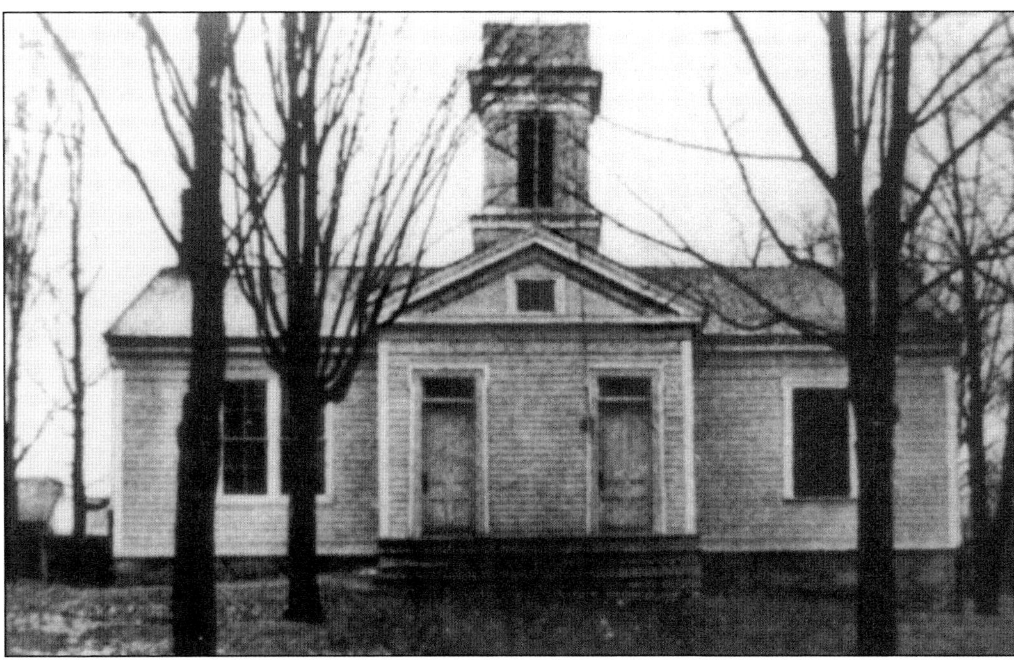

As early as 1796, Bloomfield citizens saw to it that their children had a school. Prior to 1812, they founded an academy. By 1913, West Bloomfield was divided into nine school districts. Pictured is the West Bloomfield School as it appeared c. 1913. (Courtesy West Bloomfield Historical Society.)

The First Congregational Church on the green in East Bloomfield is typical of the fine churches worshipers have established in what is truly a remarkable agricultural and industrial community. (Courtesy Historical Society of the Town of East Bloomfield.)

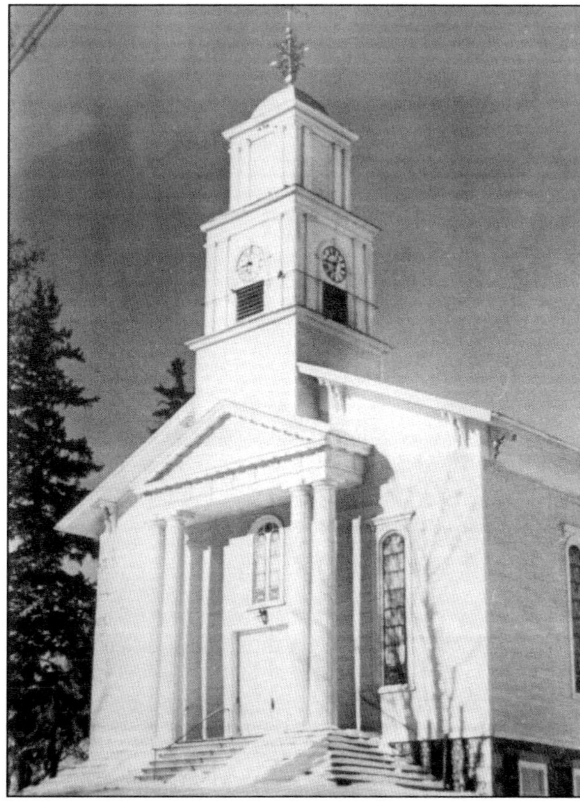

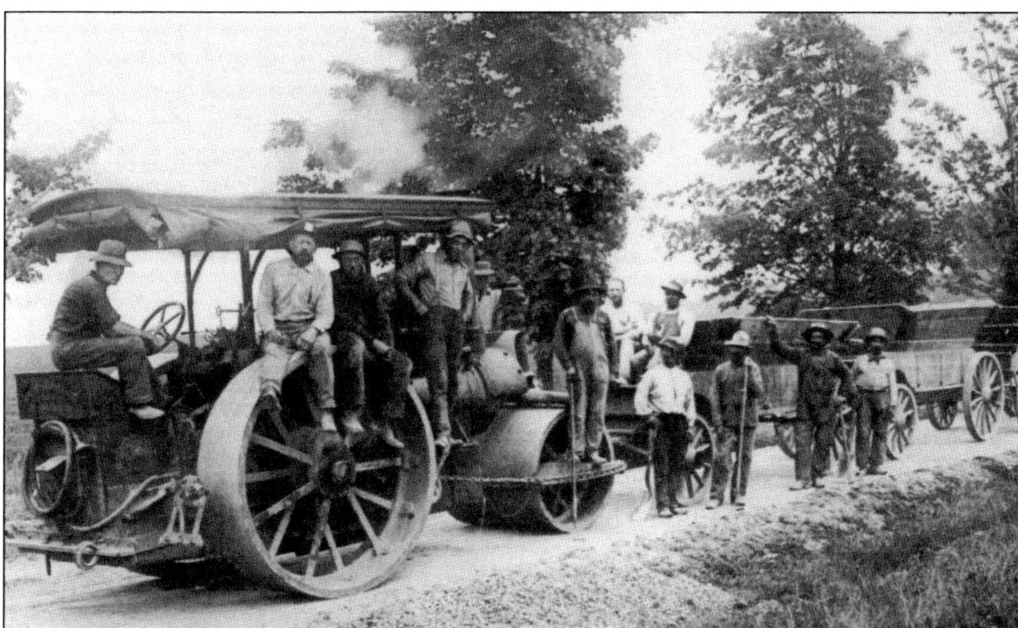

A crew prepares for a day of road improvements. The bulky tractor is steamed up and ready for rolling. A train of heavy wheeled gondolas, filled with dirt, gravel, and tools, is prepared to go. (Courtesy Historical Society of the Town of East Bloomfield.)

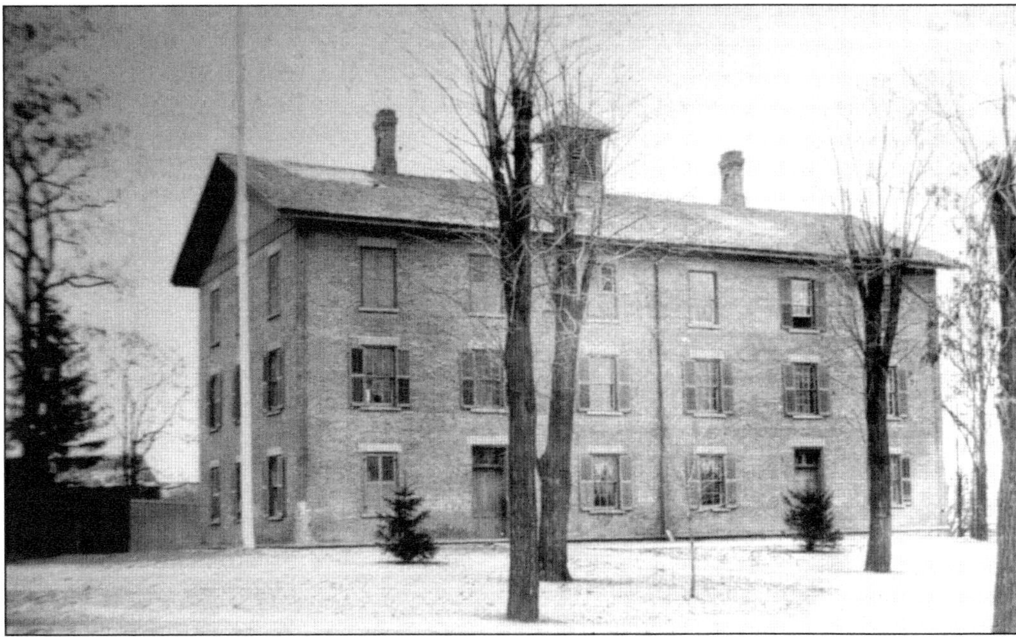

The Bloomfield Academy opened in May of 1838 "for the purpose of establishing, maintaining, and conducting a Seminary of learning for the proper education of youth of both sexes." It now houses the Historical Society of East Bloomfield and the Antique Wireless Association and Electronic Communication Museum. (Courtesy Historical Society of the Town of East Bloomfield.)

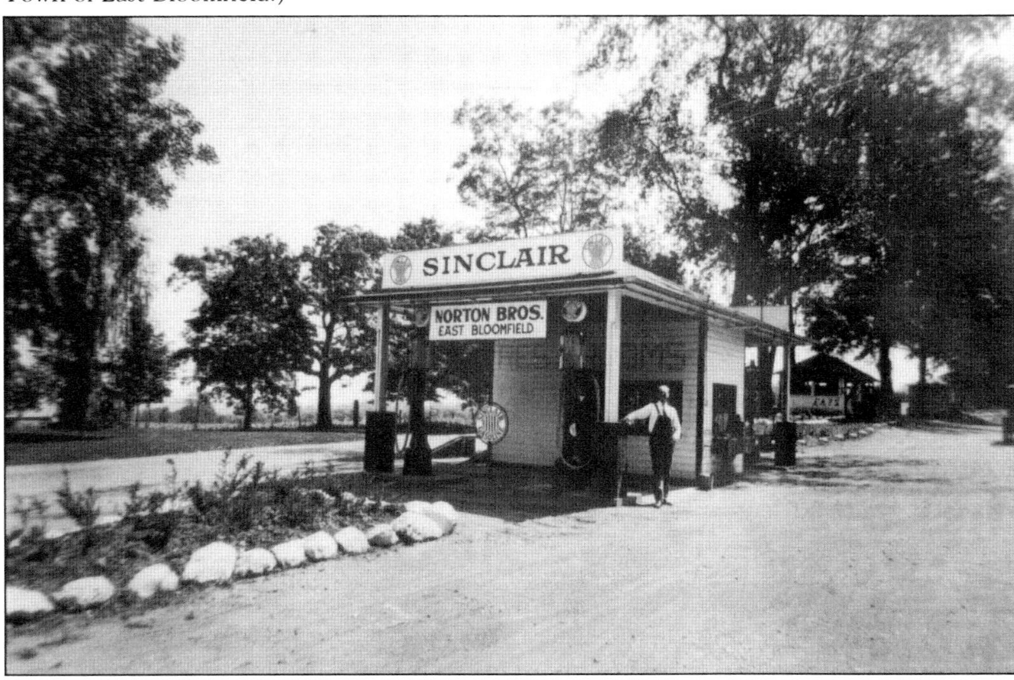

Norton Brothers Garage occupied a small triangle between Routes 5 & 20 and 20C. Along with Sinclair gas, the garage provided rest rooms. A sign on the small pavilion behind the station reads "EATS."

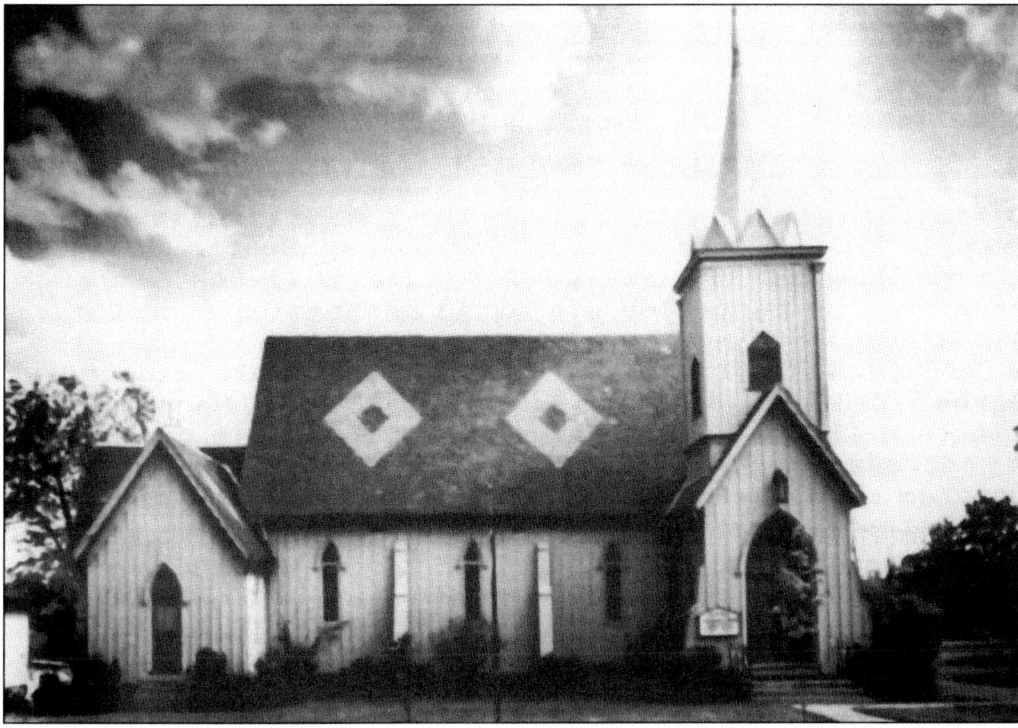

In the 1830s, individual Episcopalians took turns holding Sunday services in their homes. As the parish grew, the congregation moved to different sites. In 1871, the group began work on this lovely church. (Courtesy Historical Society of the Town of East Bloomfield.)

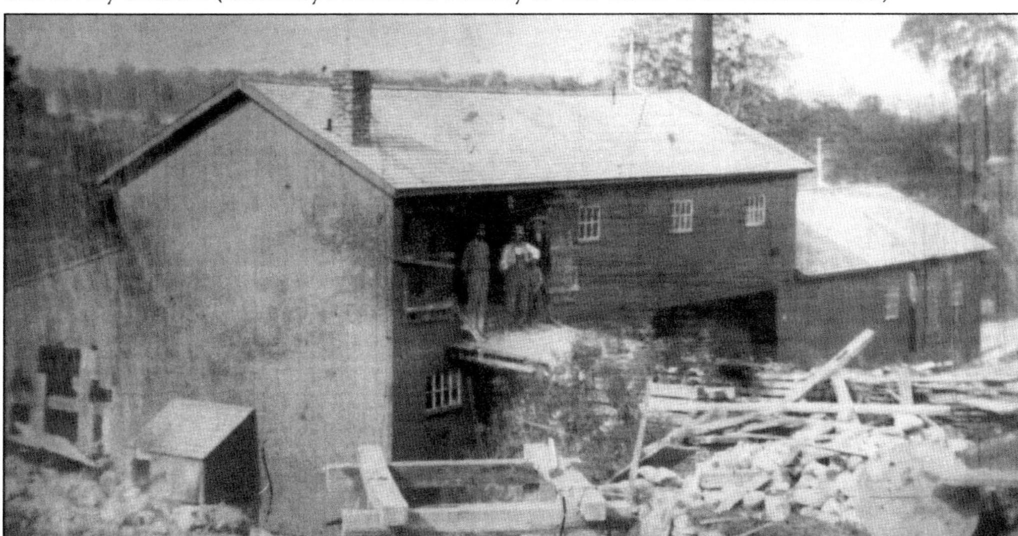

This busy sawmill was located just outside town. Along Mud Creek numerous mills kept Bloomfield on sound financial footing. "New York State soft white winter wheat," grown primarily around Bloomfield, was in demand in London and France. In fact, the world price for wheat was set not far away in Canandaigua. Wheat was shipped to the milling center of Rochester via the Erie Canal. Drop-offs were made at Palmyra and Bushnell's Basin. (Courtesy Historical Society of the Town of East Bloomfield.)

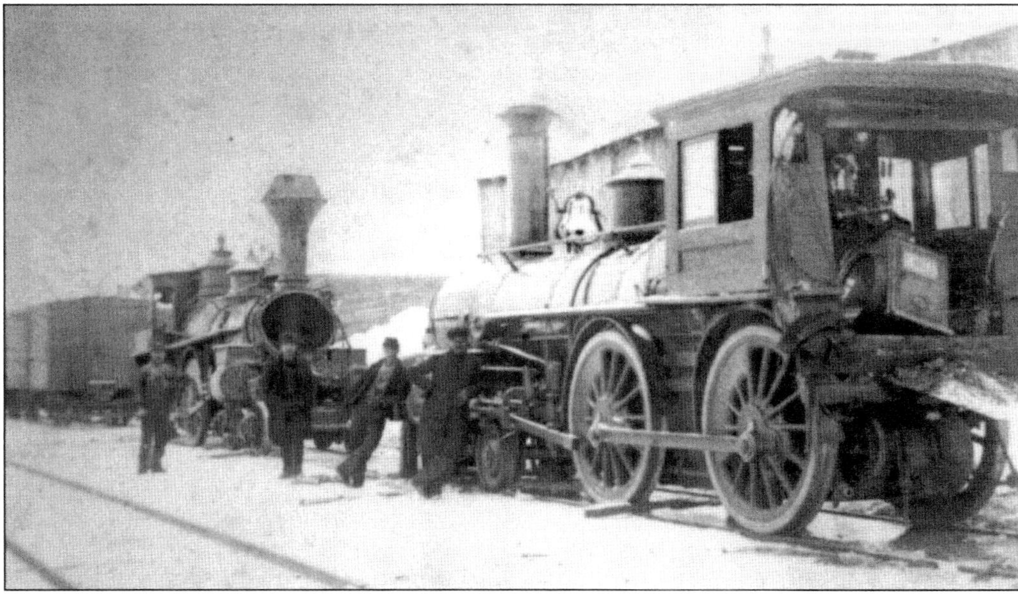

It appears that these two steam engines locked horns somewhere down the line. With the Erie Canal bypassing Bloomfield, railroads were vital to an incredibly industrious community. Threshing machines were manufactured here. There were five flour mills alone along Mud Creek. Gould hats were made here, as were clocks and carriages of such quality that Studebaker studied them. Additionally, there were chair makers, at least seven distilleries, two tanneries, two gun shops, and a potash factory or two. (Courtesy Historical Society of the Town of East Bloomfield.)

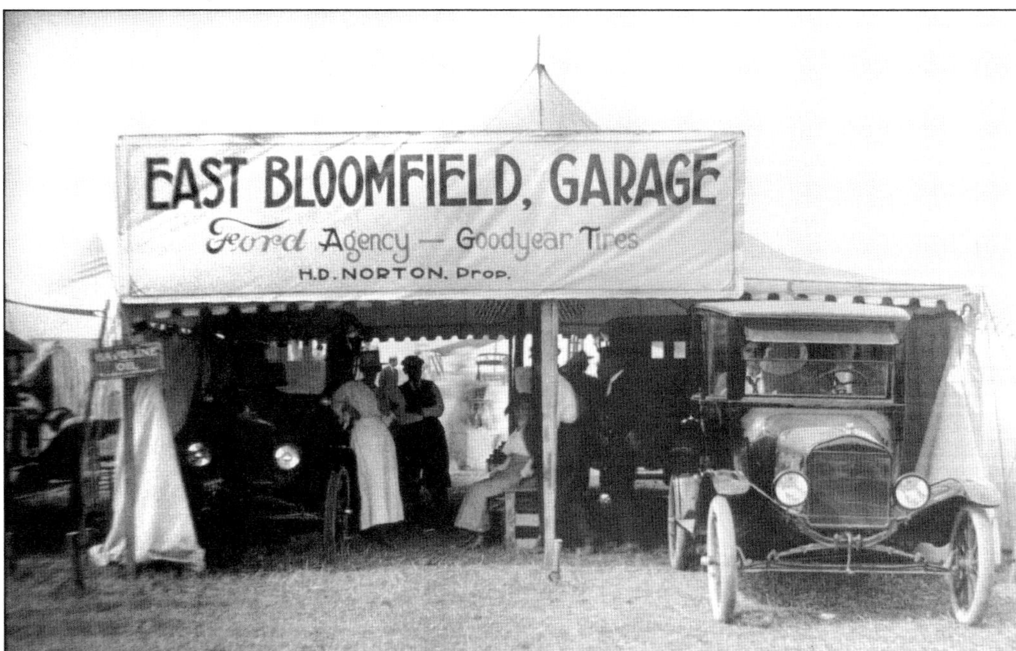

It is 1919, and Harry Norton is showing off some Fords from his dealership at the Livingston County Fair. He sold Goodyear tires as well.

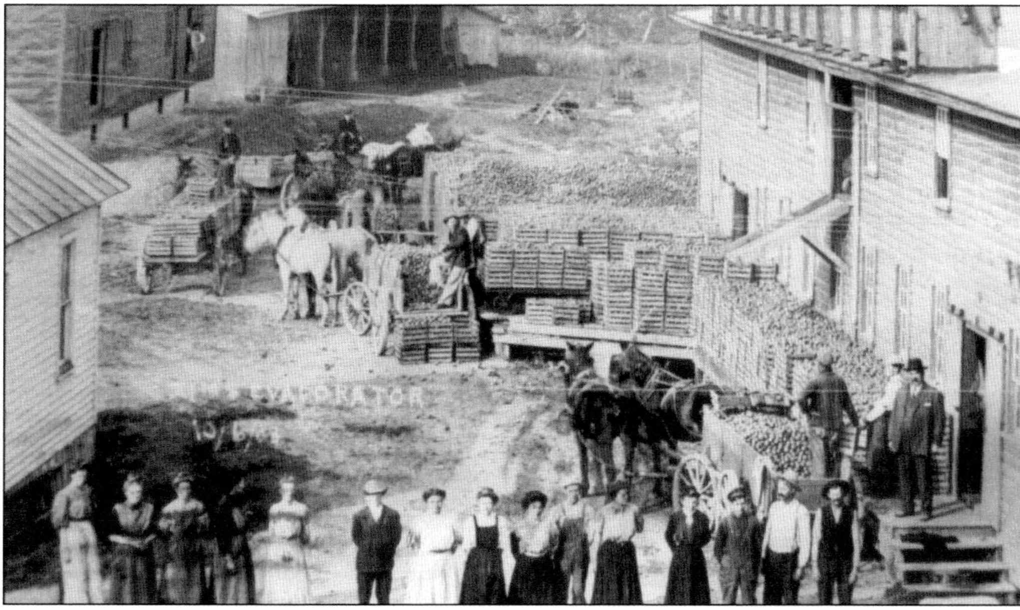

Zim's Evaporator business was located on the west side of Elm Street. Proprietor C.F. Zimerman also sold farm implements and ran an agency for Sampson tractors. The complex was later taken over by Elmer Wood, who made pickles and sauerkraut here, as well as dealing in coal and fuel oil. (Courtesy Historical Society of the Town of East Bloomfield.)

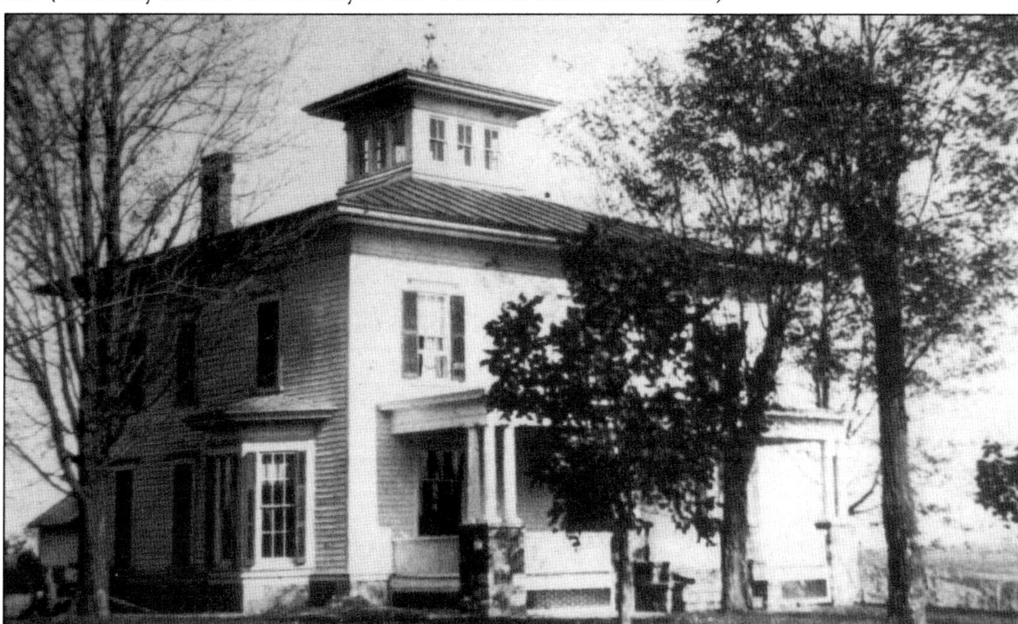

Travelers leaving the hustle and bustle of Canandaigua marveled at the sophistication of Bloomfield. The schools, homes, and churches were of the finest quality, such as the Jessie Adams house on Routes 5 & 20. When they arrived to buy or speculate on wool for their mills, New Englanders may have imagined Bloomfield as the boondocks populated by "apple knockers," but they certainly thought otherwise upon leaving. (Courtesy Historical Society of the Town of East Bloomfield.)

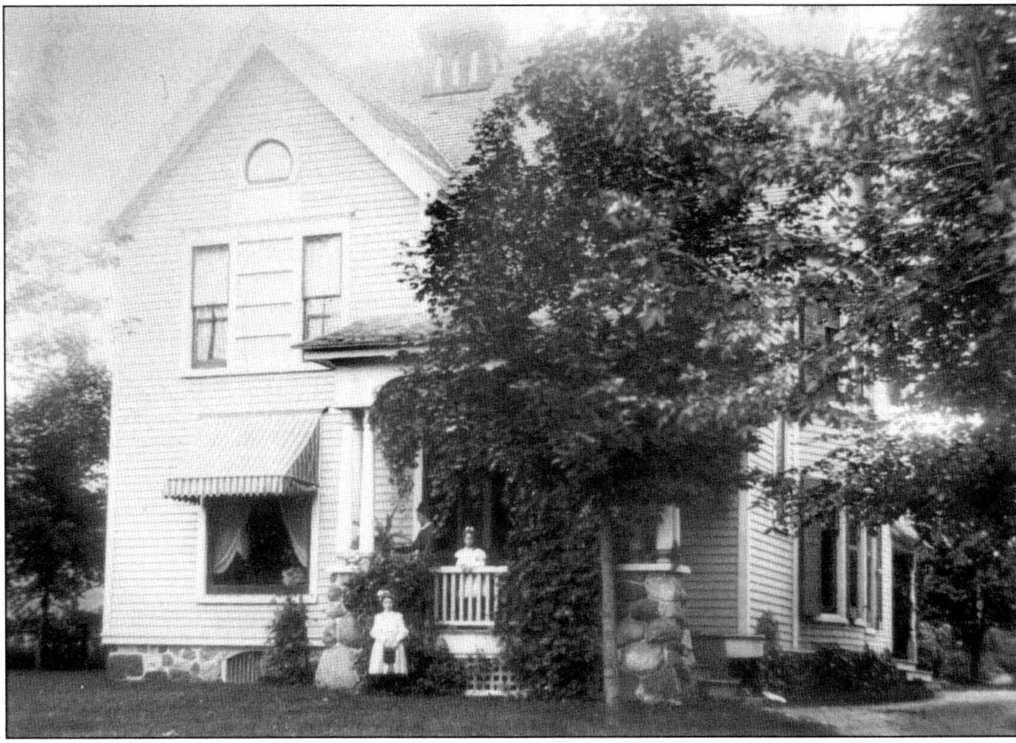

The Wheeler home on Main Street is another example of the exquisite craftsmanship found in Bloomfield homes. A small carriage stoop extends from the porch. This picture dates from *c.* 1915. (Courtesy Historical Society of the Town of East Bloomfield.)

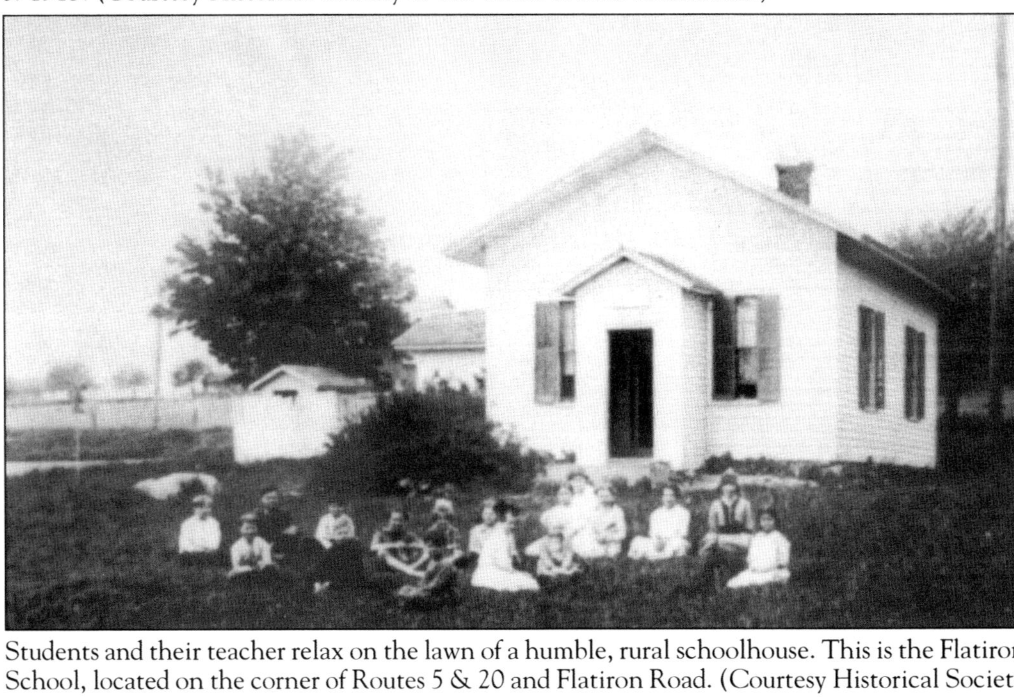

Students and their teacher relax on the lawn of a humble, rural schoolhouse. This is the Flatiron School, located on the corner of Routes 5 & 20 and Flatiron Road. (Courtesy Historical Society of the Town of East Bloomfield.)

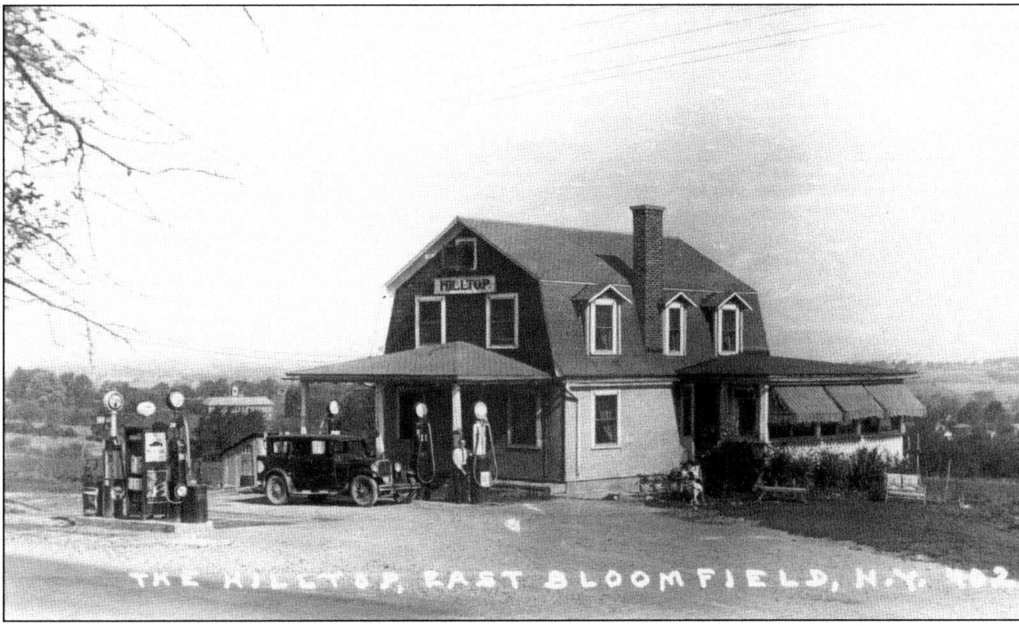

The Bloomfields had some of the most picturesque gas stations around. In those days the attendant stuck a wood ruler into the gas tank, which was located under the driver's seat. When pulled out, the ruler showed the gasoline level, indicating how much additional fuel was needed. (Courtesy Shirley Ruth.)

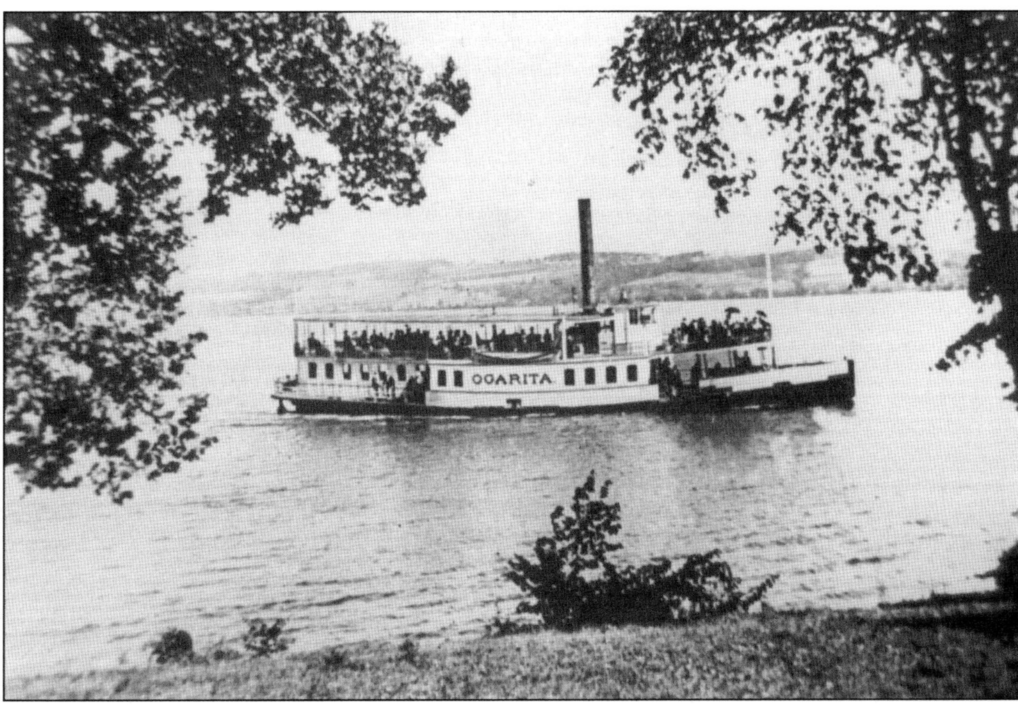

The steamer *Ogarita* takes passengers on a tour of Canandaigua Lake. The hardworking citizens of Bloomfield, deservedly, used the lake for much of their recreation.

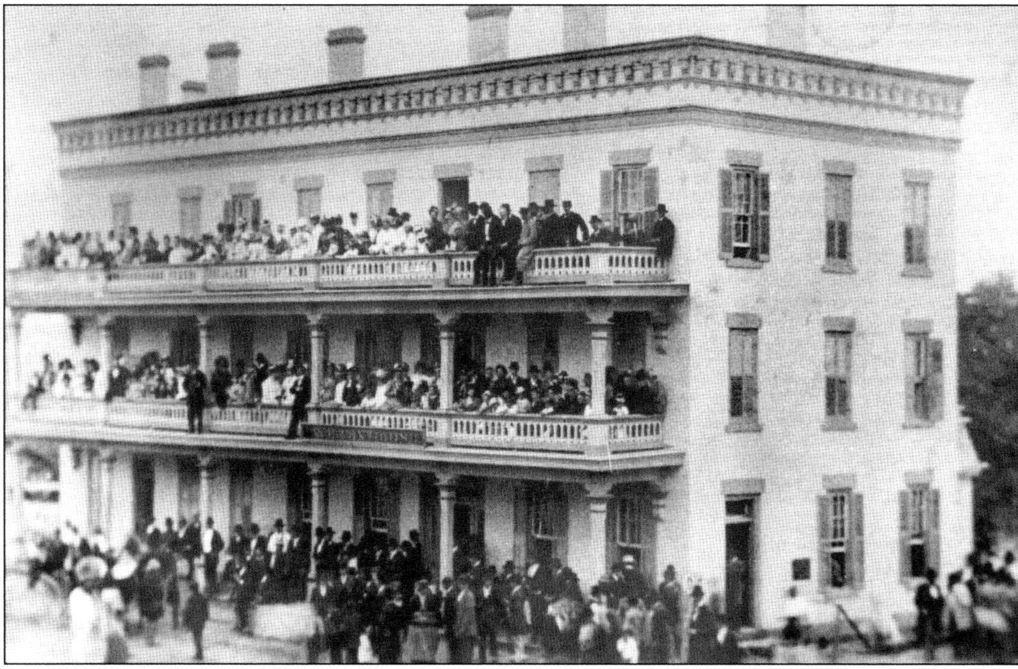

The Wilcox House in Honeoye Falls, located on the northeast corner of North Main Street, was formerly the Falls Hotel. It was enlarged and embellished by owners Sylvester Wilcox and Frederick Hubbell in 1861. The Masons acquired it in 1920. (Courtesy Honeoye Falls Village Historian Anne Bullock.)

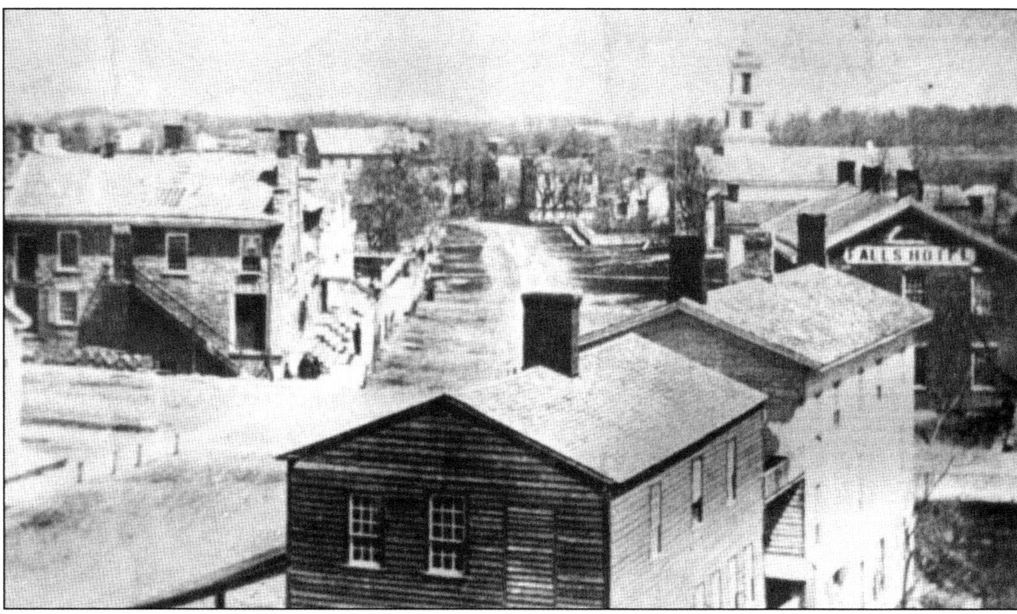

The oldest known view of Honeoye Falls is this 1858 view looking north on Main Street. It was along this road that fugitive slaves were ushered by conductors on the Underground Railroad to designated homes on Clover Street. Honeoye Falls was incorporated in 1838. Prior to then it was West Mendon and, more hesitantly, Norton's Mills. (Courtesy Honeoye Falls Village Historian Anne Bullock.)

Four

Images of Honeoye Falls

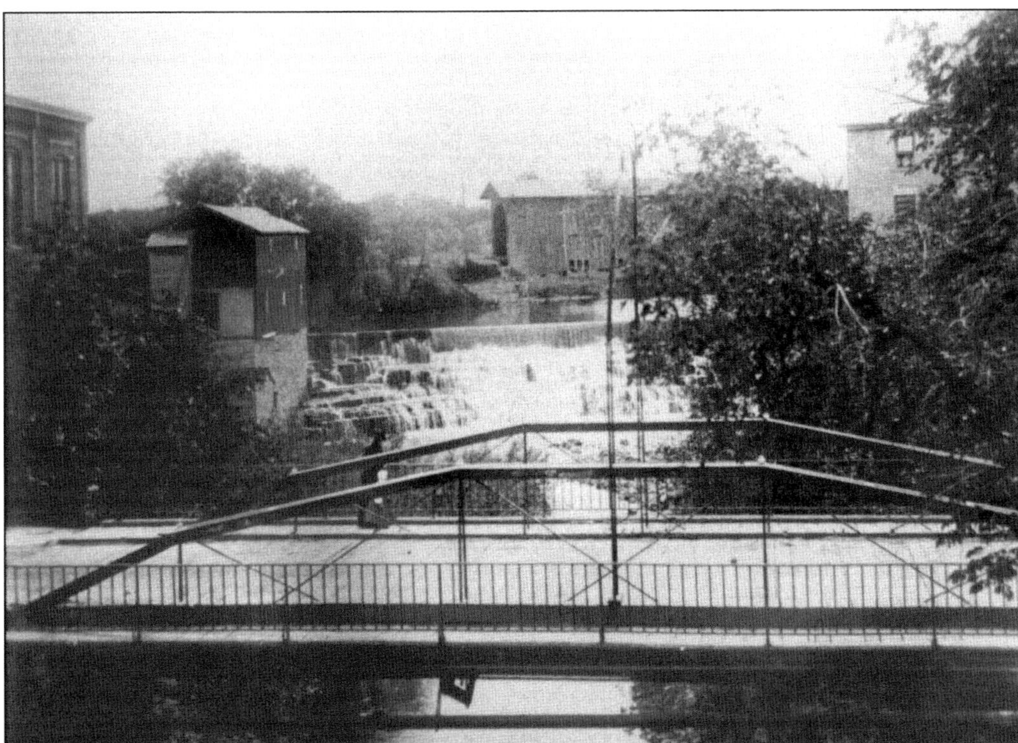

Blessed with abundant waterpower, Honeoye Falls attracted settlers from Connecticut, Massachusetts, and New Hampshire. In the distance is the *c*. 1853 covered railroad bridge that carried the New York Central over Honeoye Creek. The Upper Mill is to the right; a sawmill is across the creek.

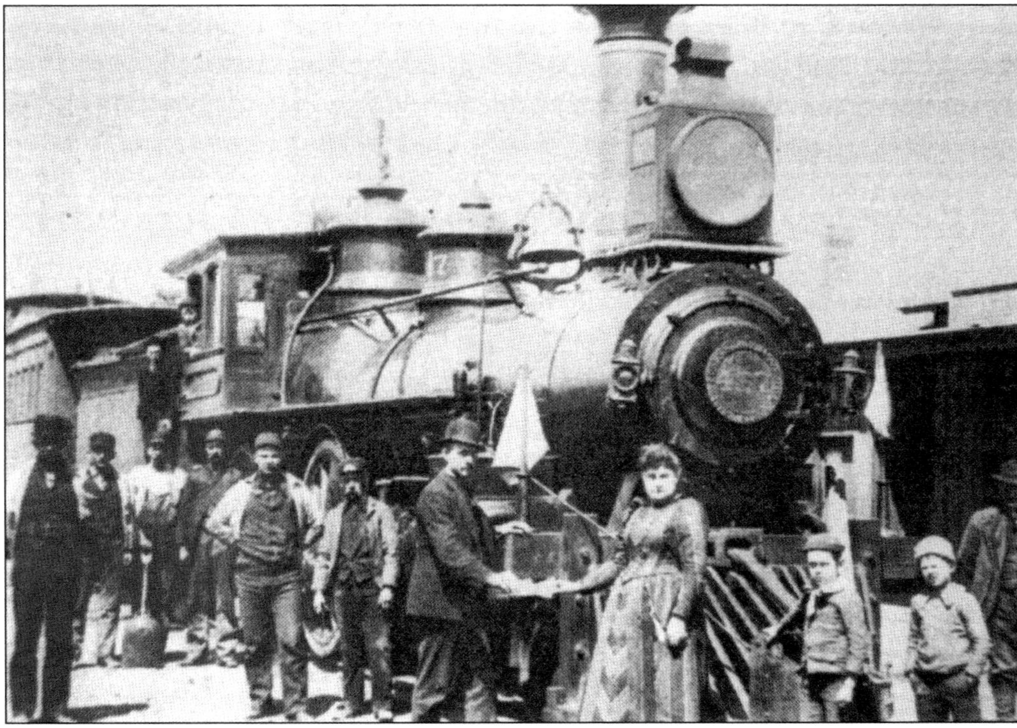

Between 1853 and 1961, with barely 2,000 citizens, Honeoye Falls was self-sufficient to the point of being serviced by three railroads. A handsome steam engine in the New York Central Peanut Branch yard is adorned with fancy ironwork and polished brass. Village streets were often congested with wagons loaded with produce, many from South Lima, lined up waiting to unload. (Courtesy Honeoye Falls Village Historian Anne Bullock.)

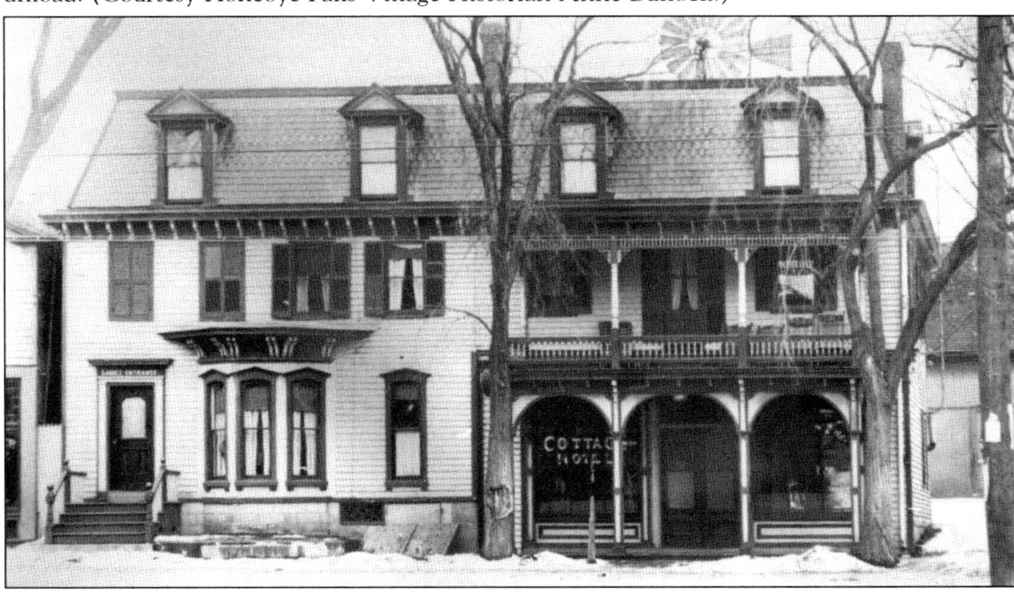

Big dormers, small porches, gingerbread, brackets, and a clumsy bay decorate the Cottage Hotel on North Main Street. Note the "Ladies Entrance" sign over door on the left. (Courtesy Honeoye Falls Village Historian Anne Bullock.)

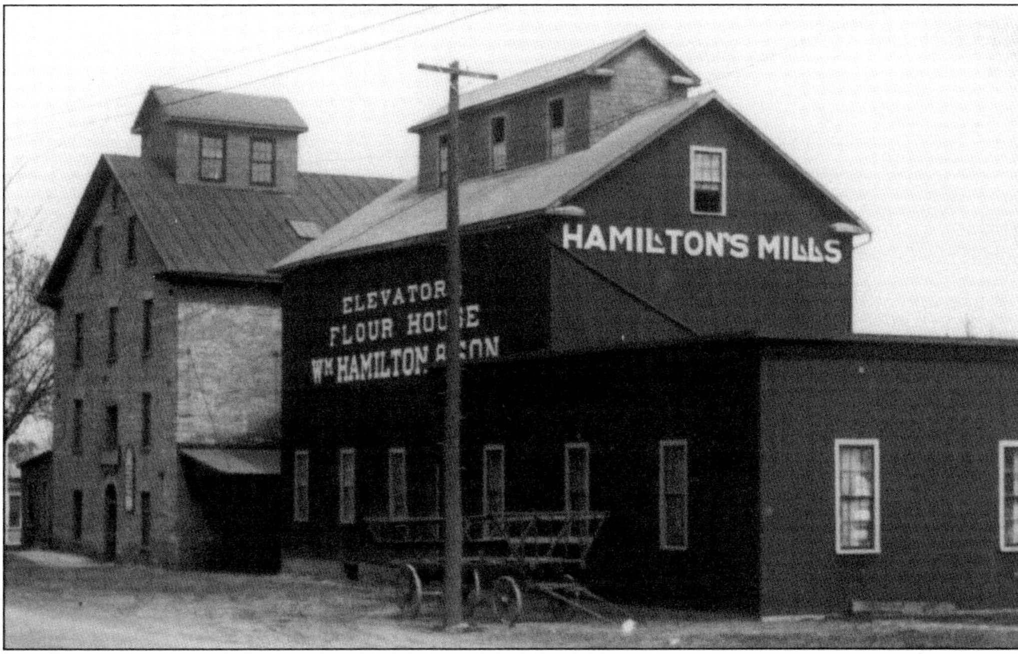

The William Hamilton & Son Elevator and Flour House along with the Upper Mill are pictured in this *c.* 1900 view. (Courtesy Shirley Ruth.)

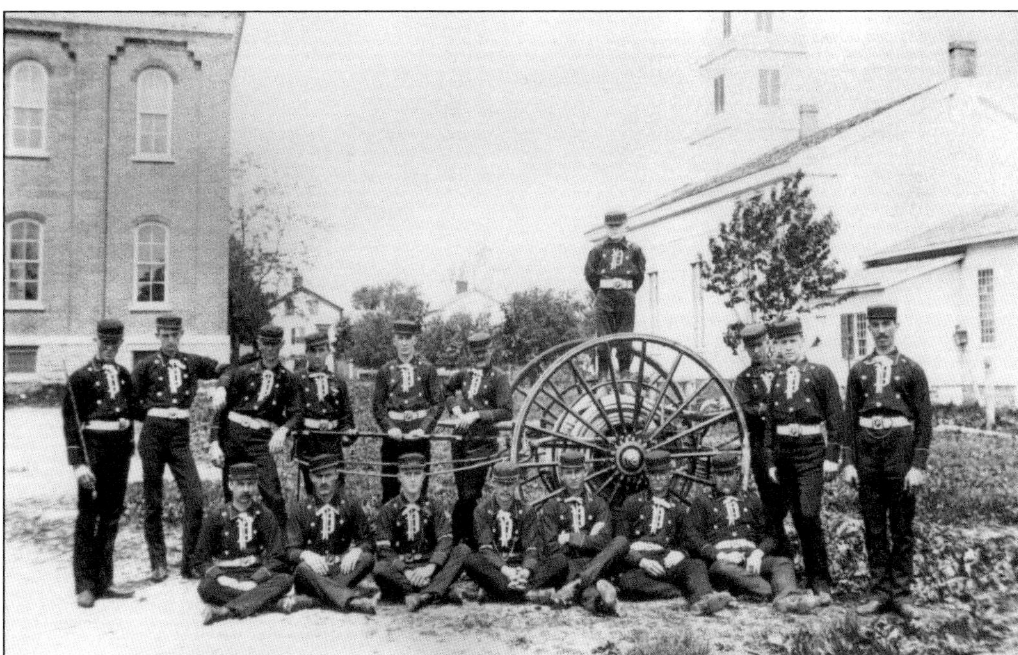

The Protectors, volunteer members of the Honeoye Falls Fire Department, pose around their hose cart in this 1888 photograph. The Presbyterian church and Honeoye Falls Free Union School are behind them. (Courtesy Honeoye Falls Village Historian Anne Bullock.)

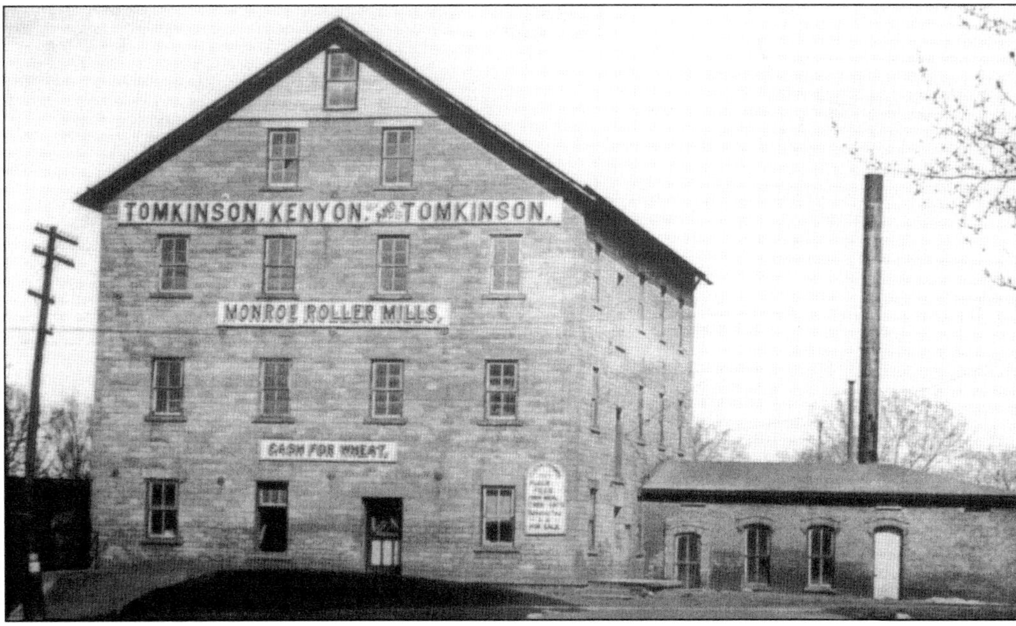

Erected between 1827 and 1837, the Lower Mill ground tons of flour that was shipped all over the world. The mill has housed several industries and businesses in its long history. It is believed the stone used to build it was from quarries north of the village. (Courtesy Shirley Ruth.)

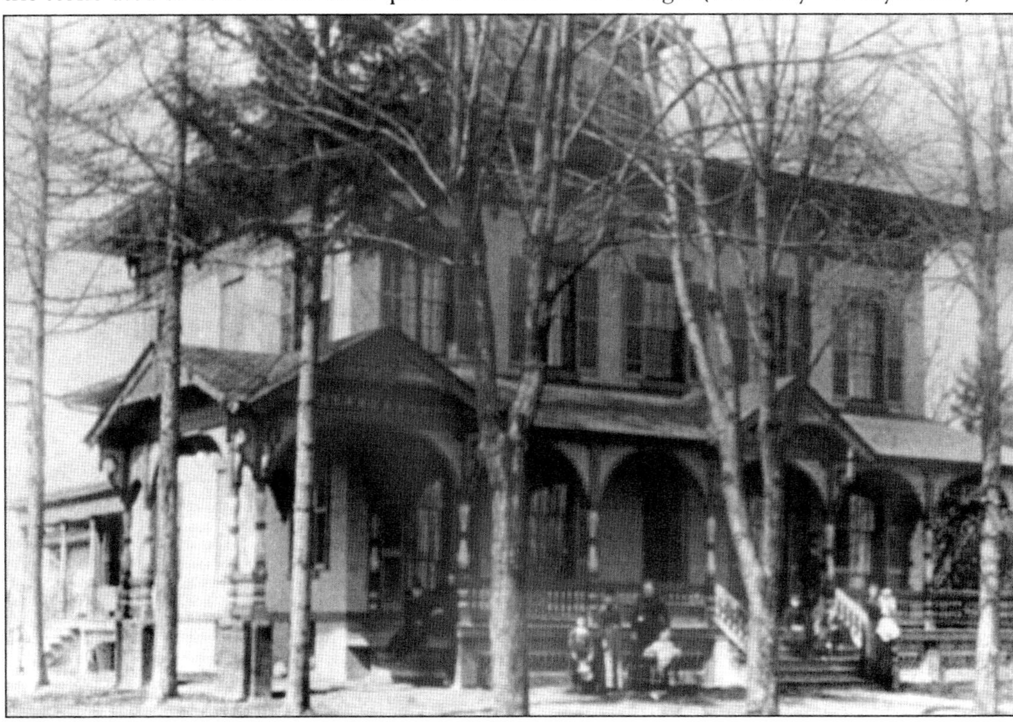

Col. Henry Culver began construction of this impressive residence on Ontario Street in 1838. Culver built the Upper Mill. When he fell on hard times, he sold the house to Hiram Finch, owner of the Lower Mill, who completed it, adding a flourish of additional embellishments. (Courtesy Honeoye Falls Village Historian Anne Bullock.)

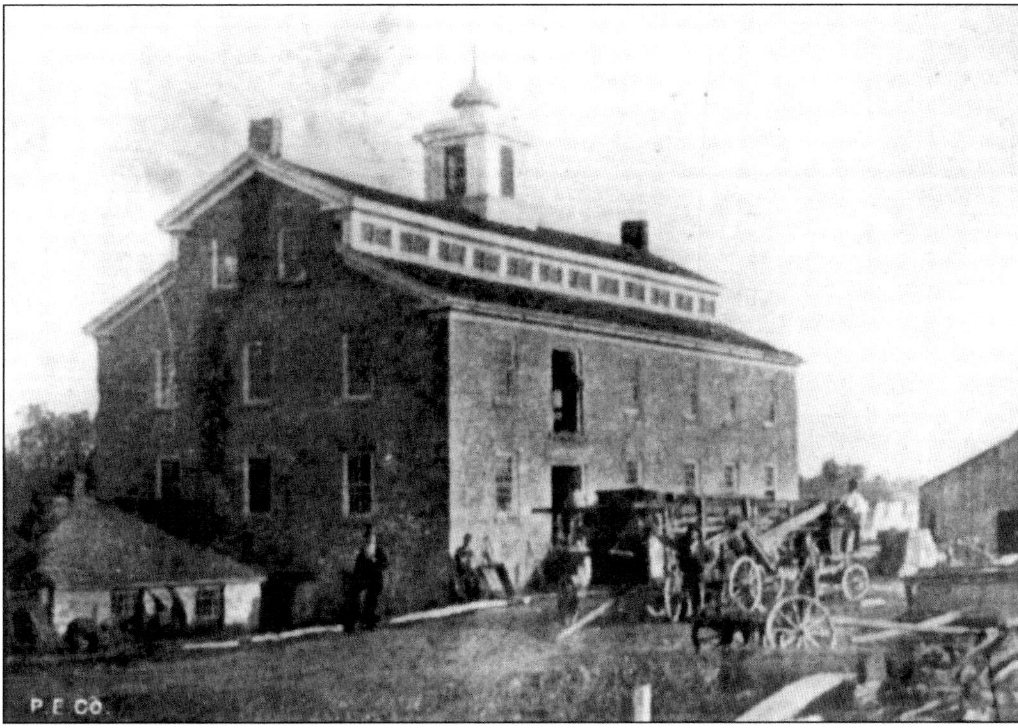

The beautiful stone York's Foundry was located on West Main Street above the falls. (Courtesy Honeoye Falls Village Historian Anne Bullock.)

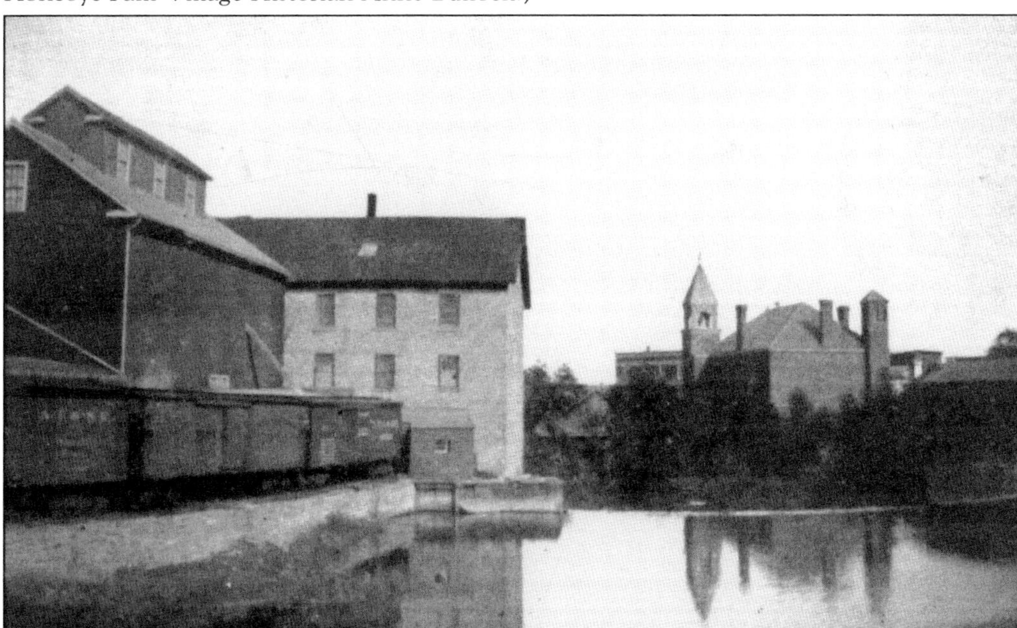

This serene view was taken looking north from the New York Central Railroad bridge. Freight cars on a spur from the Peanut Branch yard are being loaded with flour—obviously ground at the Upper Mill. Beside the car nearest the mill is the housing for the apparatus used to raise and lower the sluice gate. (Courtesy Honeoye Falls Village Historian Anne Bullock.)

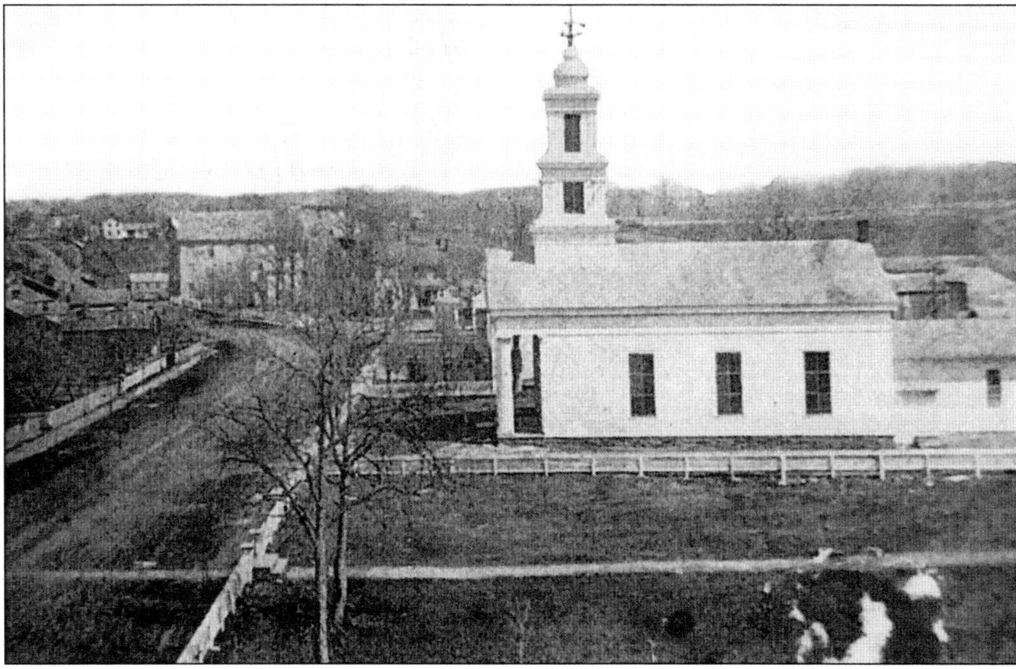

In 1831, the Presbytery of Rochester gave direction to the infant congregation here to build a church. The original section of this church dates back to July 17 of that same year. It has been modified and enlarged. In August 1943, a lightning strike obliterated the original mushroom dome. Fortunately, the fire from that strike not spread to the main structure. (Courtesy Honeoye Falls Village Historian Anne Bullock.)

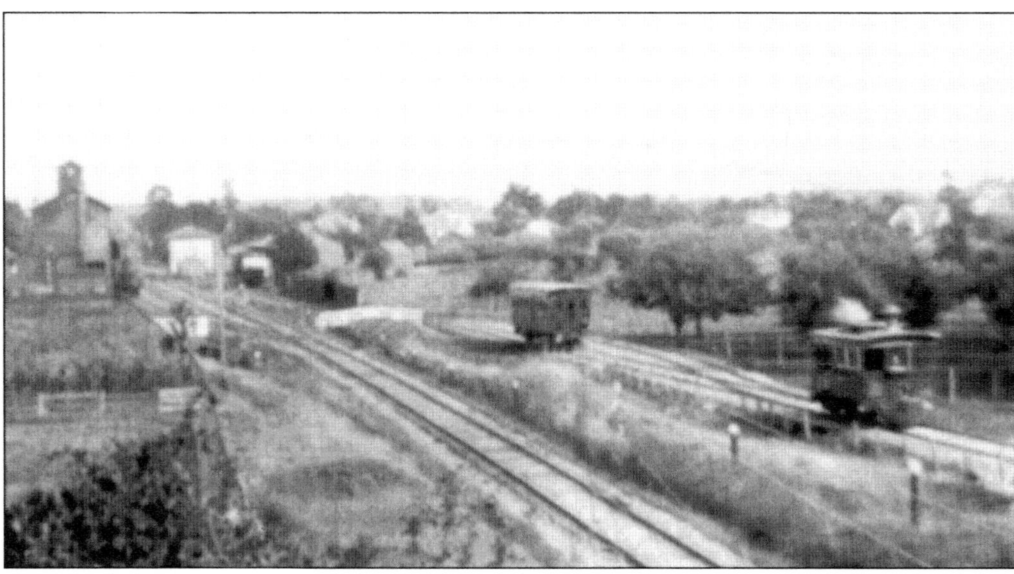

The *Motor* of the Lima and Honey Falls Railroad speeds out of the west end of the Peanut Branch yard on its return to Lima. This photograph was taken in the summer of 1895. Not long after that, the *Motor* ceased regular runs and the line slipped into inactivity. Behind the steamer is the passenger coach. (Courtesy Honeoye Falls Village Historian Anne Bullock.)

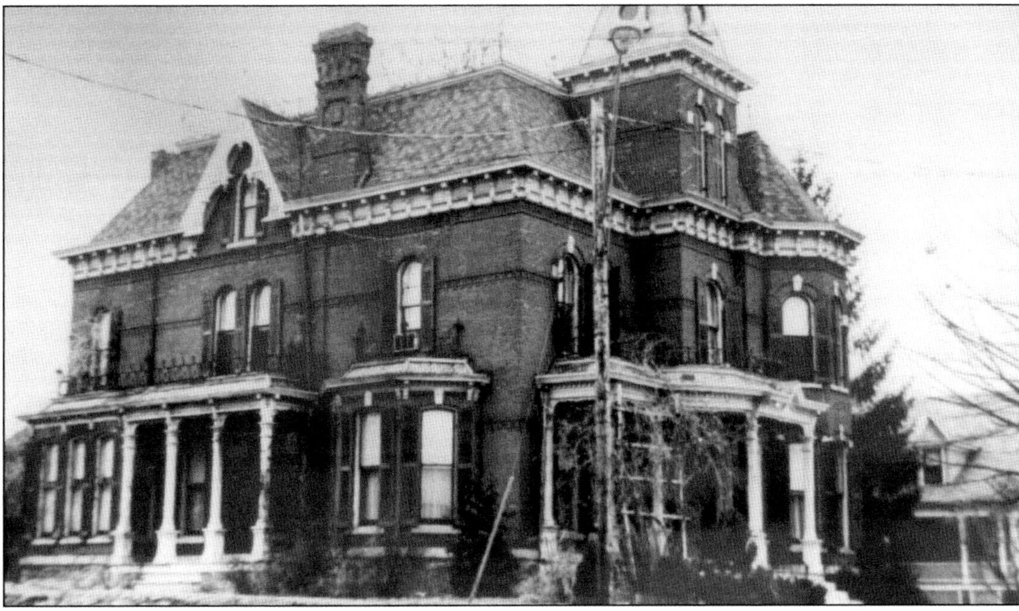

A lost masterpiece is this 1870s Victorian Gothic. Known as the Despard House, it was built by Sylvester Wilcox on Monroe Street. The architectural heritage of Honeoye Falls is one of stunning craftsmanship and unequaled beauty. To date, more than 200 applications from Honeoye Falls have been submitted to the National Register of Historic Places, and the majority of them have been accepted. (Courtesy Honeoye Falls Village Historian Anne Bullock.)

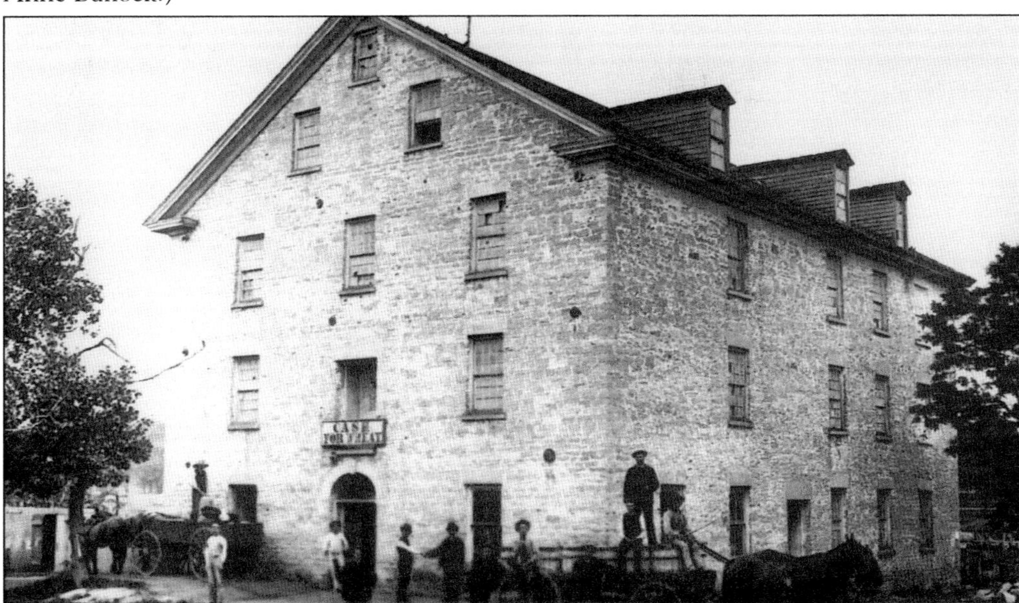

Several mills preceded this one, but none were as sturdy. Its stone walls were nearly three feet thick. Known as the Upper Mill, it was built in 1827 by Col. Henry Culver. Tradition says Hiram Finch, a later owner, sent a barrel of his best flour to Queen Victoria in hopes of entering the English market. The mill wheels were turned first by water, next by steam, and finally by electricity. The old mill now serves as the town hall.

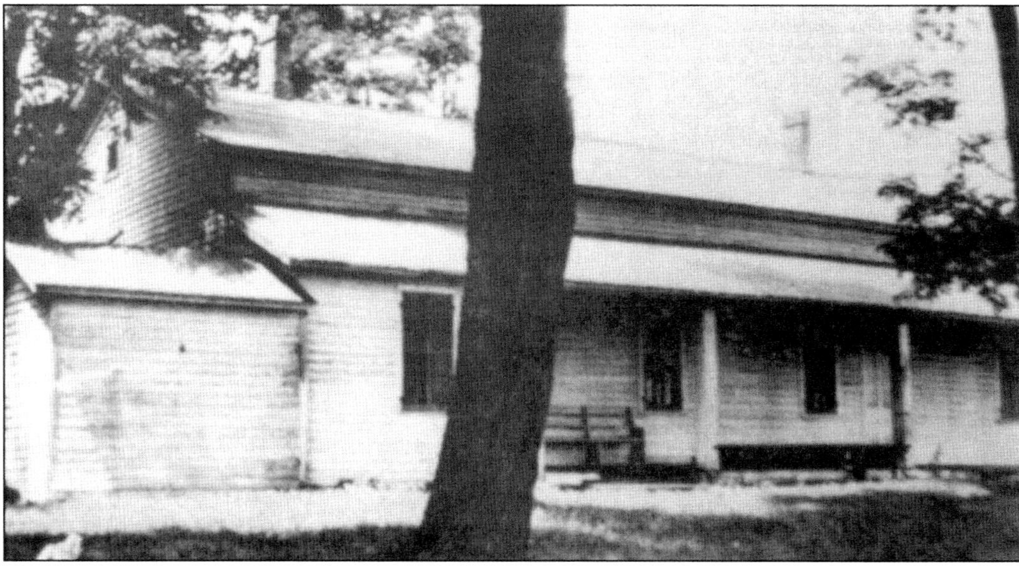

The Quaker Meeting house was built in 1833 and served about 500 worshipers in the Mendon Center area. Portable shutters divided the main hall; women sat on one side, men on the other. Many noted speakers made appearances here. The building was torn down in 1905, but the burial ground remains on Quaker Meeting House Road. (Courtesy Mendon Town Historian Diane Ham.)

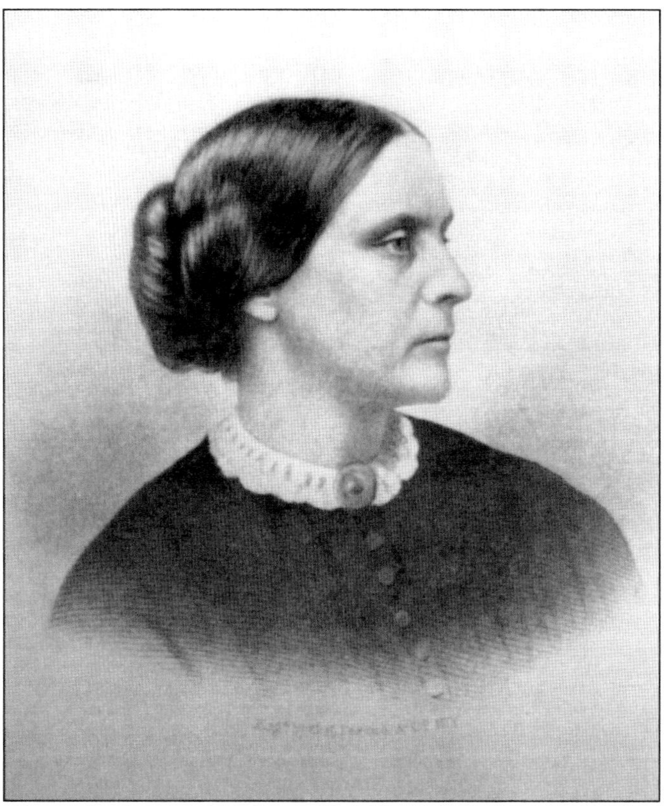

Among the many noted speakers to address the Friends Society at the Quaker Meeting house was suffragist Susan B. Anthony of Rochester.

Another national figure to address the Friends Society was Sojourner Truth, the first black woman to crusade for the abolition of slavery. The local population was actively connected with the vigorous antislavery movement in Rochester. It is interesting to note that members of the Bush family, forebears of the Bush presidents, lived in Rochester and Pittsford and were active abolitionists. In 1838, O.N. Bush was elected one of the vice-presidents of the Anti-Slavery Society and Abigail Bush helped direct the society events in western New York.

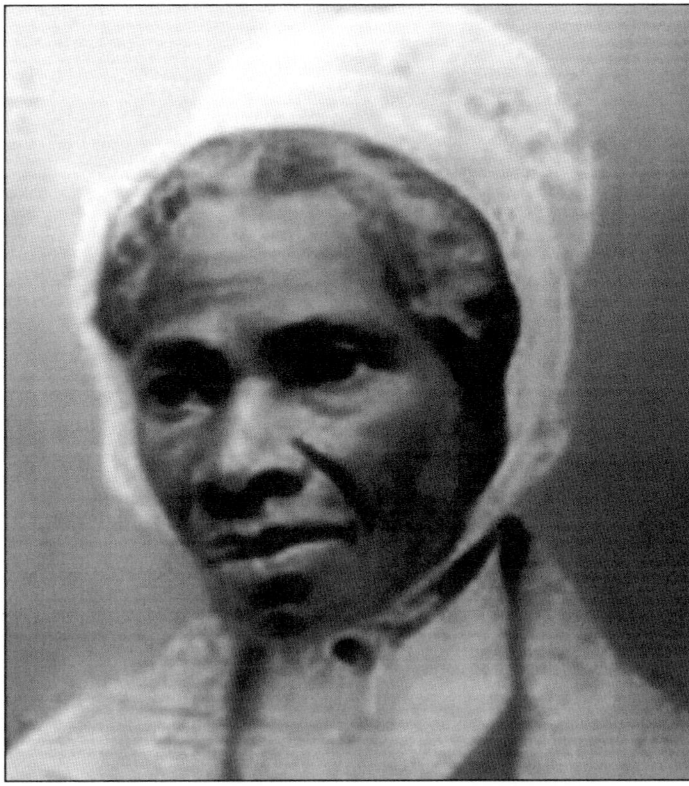

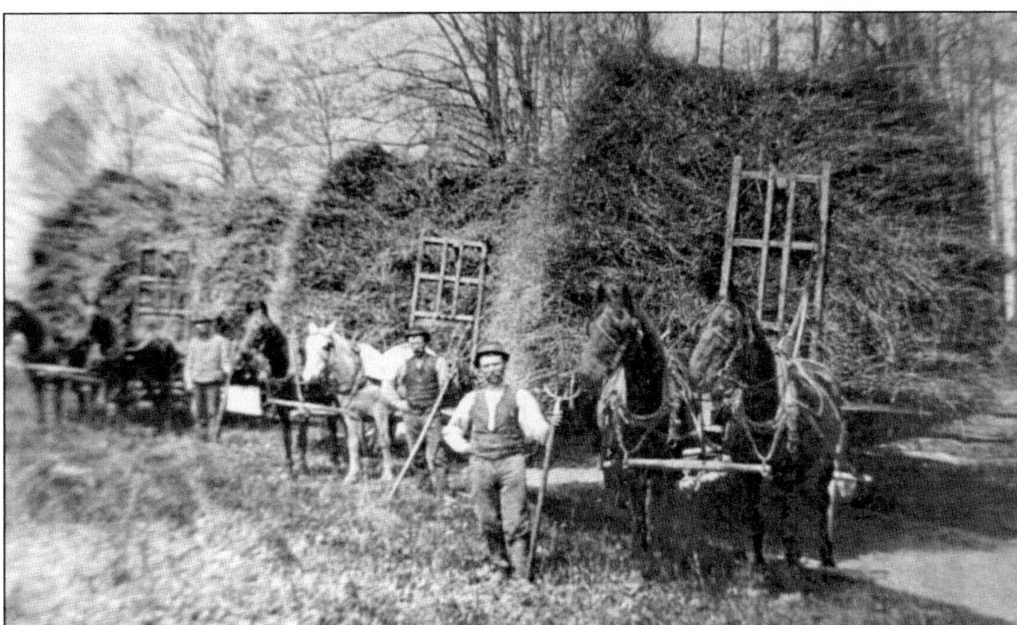

Wagons burdened with straw from Mendon farmers are bound for a paper mill in North Bloomfield. Mendon is a township, which includes the incorporated village of Honeoye Falls and the four hamlets of Mendon, Mendon Center, Sibleyville, and Rochester Junction. (Courtesy Mendon Town Historian Diane Ham.)

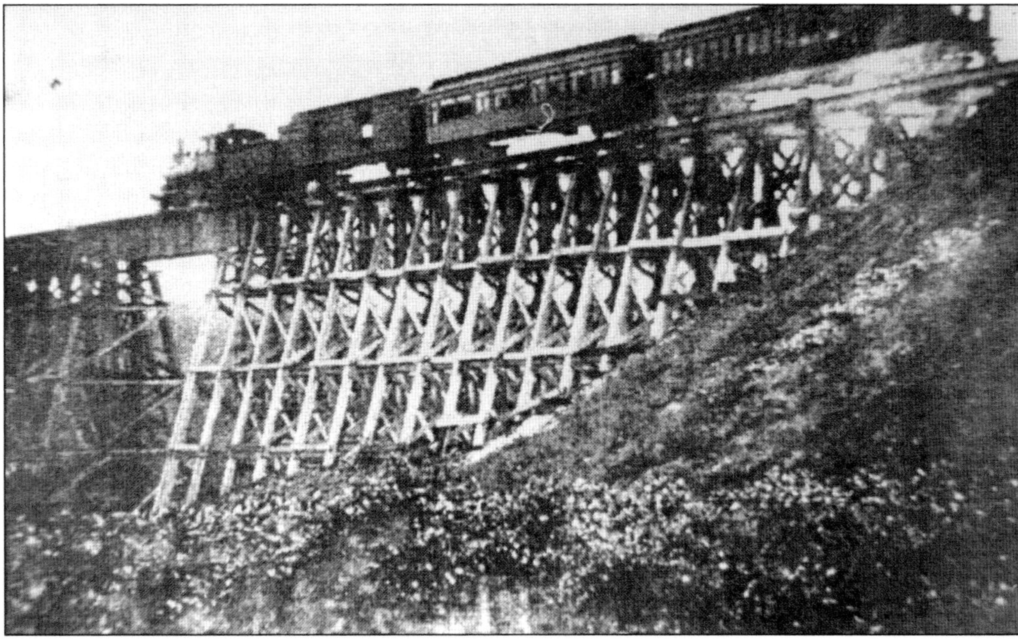

Affectionately referred to as the "Papa Trestle," this 1890s bridge carried the Lehigh Valley Railroad over Honeoye Creek about one-half mile north of the Honeoye Falls Monroe Street crossing. (Courtesy Mendon Town Historian Diane Ham.)

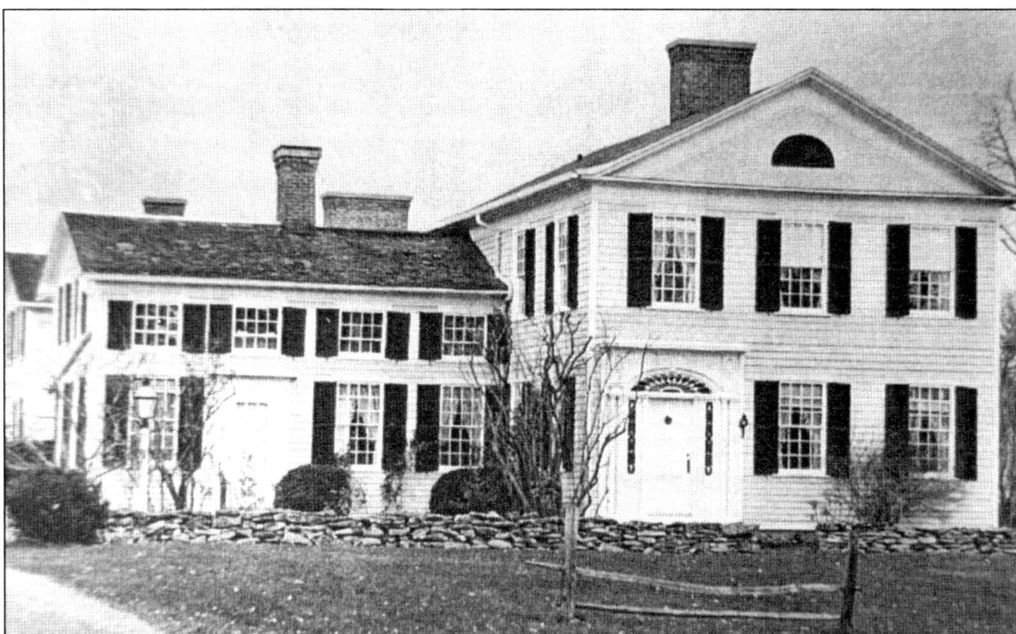

A thriving pioneer community formed in the woods beside Honeoye Creek near a crossroads linking Clover Street and the Rush-Mendon Road. It got its name, Sibleyville, from founder Col. Timothy Sibley. The founder's son Hiram Sibley, who moved to Rochester where he helped found the Western Union Company, built this house in 1833. (Courtesy Mendon Town Historian Diane Ham.)

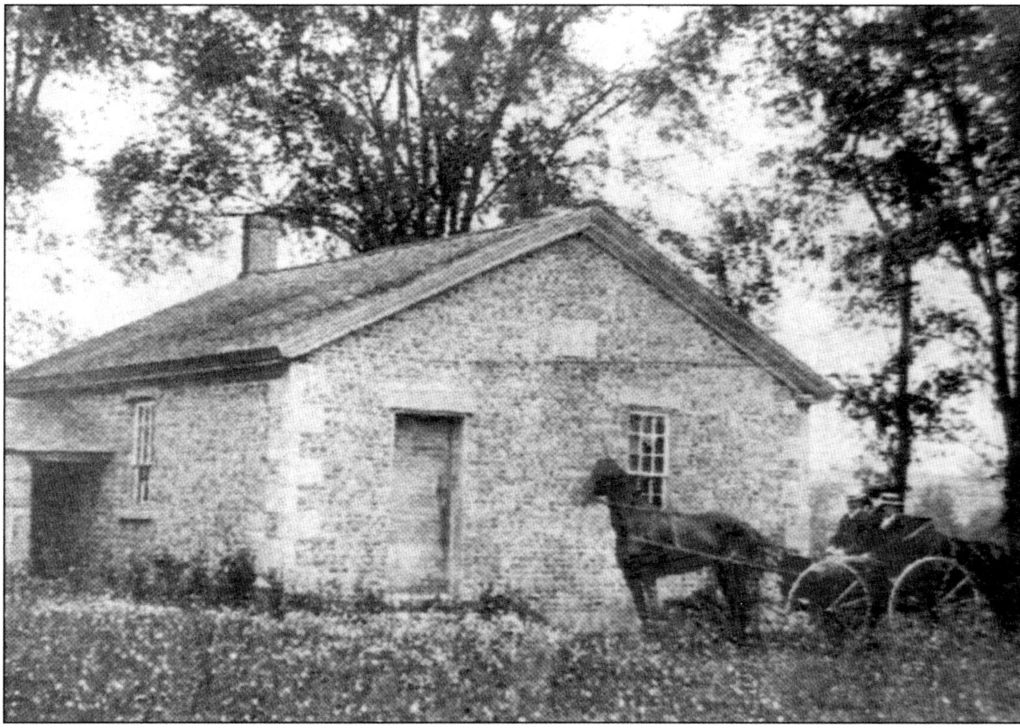

As early as 1821, Sibleyville had a machine shop, a gun shop, tailor and blacksmith shops, a cooper shop, a gristmill, and a sawmill. In 1840, this cobblestone meetinghouse was built. It became Mendon District School No. 12 and serves as a residence today on the Rush-Lima Road. (Courtesy Mendon Town Historian Diane Ham.)

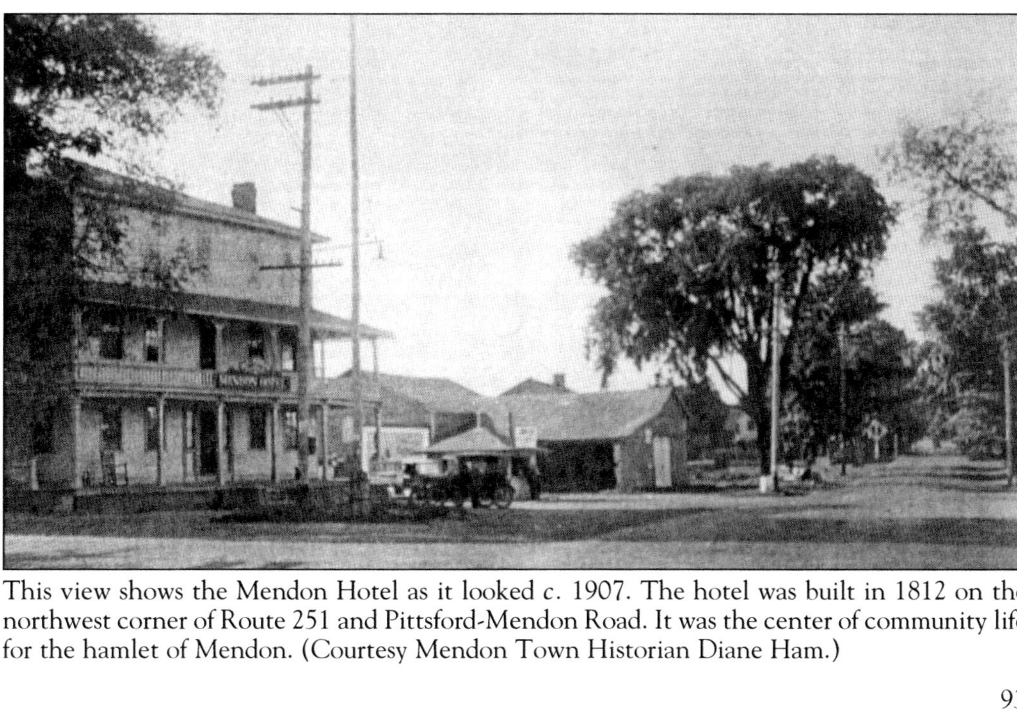

This view shows the Mendon Hotel as it looked *c.* 1907. The hotel was built in 1812 on the northwest corner of Route 251 and Pittsford-Mendon Road. It was the center of community life for the hamlet of Mendon. (Courtesy Mendon Town Historian Diane Ham.)

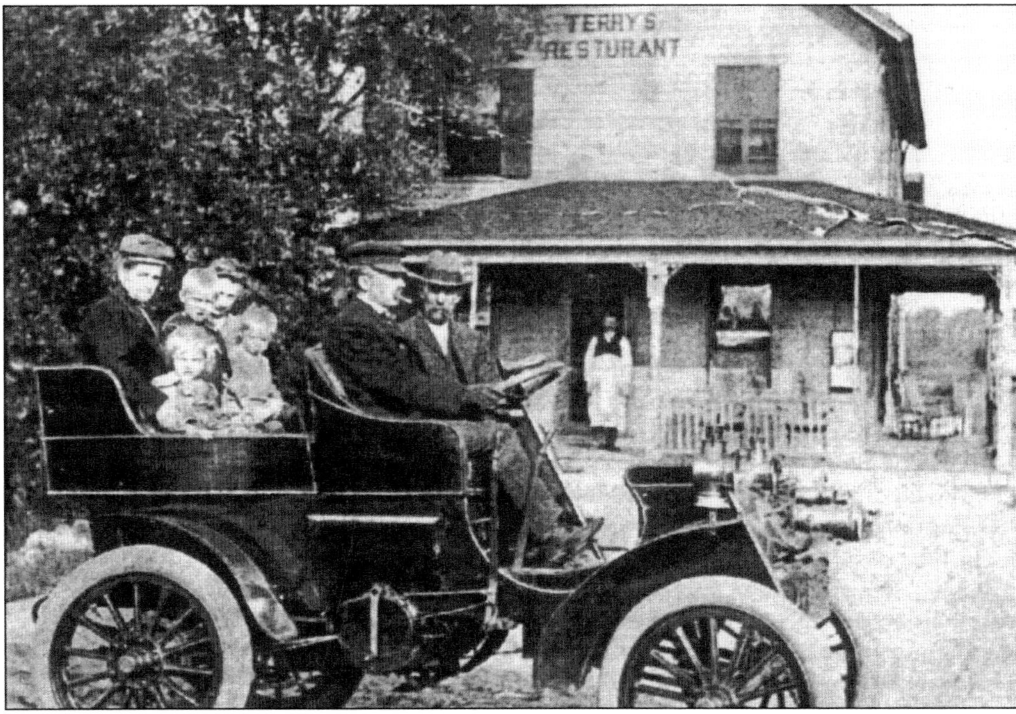

Terry's hotel and restaurant was located on the west side of Plains Road in Rochester Junction. This view dates from 1902. The hotel has been converted to a residence. (Courtesy Mendon Town Historian Diane Ham.)

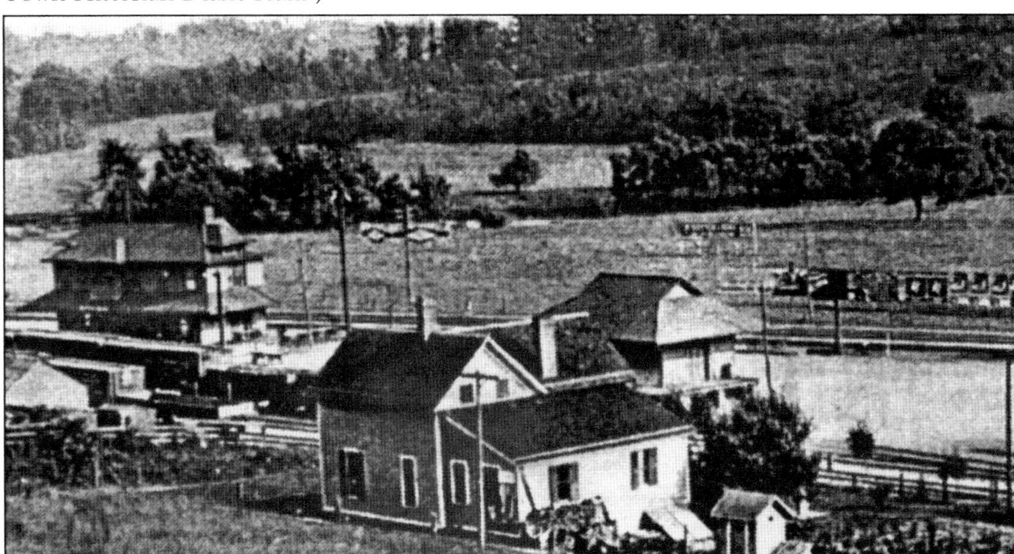

The Rochester-Hemlock Branch of the Lehigh Valley Railroad joined with the Lehigh mainline here—thus, the name Rochester Junction. At least four trains from Rochester to Honeoye Falls, Lima, Livonia, and Hemlock left here daily. The *Black Diamond*, considered the handsomest train in America, stopped here on its Rochester run. Many people who grew up in this area can remember seeing the colorful Ringling Brothers and Cole Brothers Circus trains roll in. (Courtesy Mendon Town Historian Diane Ham.)

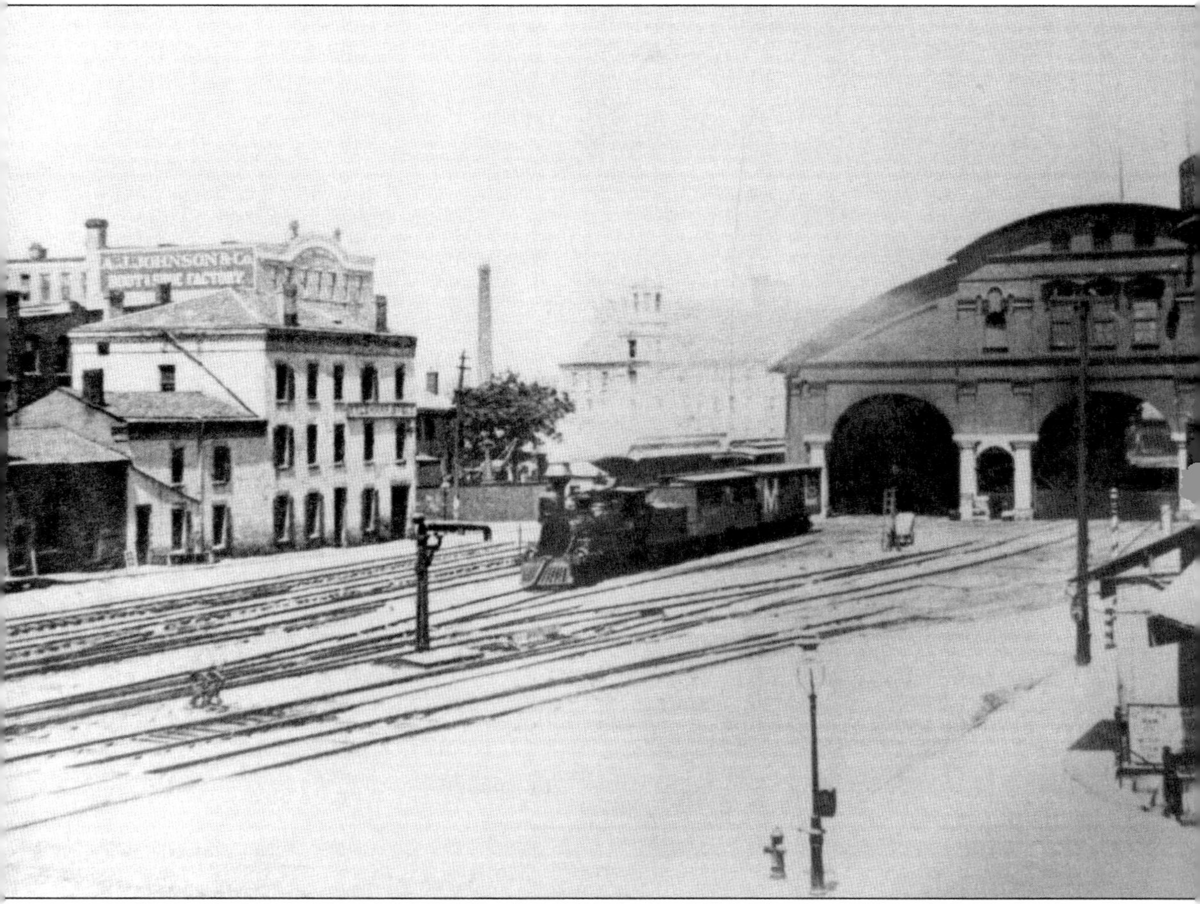

Kenneth Alling recounted how, in the predawn darkness of February 18, 1861, sleighs, cutters, and trains set out from rural villages. Nearly 15,000 citizens, desperate about the country's future, watched Pres. Abraham Lincoln's inaugural train roll into the New York Central station on Mill Street in Rochester at 7:30 a.m. Alling, a boy at the time, worked through the crowd until he reached the new president's coach. He even climbed onto the bumper just as Lincoln came out to speak. The president looked right at him, smiled, said, "Good morning, little boy," and shook his hand. On a rainy April 27, 1865, a crowd gathered at the station again to see the train carrying the dead president's body to Illinois.

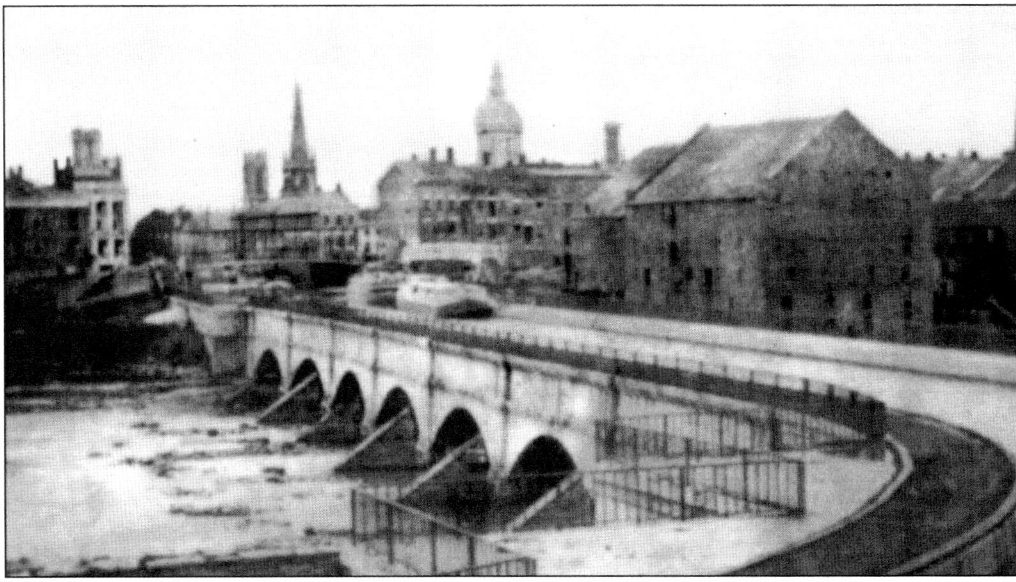

The Erie Canal is carried over the Genesee River in Rochester via a magnificent aqueduct. The Erie meandered whichever way the political winds blew, and when it swung north instead of south through the Lima area, residents were not long dispirited. The canal brought a level of prosperity to the entire region. The Genesee Valley Canal, which came through Avon, connected with the Erie in a basin just west of here.

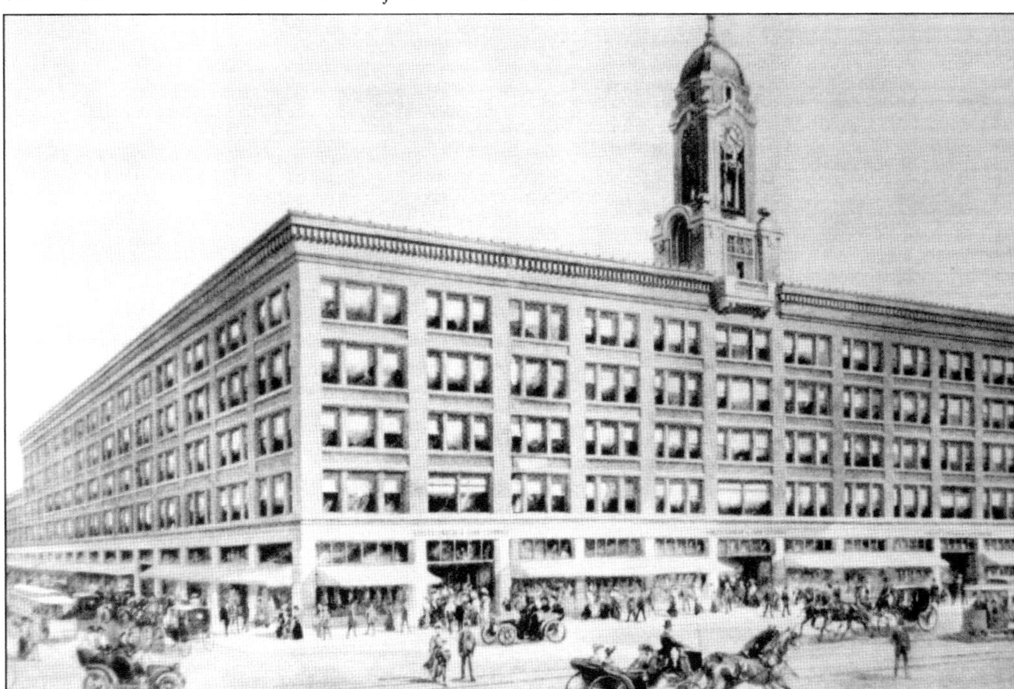

Growing prosperity and improved transportation made shopping a major diversion for all classes. Sibley, Lindsey, and Curr ran promotions, even train excursions, to attract rural families who would often spent the day. Sibley's had a European elegance by design to make shoppers feel important, but it wisely remained a bargain hunter's mecca.

Five

The Glorious Season of Avon Springs

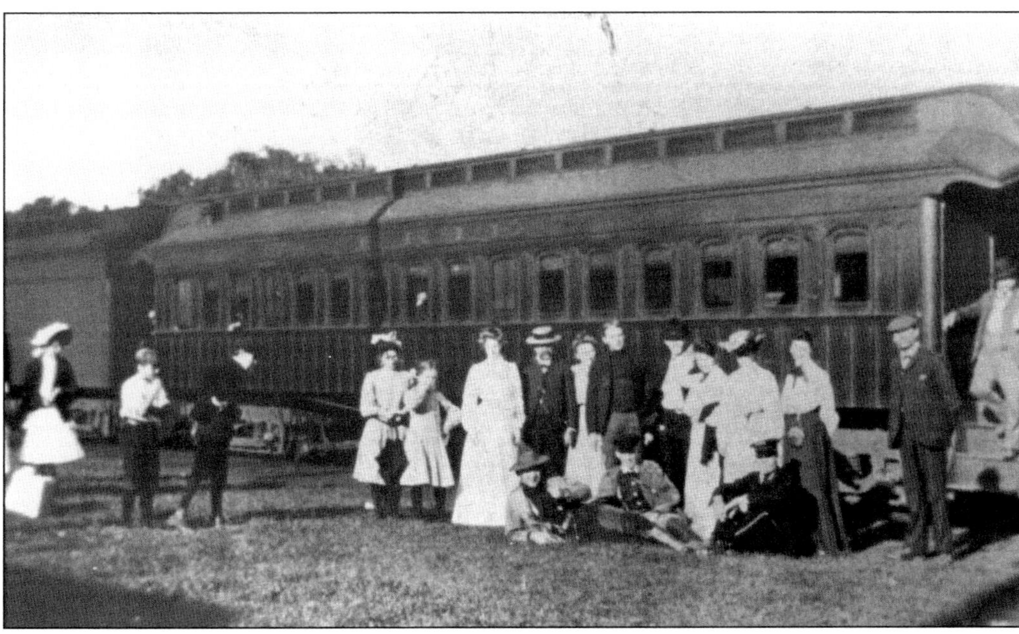

Visitors from all over America, Canada, Europe—even Cuba, the West Indies, Honduras, and Nova Scotia—arrived daily in Avon Springs at the height of its spa days. It rivaled and possibly surpassed in some ways Saratoga Springs, near the Adirondacks. Avon had numerous mineral springs, and it capitalized on them at a time when water treatments were believed to have special healing powers. It was a colorful era with a singular appeal capable of attracting more visitors than all the Finger Lakes combined.

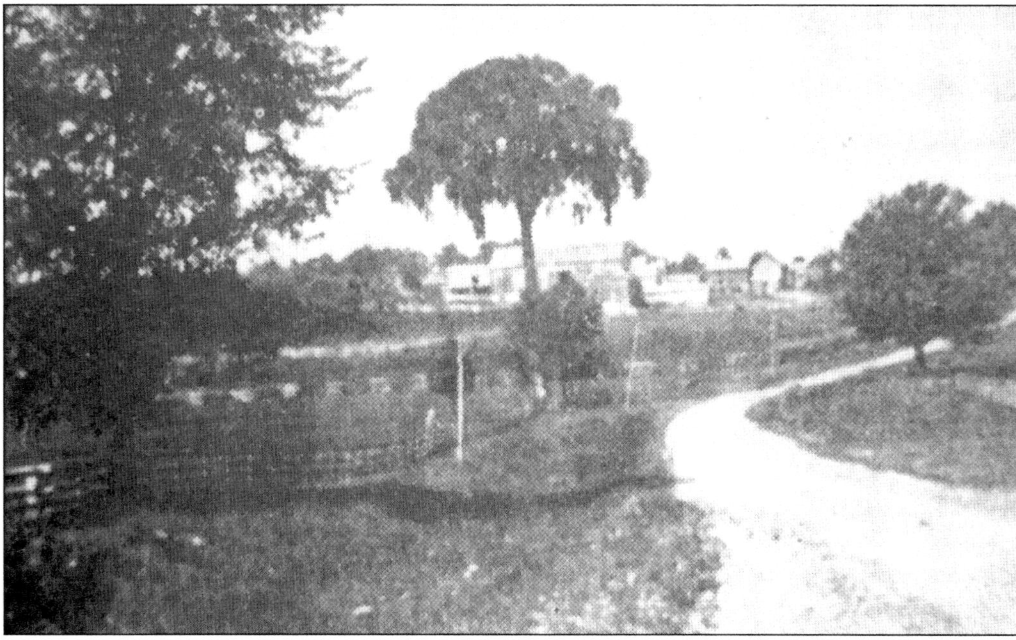

A noted landmark for travelers heading to Avon on the old State Road was the "Umbrella Tree." Men from Hemlock recounted for historians how, as boys, they rode hay wagons with concealed slaves from Harvey Blackner's hemlock farm, a busy depot on the Underground Railroad, to East Avon. There, the Taintor homestead was a depot, and conductors used the north road to reach Rochester. This road allowed travel east to Lima, where slaves could then head north on Rochester Street or continue through Bloomfield to Canandaigua and then go north to the port at Pultneyville. (Courtesy Town of Avon Historian.)

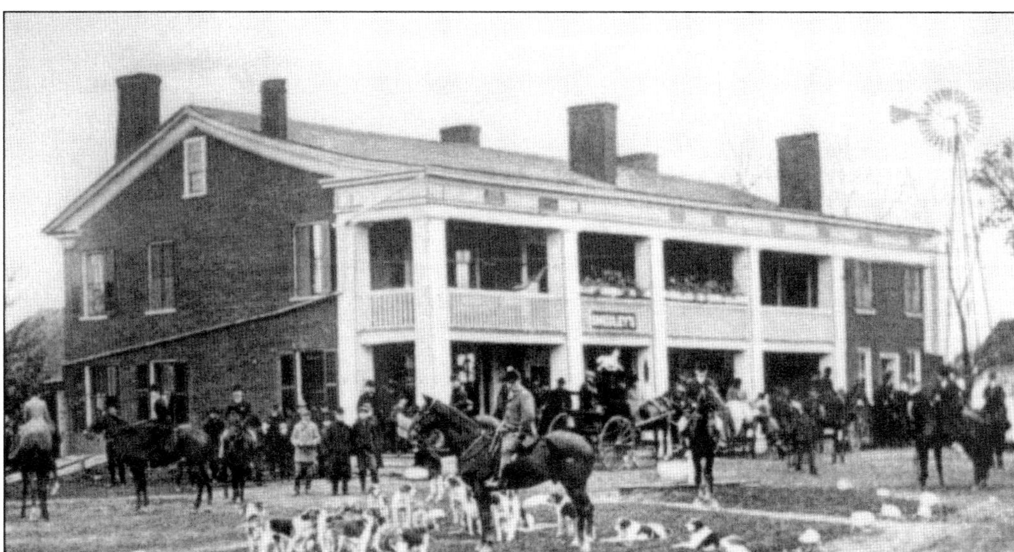

The White Horse Tavern in East Avon, built by John Pierson, is hosting a Genesee Valley Hunt. (Courtesy Town of Avon Historian.).

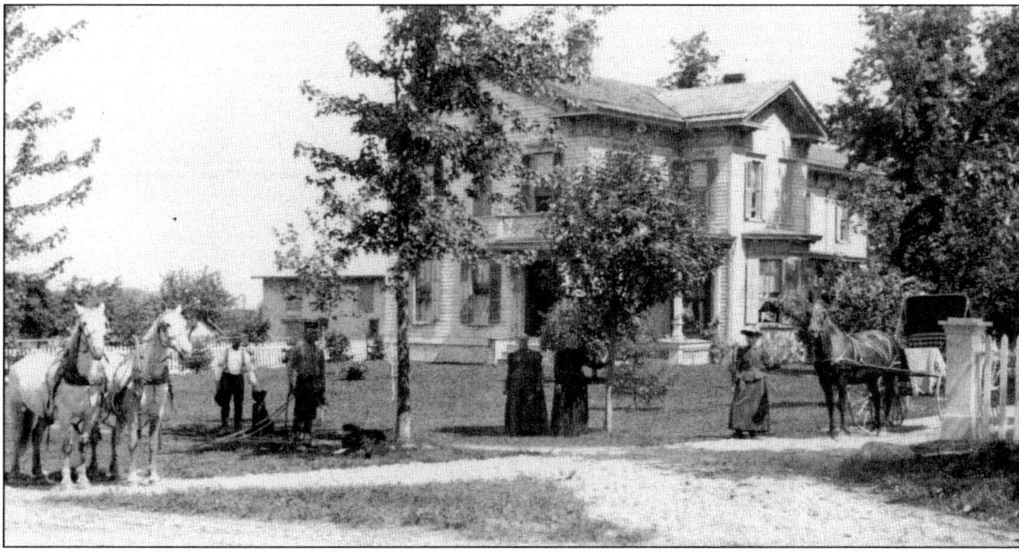

Located on the north side of the State Road was the John Smith farm, pictured here in the 1870s. Almost 100 years later, it was the Jolley Farmer tearoom and antiques establishment.

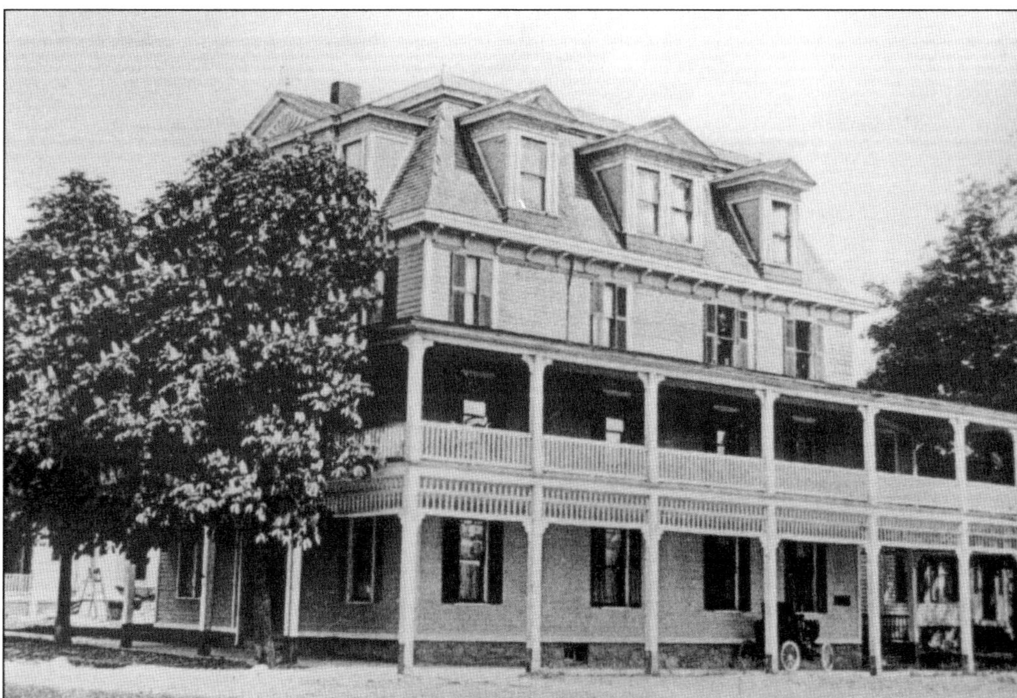

William Radford built Radford Hall as a hotel c. 1877 on the corner of East Main Street and Park Place. The back-to-nature movement was in full swing. Parents in cities lived in constant dread of losing children to diseases. A trip to Avon Springs gave them some peace of mind. This property was later the residence of Dr. F.A. Strasenburgh. (Courtesy Avon Preservation and Historical Society.)

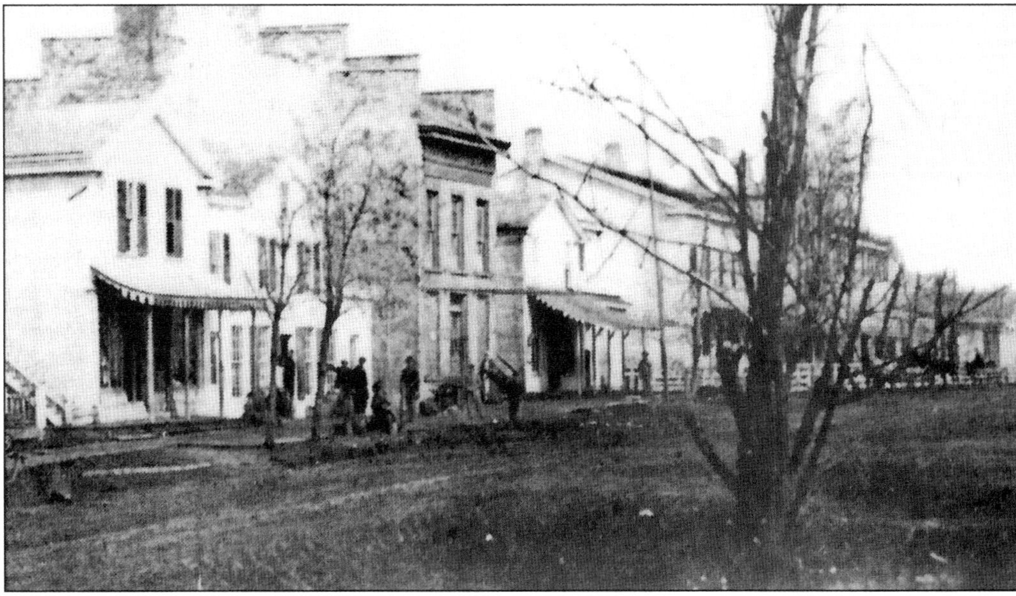

This view shows Genesee Street in is more rustic days. It did not look like this for long. The arrival of resort days transformed it. (Courtesy Town of Avon Historian.)

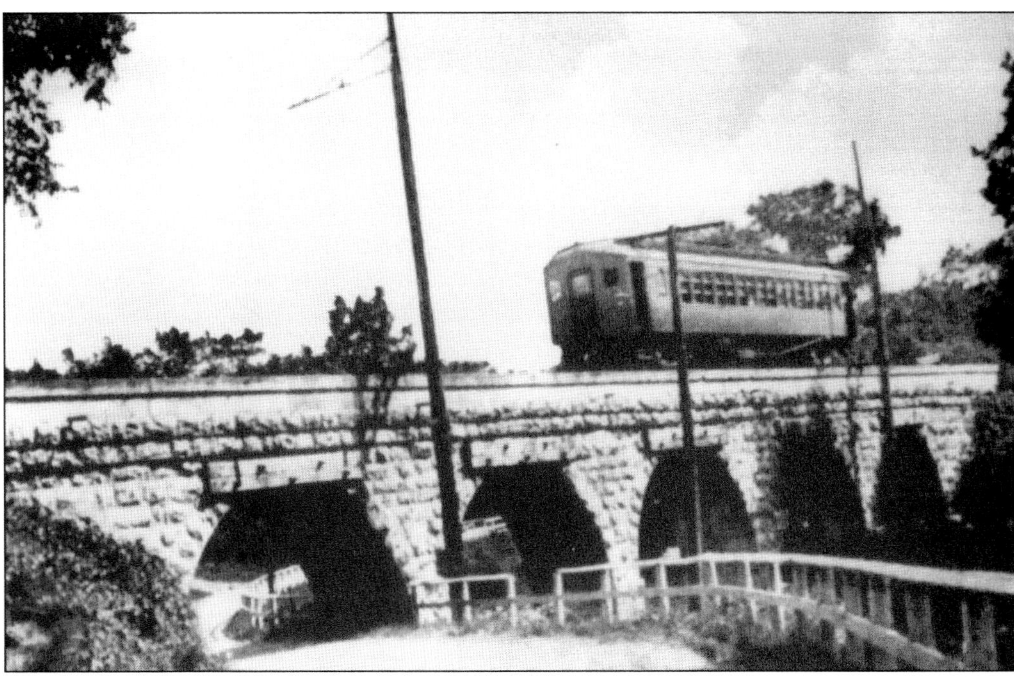

The five arch bridge, built of limestone in 1856, carried the Genesee Valley Railroad over Conesus outlet at Ashantee. In this photograph an interurban crosses on an electrified hub of the Erie Railroad that ran from Rochester to Mount Morris. (Courtesy Avon Preservation and Historical Society.)

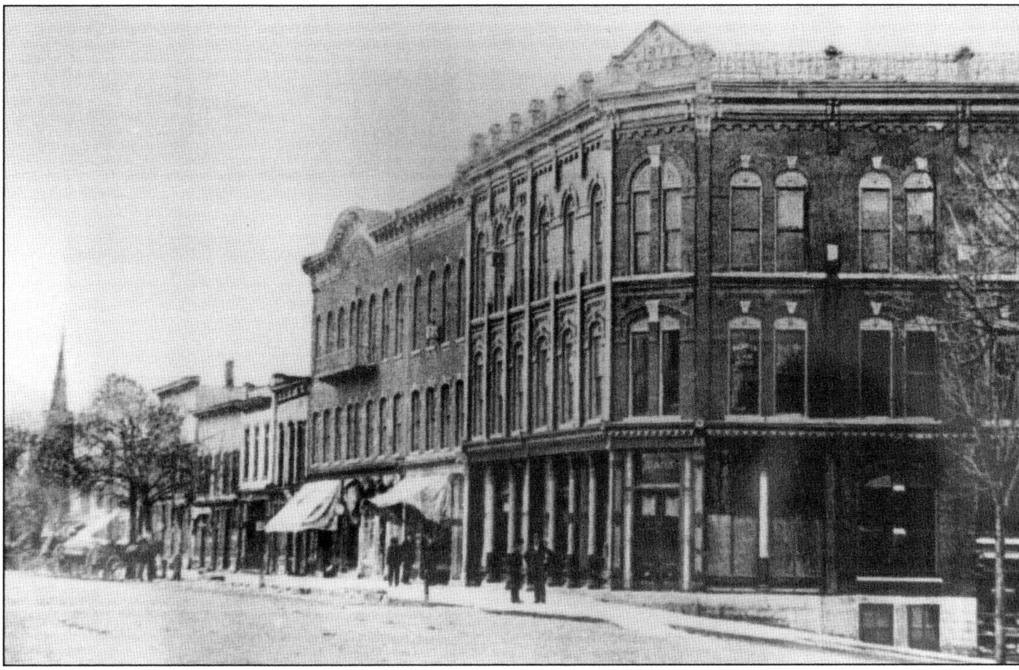

Genesee Street appears much improved in this *c.* 1910 photograph. The Whiting Block fills the corner where the United States Hotel once stood. Beside it is an opera house. (Courtesy Town of Avon Historian.)

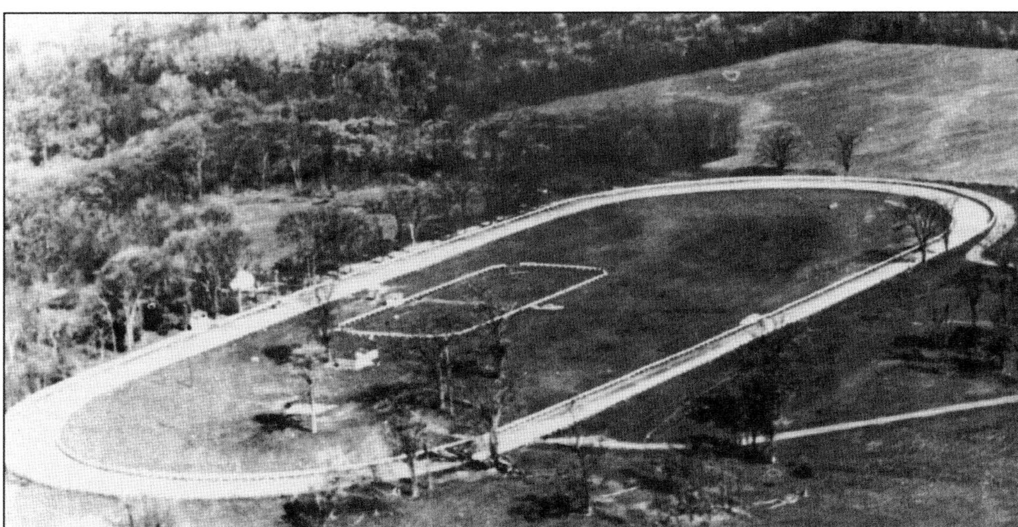

Asa Nowlen laid out Avon Springs Park, with its large racetrack, in 1836. Many of the resort hotels and baths were built in the shady groves around it. Avon has always been nationally famous for its breeding of excellent horses. The Erie Railroad ran excursions from Rochester for vacationers eager to place bets on the many races held here. (Courtesy Town of Avon Historian.)

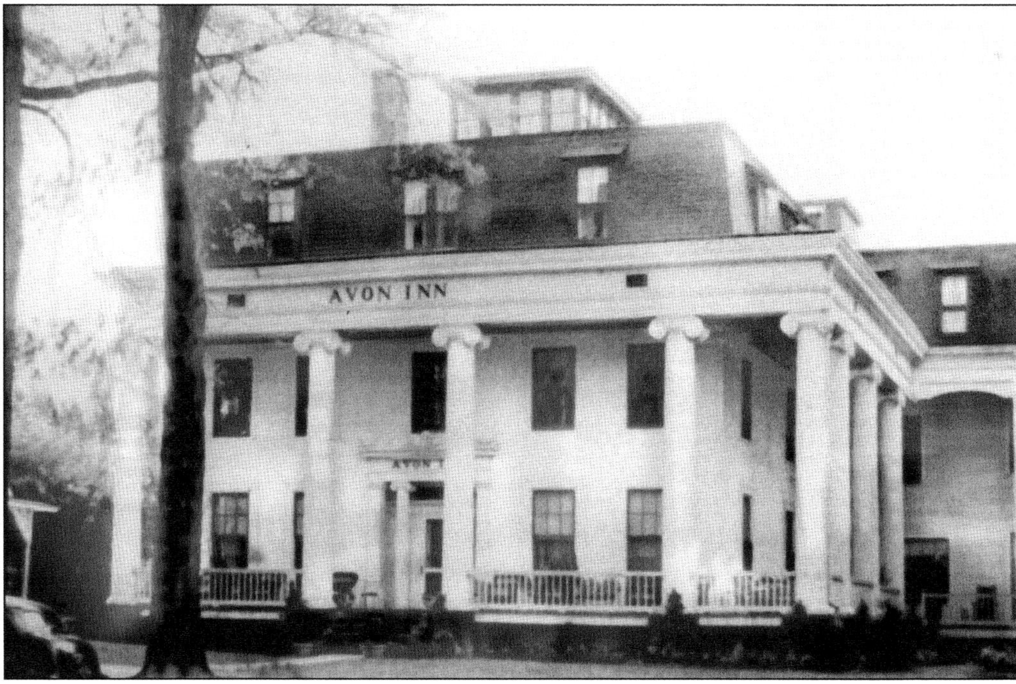

Jonathan H. Gerry began construction on his new home in the 1820s but went broke before it was completed to his liking. Subsequent owners modified, altered, and enlarged it, but it has always been impressive. It was called the Sanitarium during the resort seasons and provided mineral baths for invalids. Many social functions took place in its spacious room. For years it has been the Avon Inn. (Courtesy Shirley Ruth.)

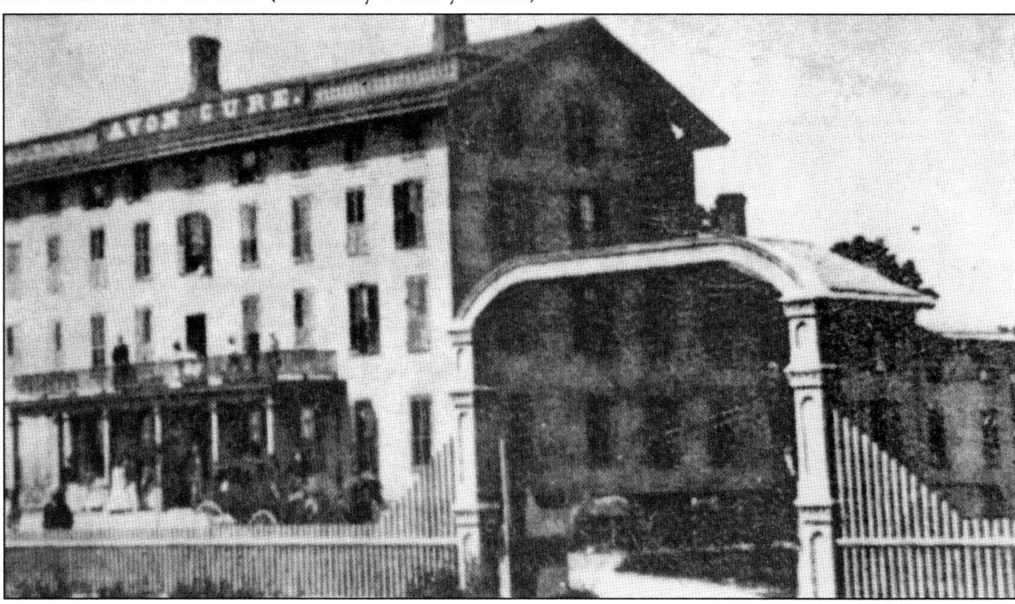

The Avon Cure was located on Wadsworth Avenue (formerly Center Street). The Cure could accommodate up to 100 guests; mineral water for the baths came from two springs on the property. In 1904, it was dismantled and moved to McPherson Point on Conesus Lake and rebuilt as the Livingston Inn. (Courtesy Avon Preservation and Historical Society.)

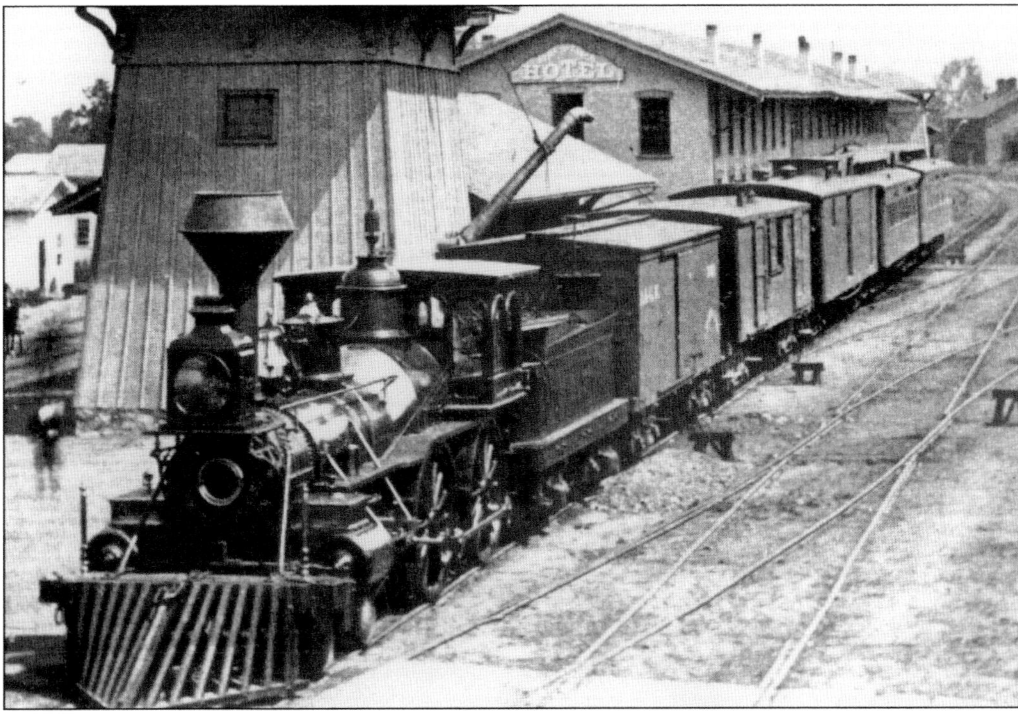

A 4-4-0 coal-burning steam locomotive waits to depart Avon's Erie Railroad terminus. The rail gauge is wider than that used today. The waterspout on the adjacent water tower would fill the tender of the locomotive with water. This photograph dates from the 1870s, when coal burners were replacing the old wood-burning locomotives.

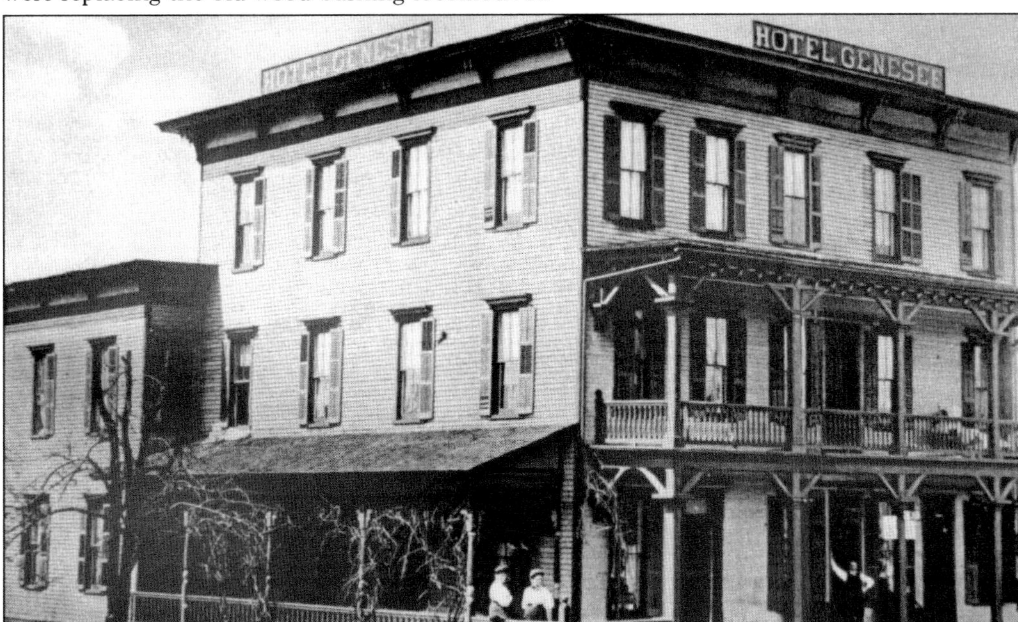

The Hotel Genesee stood opposite the Erie Railroad station. Run by William Pattee, it dates back to 1876. It was destroyed by fire in 1926. (Courtesy Town of Avon Historian.)

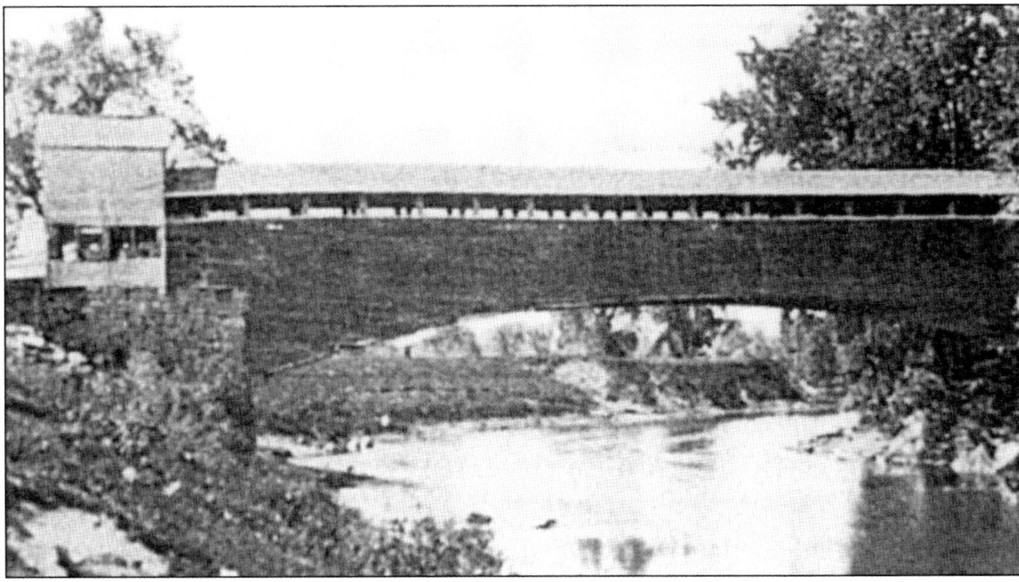

This covered bridge carried the State Road over the Genesee River. It was built in 1816 and was operated as a toll bridge. An 1812 law prohibited crossing the Genesee River within a mile of the bridge without paying a toll unless you crossed by boat or on ice in the winter. (Courtesy Town of Avon Historian.)

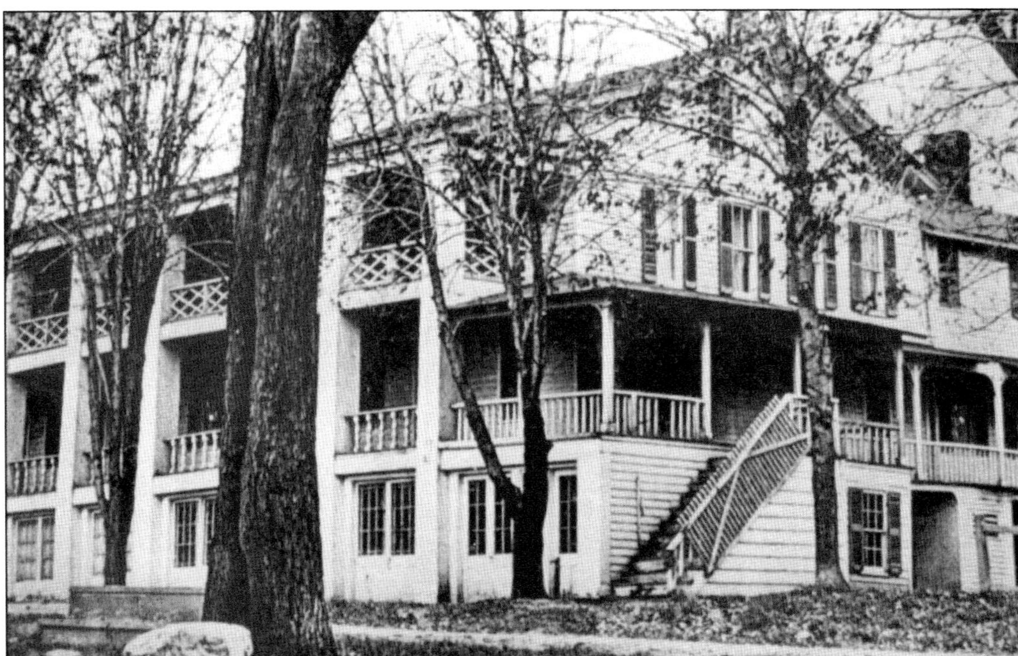

Many of the hotels that accommodated guests at Avon Springs went through several owners and name changes. This was at one time Congress Hall and then became the American Hotel. It was built in 1827 near the Upper Spring on Spring Street in Avon Springs Park. From its verandas, guests could inhale the pungent mineral waters bubbling in springs around the hotel or they could use the bathhouses on the first floor. (Courtesy Town of Avon Historian.)

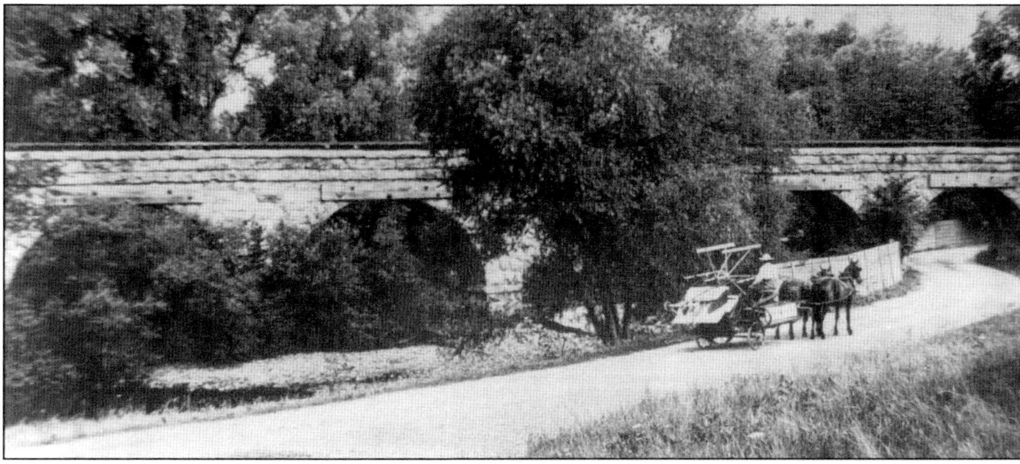

This is an earlier view of the five arch bridge, before electrification of the railroad. The horses are pulling a folding McCormick twine binder along the Geneseo Road. (Courtesy Avon Preservation and Historical Society.)

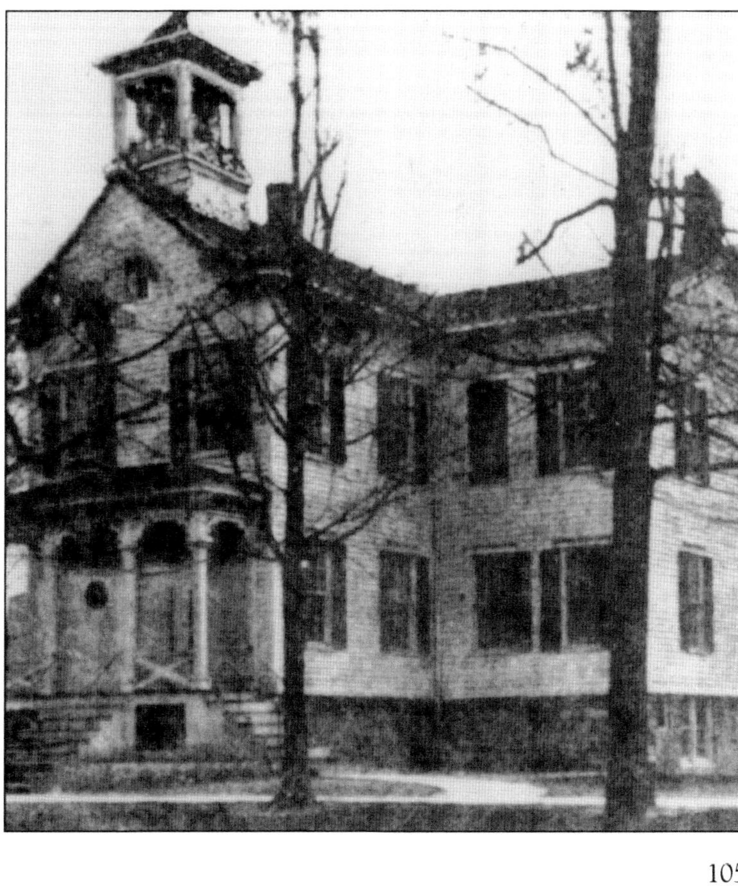

The Avon Academy was built in 1836 on Temple Street. It was later remodeled as Avon High School and served as such until 1907. (Courtesy Town of Avon Historian.)

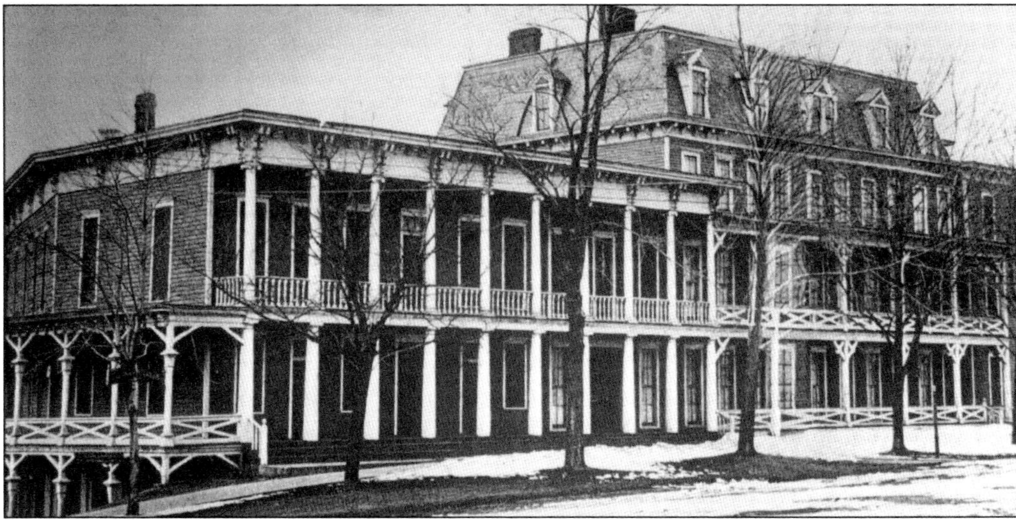

One of the grand old hotels was the Livingston. It was across from the United States Hotel and faced the village park on the corner of West Main and Prospect Streets. Built *c.* 1861, its flier boasted, "This is the largest and best hotel at Avon Springs. It is furnished with gas, steam heat, hot and cold water . . . Its appointments and cuisine are of the best . . . To supply a much felt want an elegant and convenient Bath House not in the Hotel but immediately adjoining it and shown in the picture, has been erected by the proprietor. The building is steam heated and baths may be enjoyed with perfect surety and benefit, regardless of the weather . . ."(Courtesy Avon Preservation and Historical Society.)

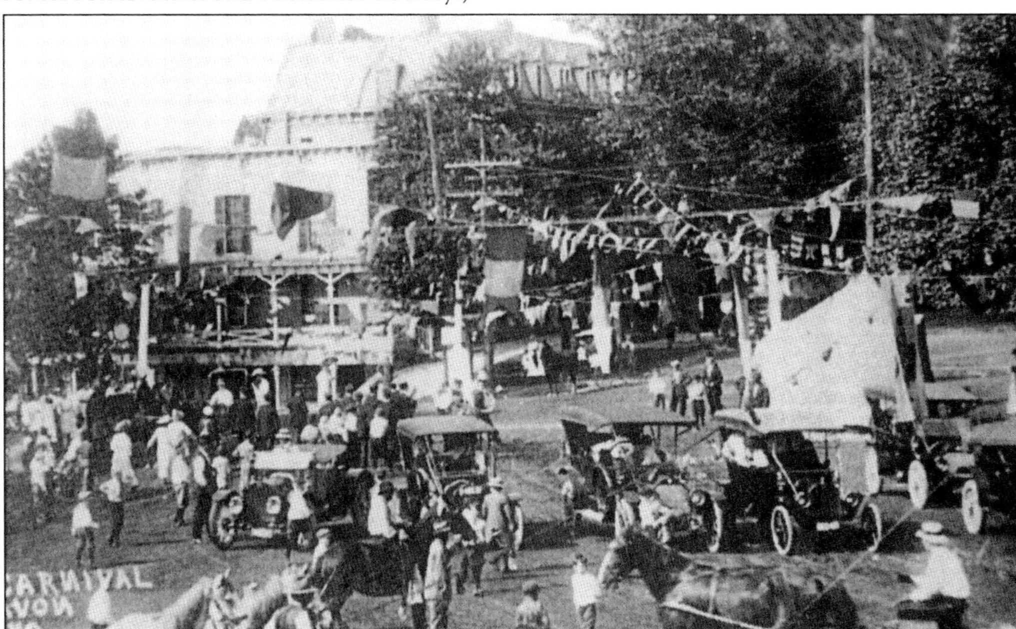

A carnival is under way on the green in 1912. The Livingston hotel is in the background. This postcard shows that it did not take long for the automobile to catch on. Note the writing on the lower left of the card; the N is backward. Reversed letters are common on postcards because the photographer had to write his caption backward on a glass negative so that it would read correctly when processed. He had to scratch the letters in with a stylus, making the task harder.

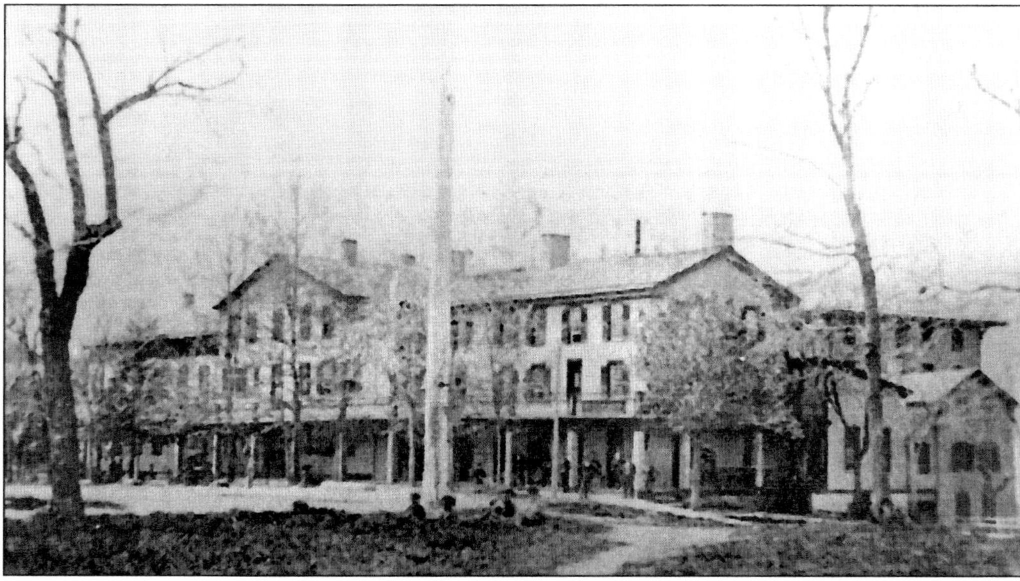

The United States Hotel was built in 1806 and stood on the corner of West Main and Genesee Streets. A massive, rambling affair, it was a favorite summer home to many wealthy and distinguished visitors to Avon Springs. Before and after the Civil War, smart carriages arrived from the railroad station to drop guests off at the front entrance. At dusk lamplight and music filled the long porches. (Courtesy Avon Preservation and Historical Society.)

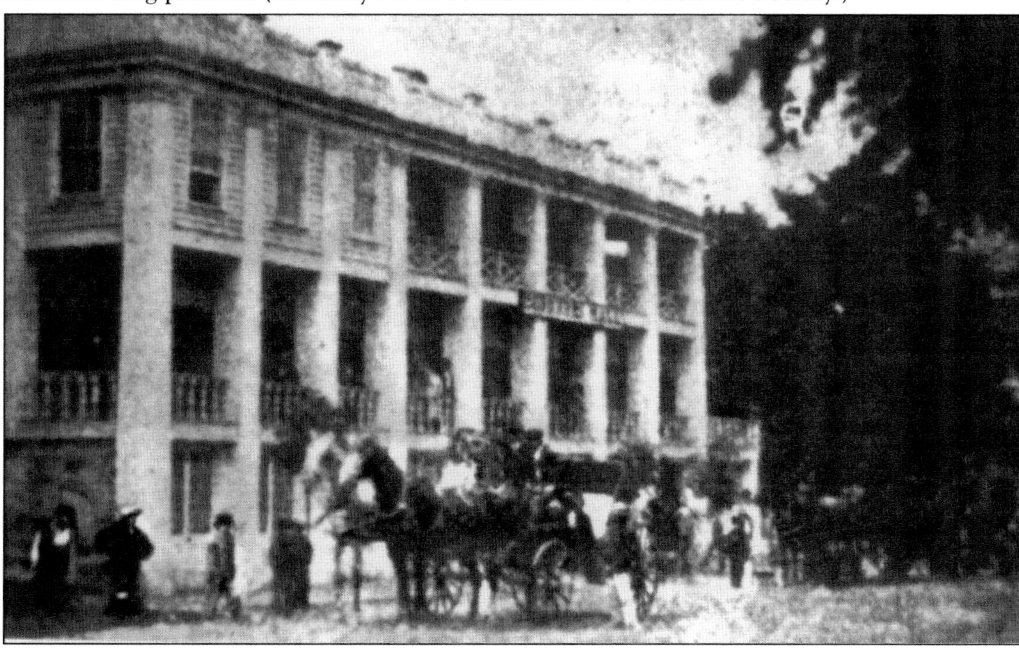

The sign over the entrance reads Congress Hall, the name of establishment when this photograph was taken. At different times in its history, the place was called the Pavilion and Nowlen House. Servants approach carriages to attend the fashionably dressed visitors. Good meals and health-related activities awaited all. If guests did not use the mineral baths, they could stroll the many garden-lined paths or simply relax in the wicker chairs along the verandas and inhale the mineral-rich breezes from the springs. (Courtesy Town of Avon Historian.)

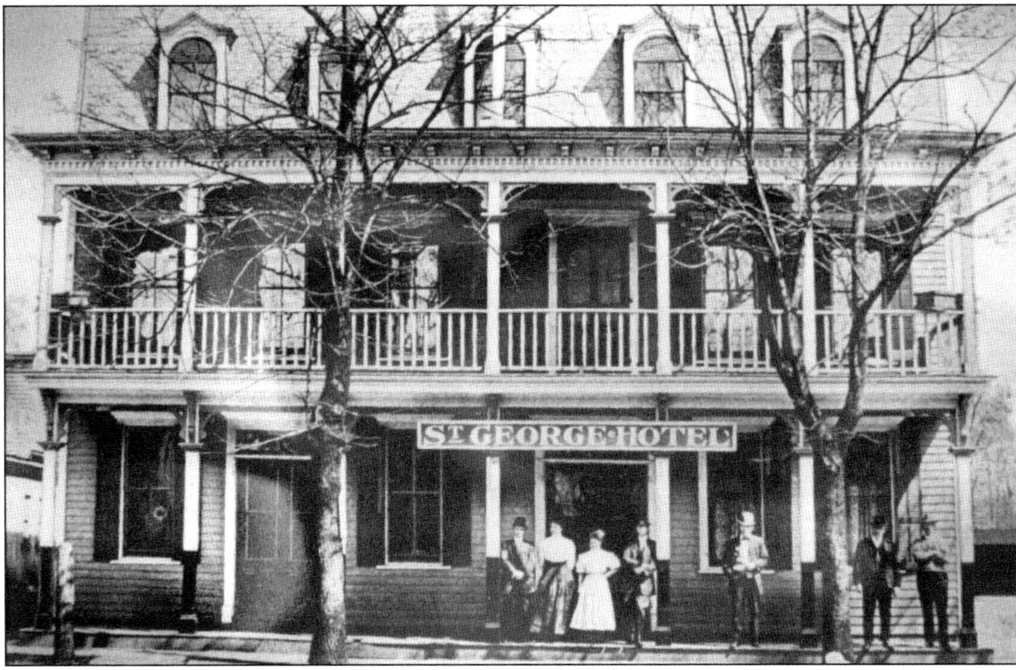

The St. George Hotel offered decent accommodations and was considered homier by those guests unimpressed by the rambling giants across from it. Guests pose in front of its welcoming entrance. Emmett Jennings drove the renowned Red Jacket Tally-Ho coach between Rochester and Avon, using the hotel as its station. (Courtesy Avon Preservation and Historical Society.).

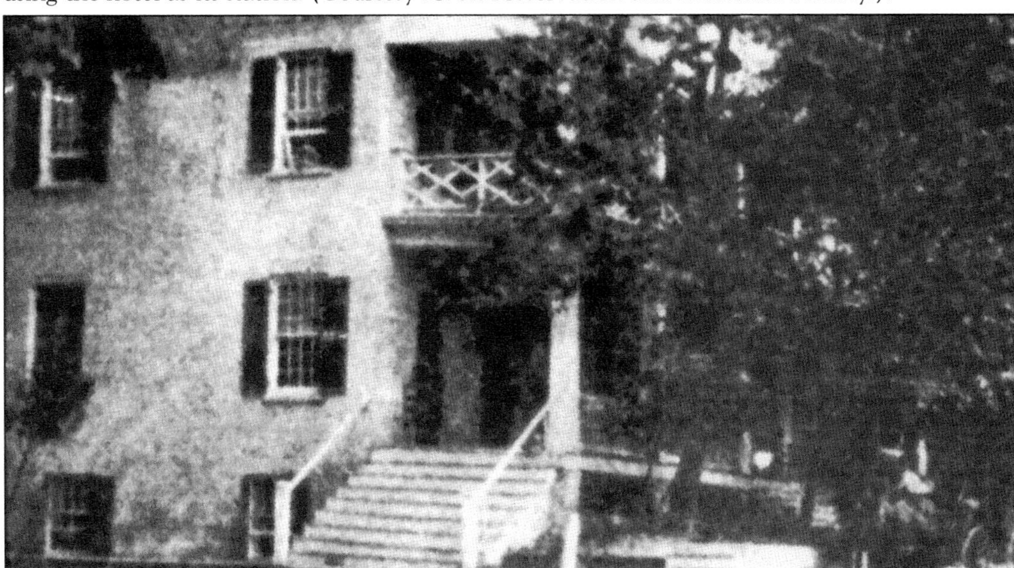

Nestled in a wooded ridge between the Upper and Lower Springs, Knickerbocker Hall was preferred by invalids incapable of flocking to the bathhouses. The air was so ripe here that visitors believed it was medicated enough to provide healthful benefits simply by inhaling. One visitor wrote of Avon in 1853 "Her health restoring waters, her delightful country which surrounds will drive away the blues and renew your age and vigor!" Avon Springs began to decline after 1900 when it was revealed that mineral waters were of limited value.

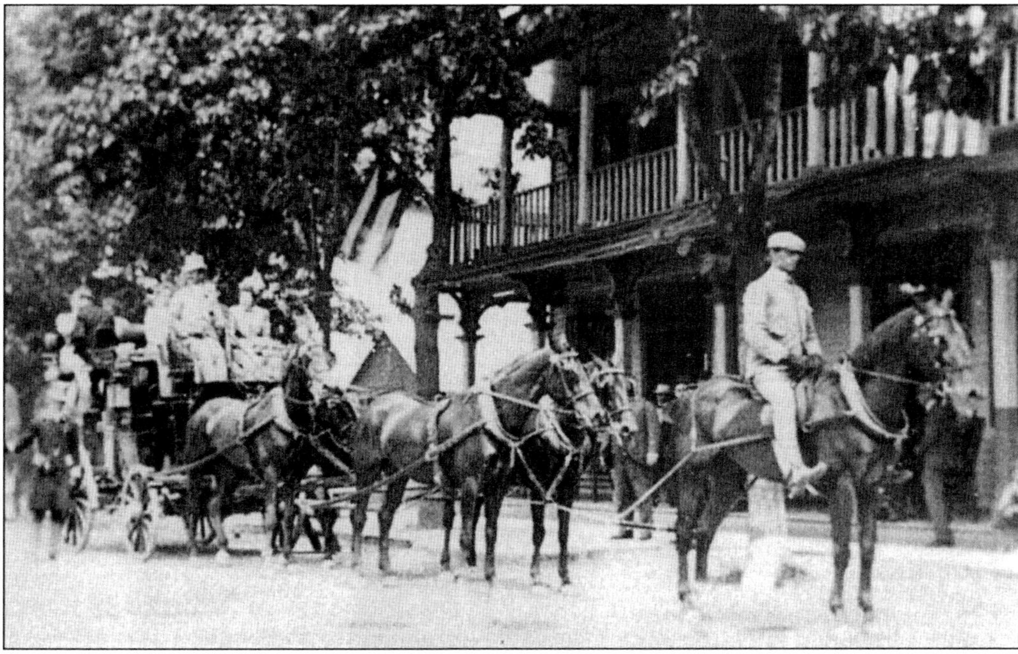

The Red Jacket Brewster is pictured in front of the St. George Hotel. It carried passengers back and forth to Rochester during the height of the resort season.

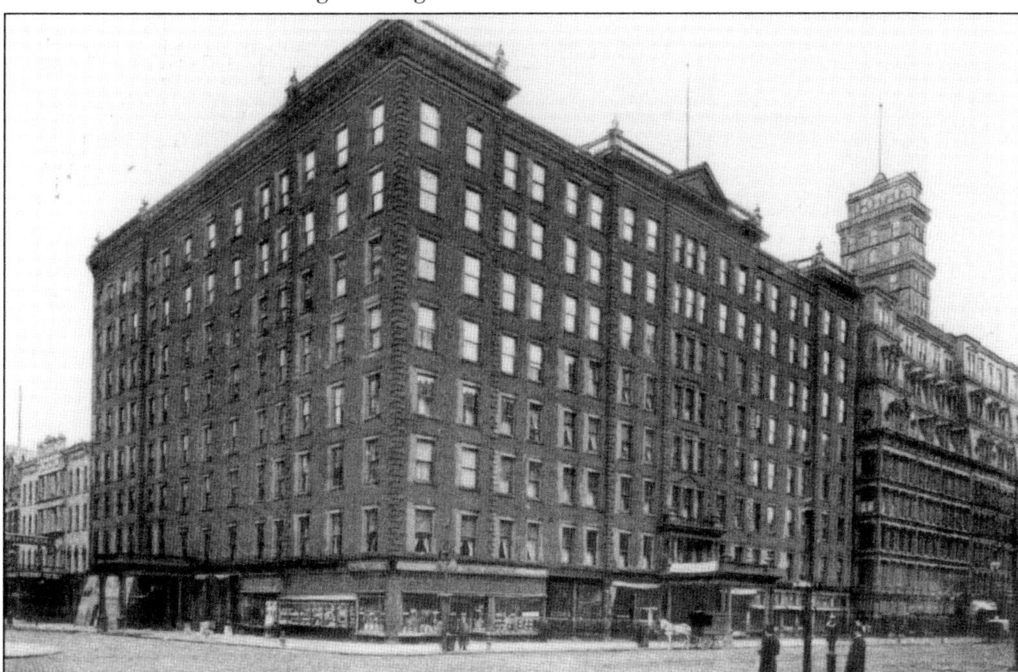

The Red Jacket left the Powers Hotel in Rochester (above) at 10 a.m., traveled up East Avenue, passing the city's finest residences, and then turned onto Highland Avenue. The first change of horses was made at Ballantine's Bridge; the second was at Scottsville, after traveling through the beautiful Genesee Valley. The coach arrived at the St. George Hotel at noon, just in time for a delicious lunch.

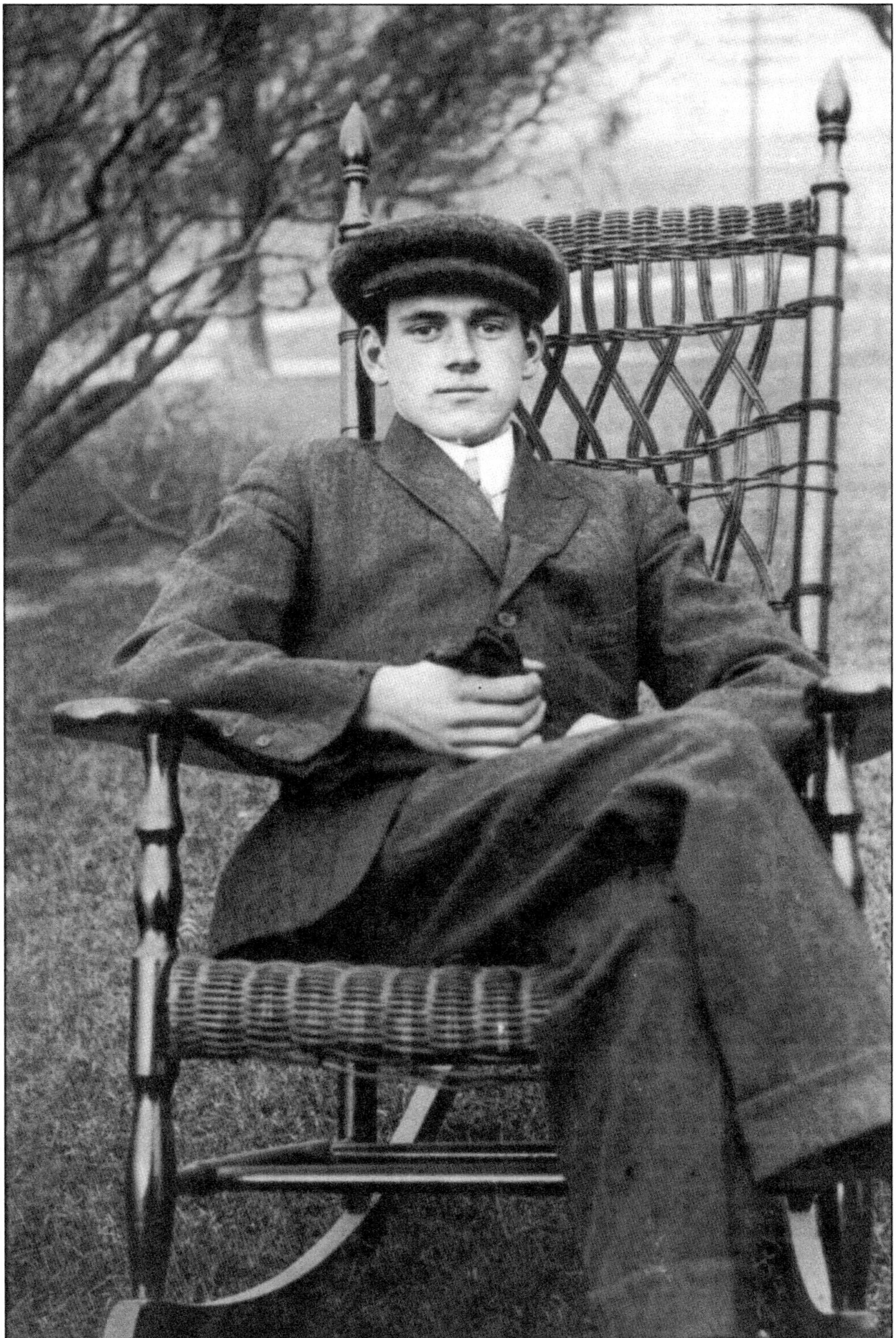

At a time when few people owned cameras, George Corby of the Corby homestead in Lima took and processed hundreds of photographs of this area. He is pictured here as a teenager c. 1910. He unknowingly left behind an unprecedented photographic history, examples of which follow. Cathy Gardner has made her great uncle's collection available to the public for the first time.

Six

Touring with George Corby

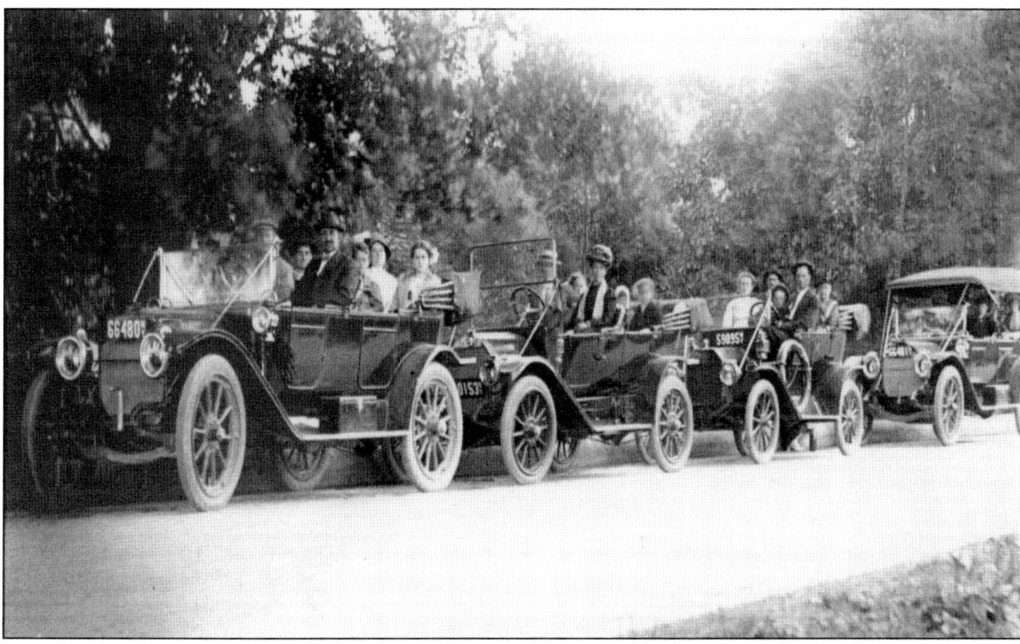

A well-educated boy with respect for hard work, born of his own farm labors, George Corby was as worldly as a small-town boy could be. He was extremely likable and had many friends. Here he has photographed family and friends as they anxiously begin a day of touring in the Finger Lakes.

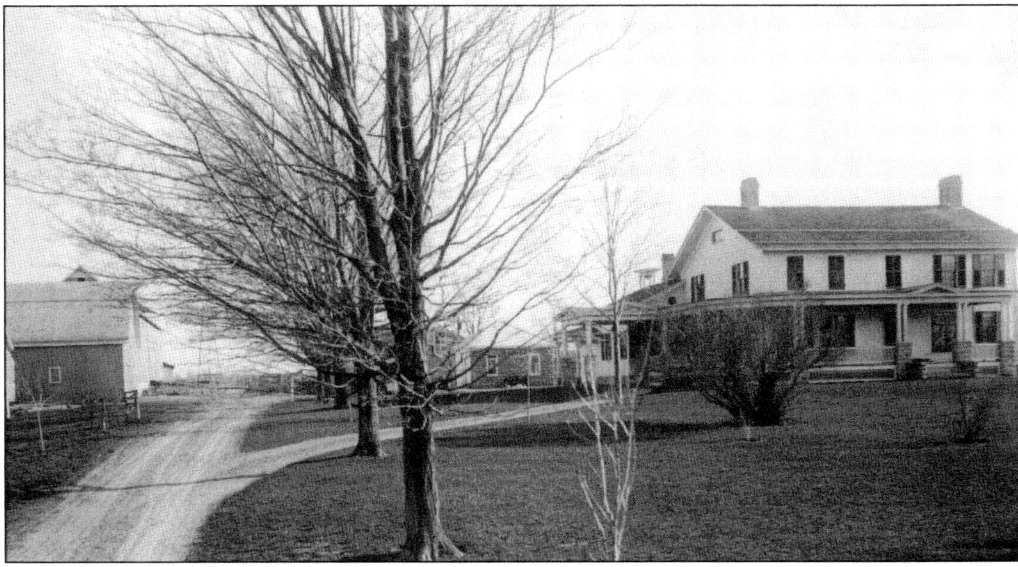

On April 23, 1914, George Corby captured this scene of the family farm on Corby Road. It is morning, and spring shadows fall across the lawn. On the left are the earlier barns.

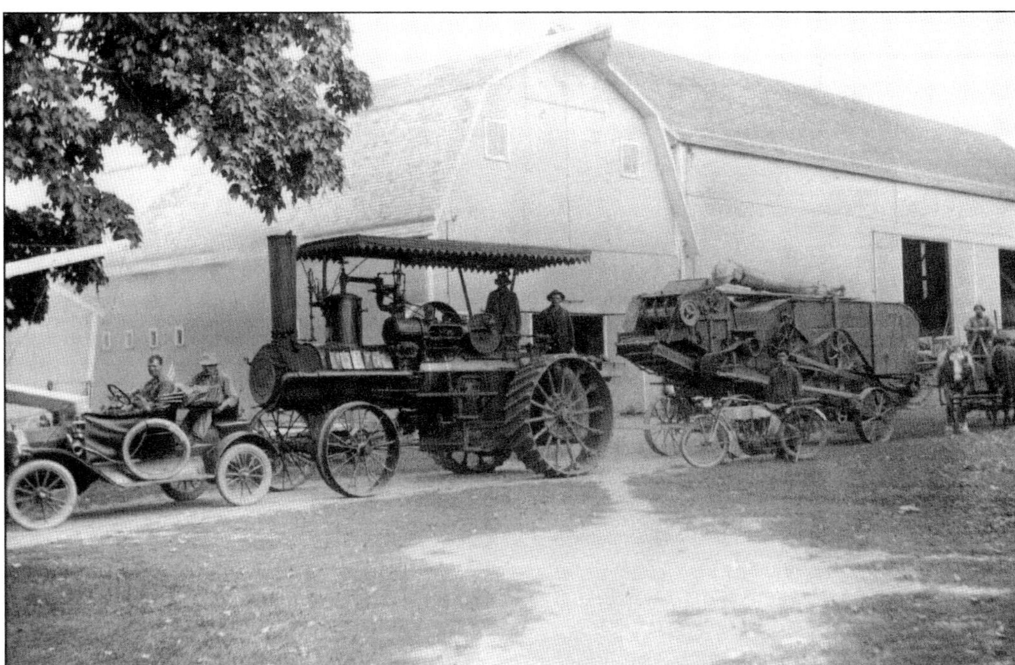

With massive barns as a backdrop, the farm's motive power is paraded down the main drive. There is a gas-powered car, steam-driven tractor and thresher, and even a horse-powered wagon for drawing hay. Note the early motorbike beside the thresher.

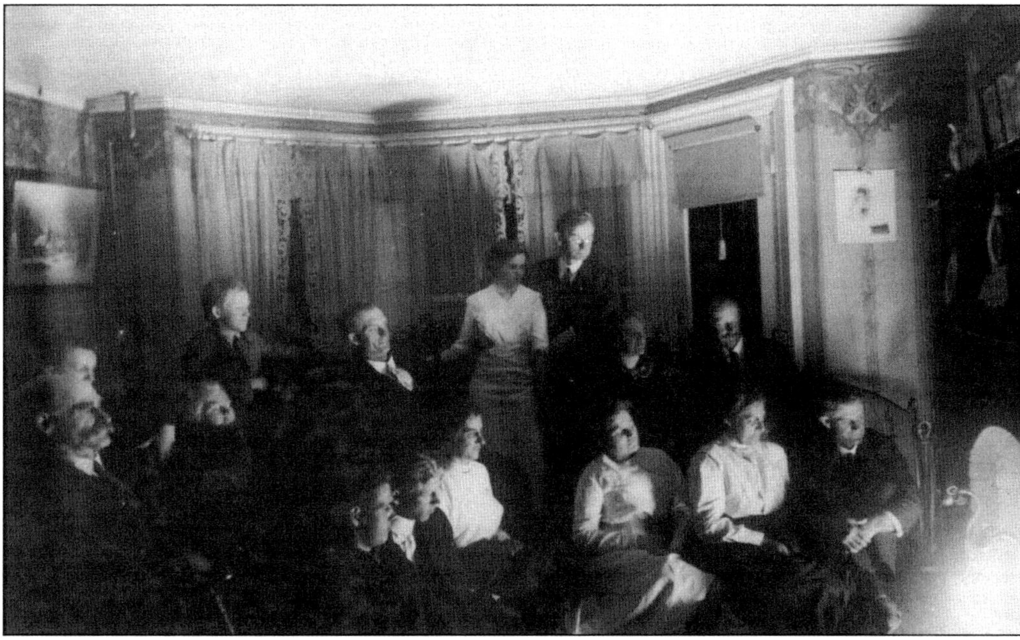
A warm glow from the parlor fireplace illuminates family members in this 1910 photograph.

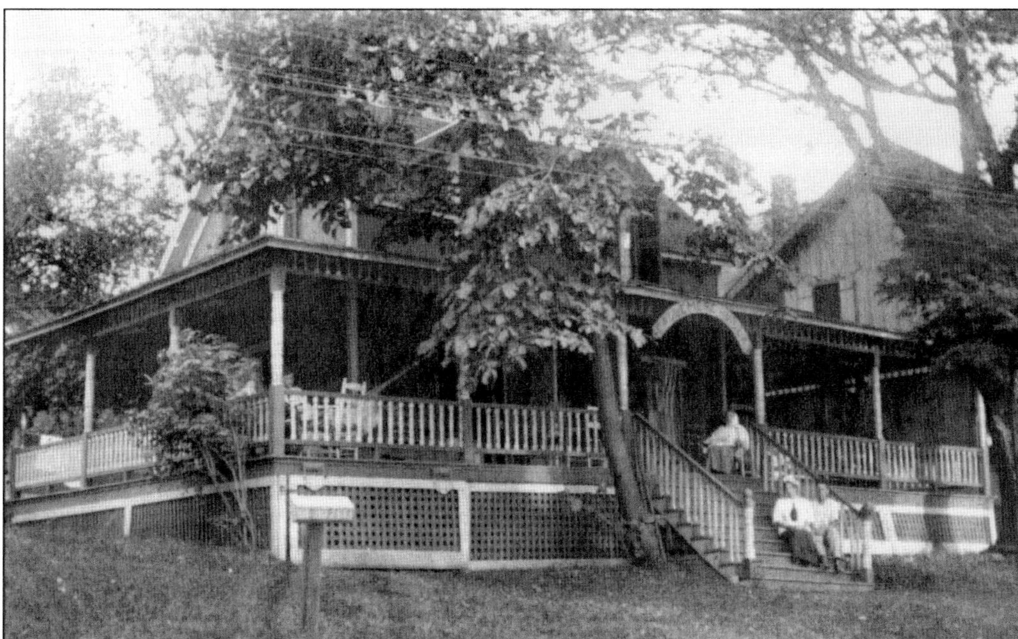
The Finger Lakes provided families a profusion of delights, from scenic wonders to recreation. A weekend outing to one of the lakes left cherished memories that lasted for years. The Corbys stayed at this cottage from August 26 to September 9, 1912. They had, as photographer George Corby records, "bully times."

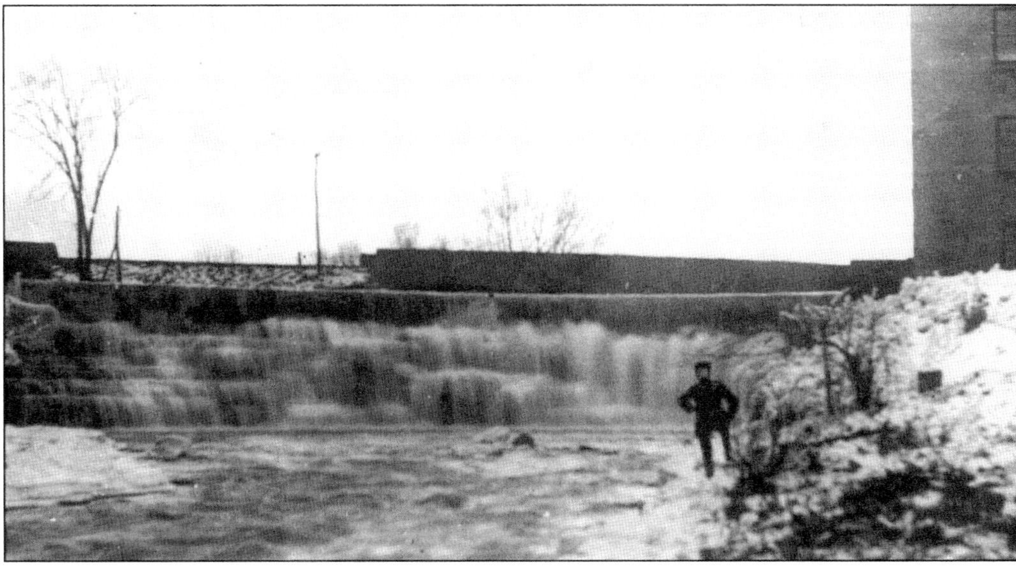

Although the farm was in Lima, Honeoye Falls was closer to George Corby's heart. A mere bike ride away, Honeoye Falls offered railroad yards with hissing steam engines, waterfalls, mills, and at least 100 adventures to be had with buddies. In this November 1910 scene, Corby has a young friend pose at the foot of the falls. On the right is the Upper Mill.

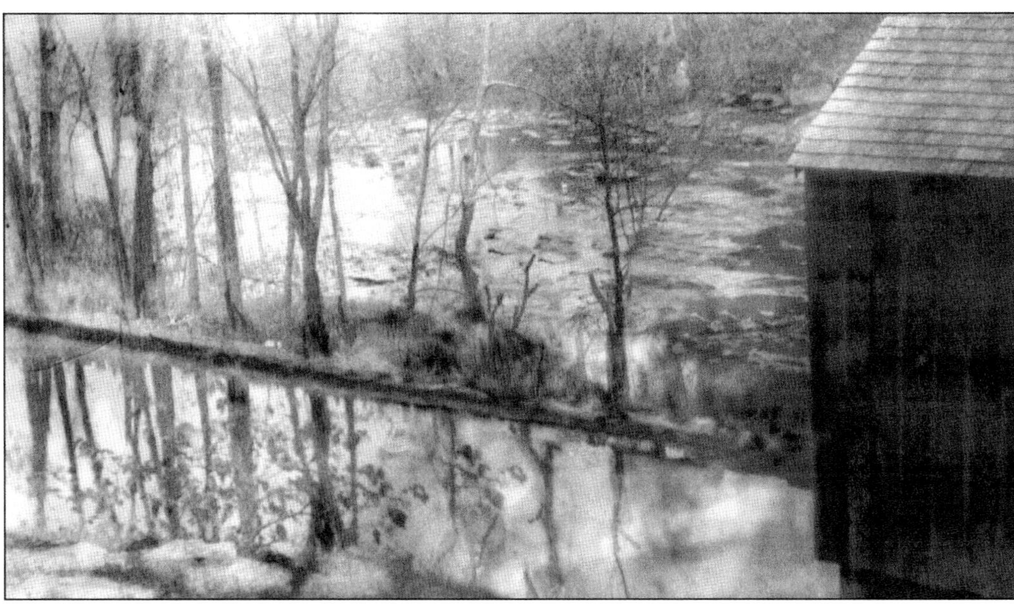

This photograph entitled "Our Swimming Hole" was taken that same November day. It is unique because it shows the millrace that supplied water to the Lower Mill. Beyond is Honeoye Creek.

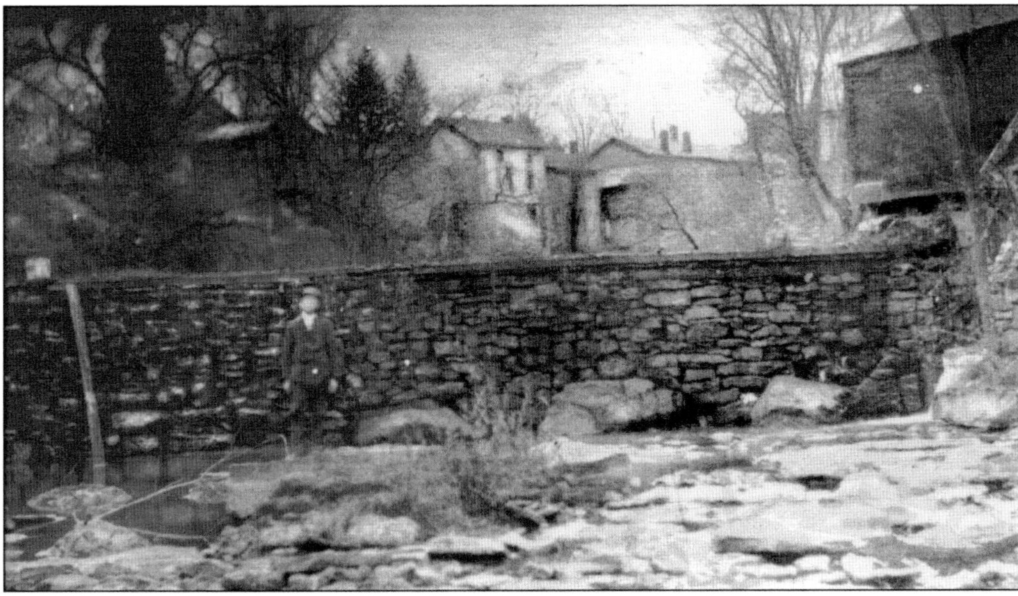

On that same bleak November day, George Corby captured this rare image of the Lower Mill dam. The view is southward. On the right is the millrace housing. By raising a gate, the race would flood, sending a torrent to turn the mill wheel. The rubble-built dam was one of four along the creek, which extended south through Bloomfield and Lima. More mills are visible behind the dam. When Rochester acquired the water rights to Hemlock Lake, from whence Honeoye Creek originates, the water flow was diminished, which doomed the mills.

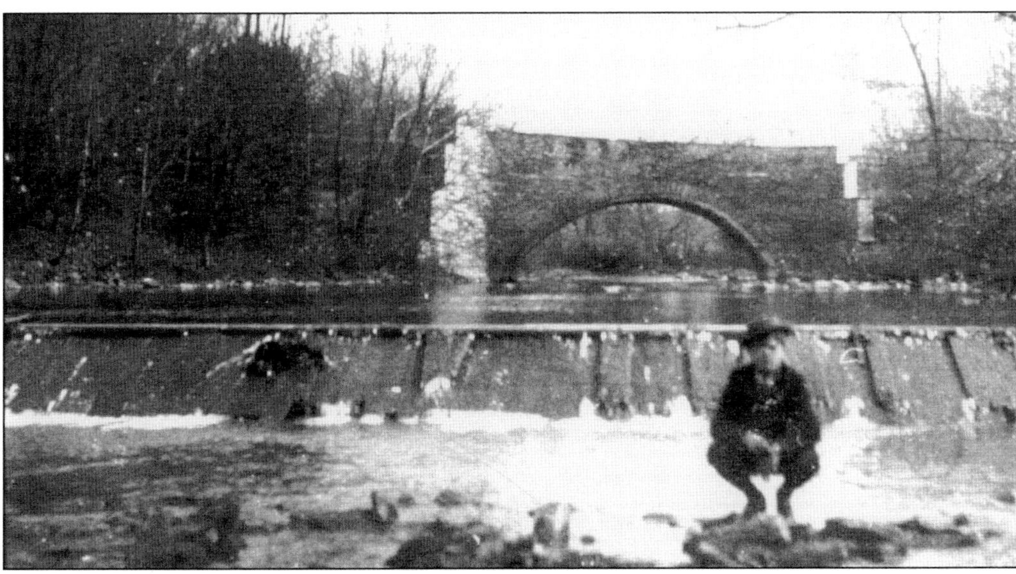

A bit farther up the creek that same day, a boy obliges the photographer. Captured is a view of the *c.* 1836 arc bridge, which carried North Main Street over the creek, and a small steel dam (foreground) used by a woolen mill.

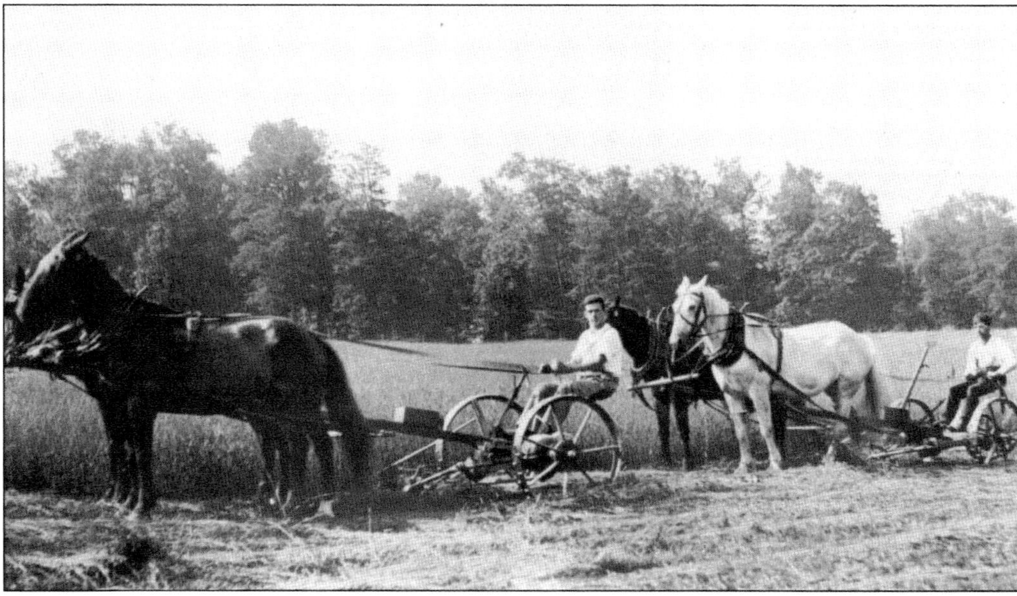

Haying was a vital—and dangerous—activity. This 1911 series of photographs offers a rare insight into the four-stage process. First came the "cutting" stage. George Corby is in the center. He managed to set up numerous self-portraits.

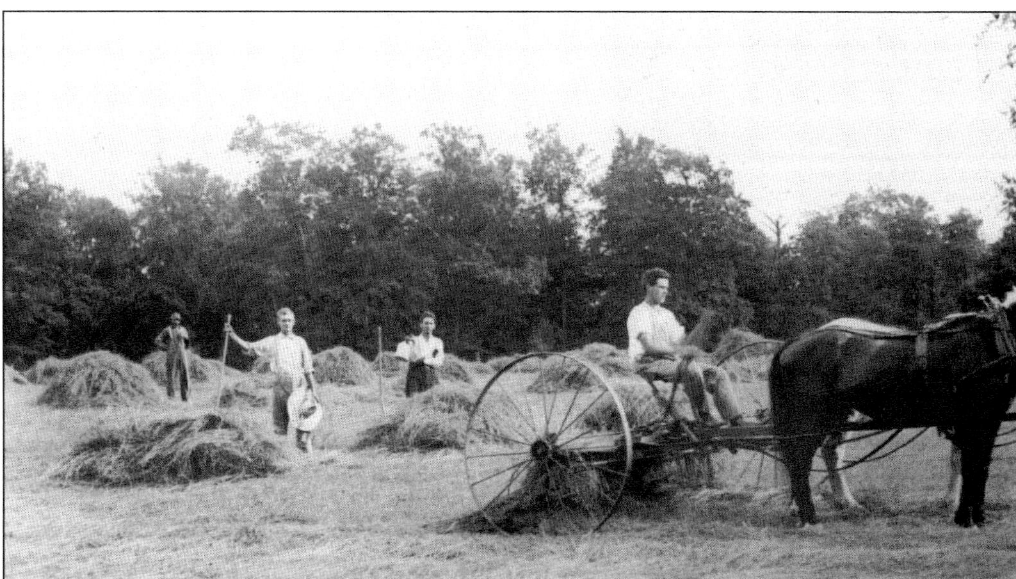

Step two of the haying process was "raking and bunching."

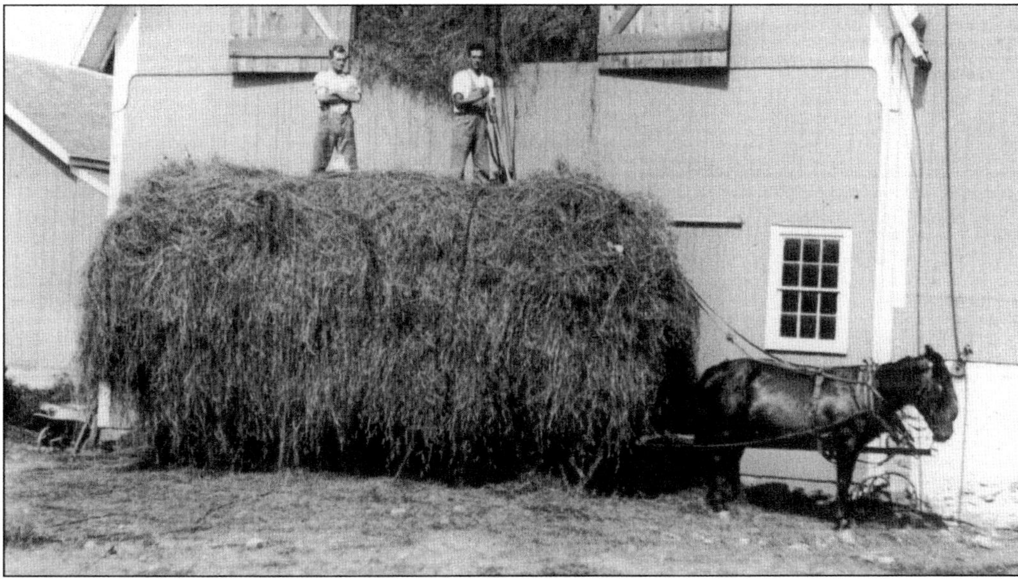

The process of "drawing" involved using heavy wagons to get the ton-loads of hay to the barn for storing.

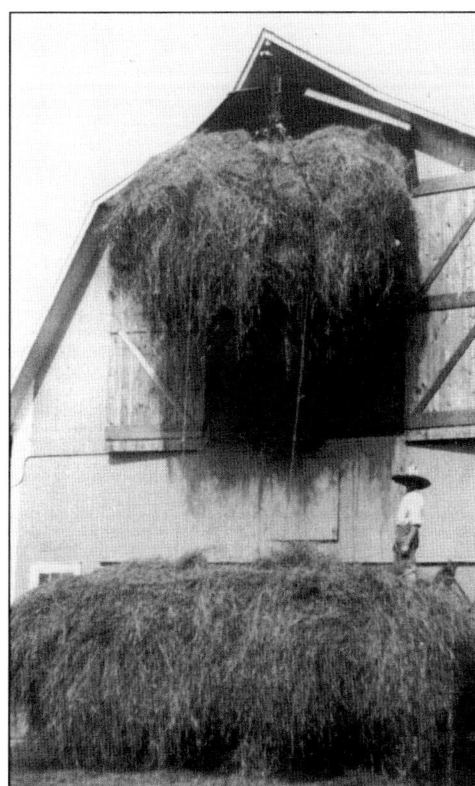

"Going in the barn" was the most difficult and dangerous stage. As the hay was hoisted up to the loading bay, it shook and dropped lots of dust and spores that thrived in human lungs. Many a farmhand developed respiratory problems because of this.

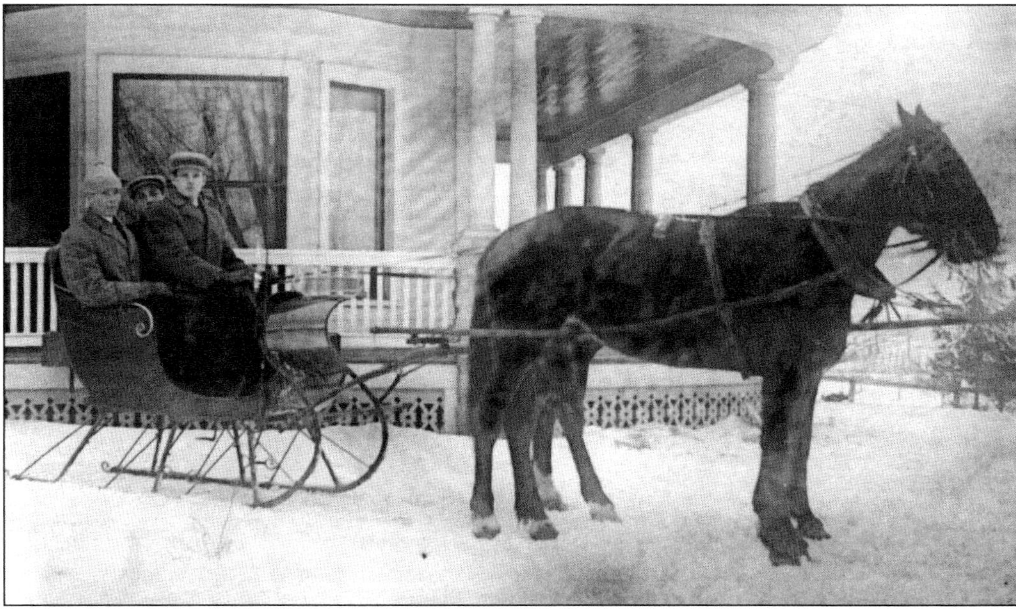

A matched team waits for a flick from the buggy whip to start a sleigh ride. This scene is on the front lawn of the Corby Road farm.

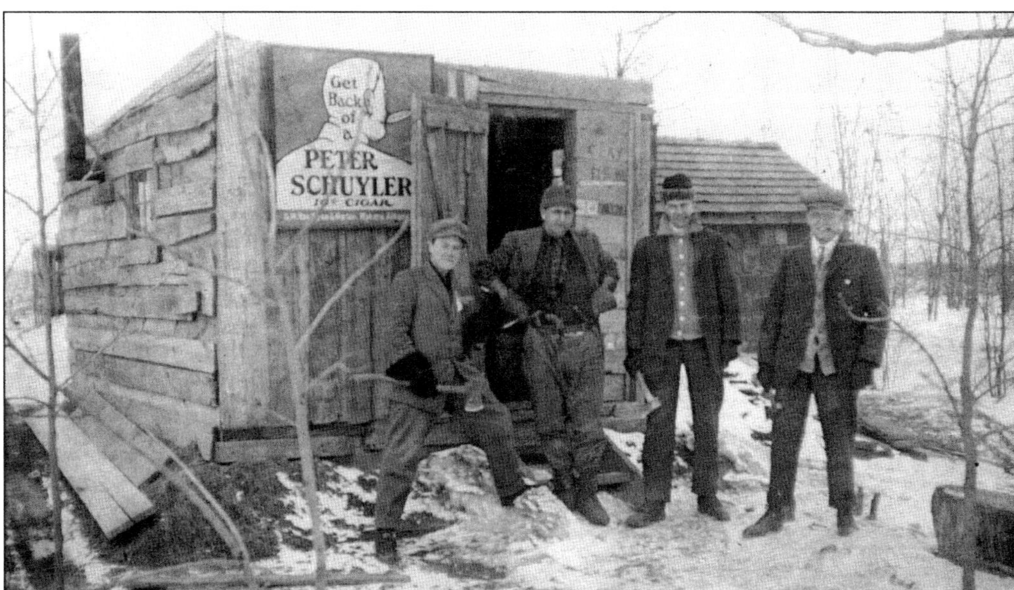

A group of farmhands called the "round-up gang" stand outside their "den." They tended cattle, chopped wood, and did their best to keep warm in their outland shack.

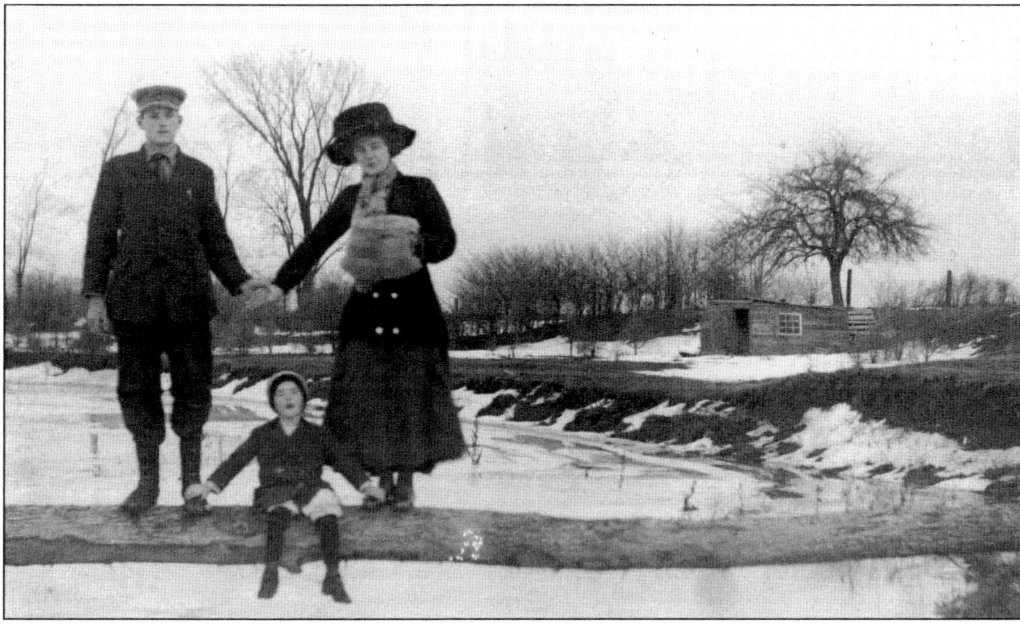

A visit to the farm by relatives on January 2, 1911, could not end without snapshots. The fashion-minded one is cousin Ida Firkins, with her fur muff. In the distance on the right is the round-up gang's den.

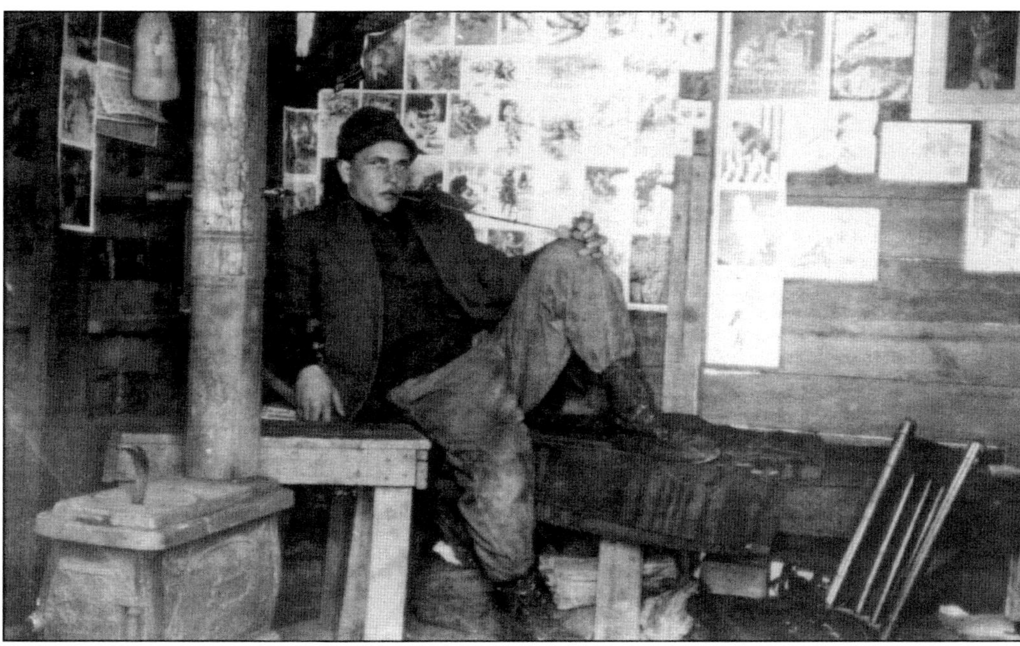

The captain of the round-up gang takes a few puffs from a long clay pipe in his den. On the wall are mostly fashion illustrations from magazines provided by George Corby. Before photographic processes were easily achieved, magazines employed talented illustrators such as Norman Rockwell, Howard Pyle, and Maxfield Parrish to produce magazine covers and fashion pictures. Most notable were Arrow shirts with detachable collars.

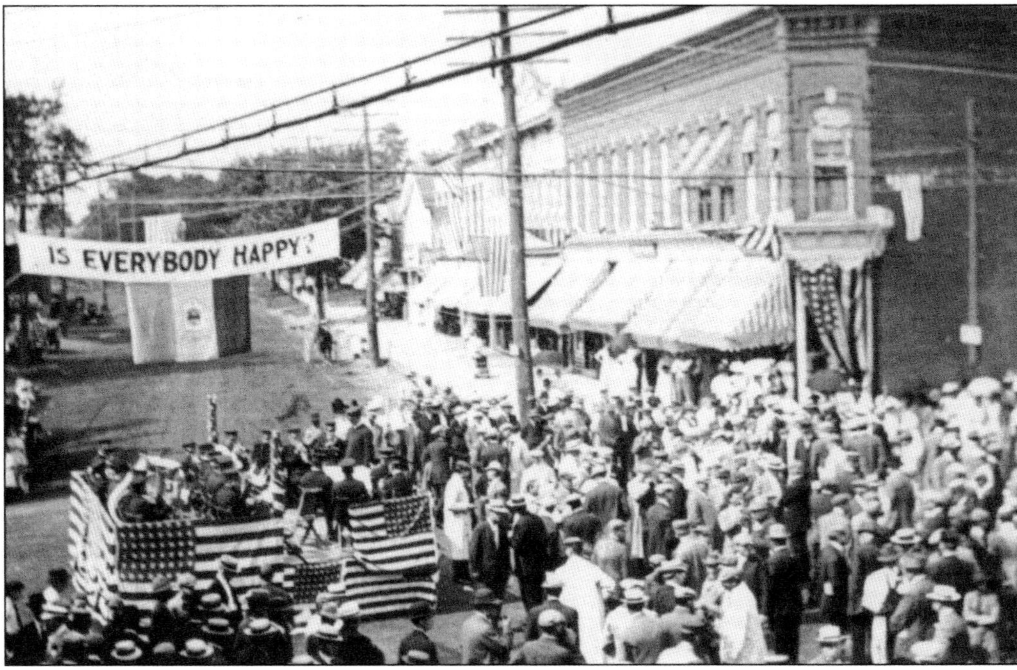

The band plays on as a crowd enjoys a Rochester Chamber of Commerce tour through Honeoye Falls in 1911.

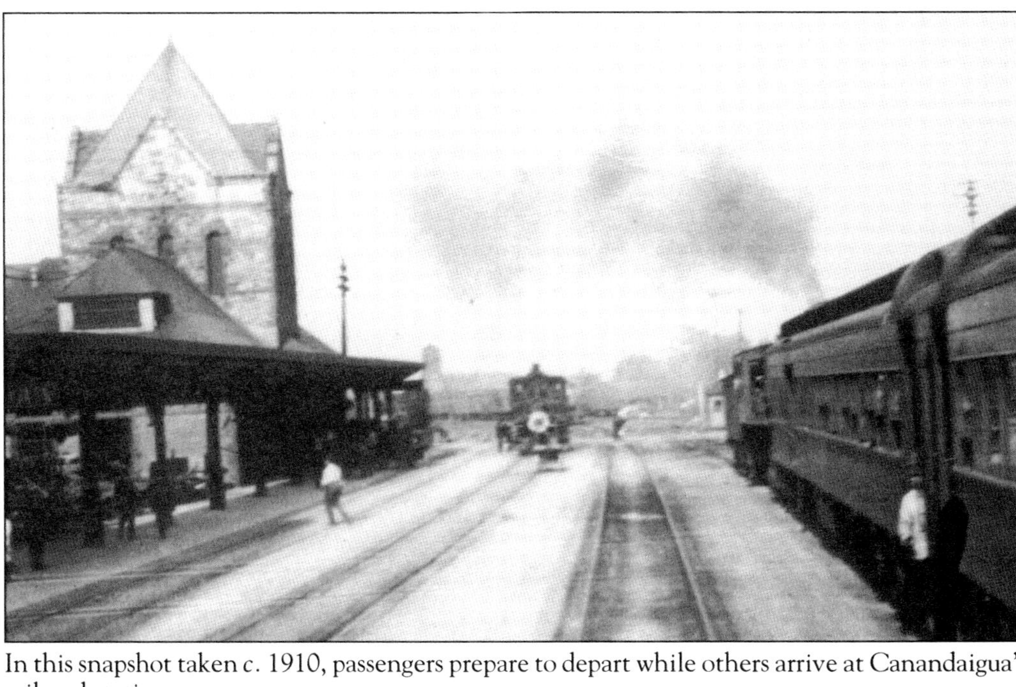
In this snapshot taken *c.* 1910, passengers prepare to depart while others arrive at Canandaigua's railroad station.

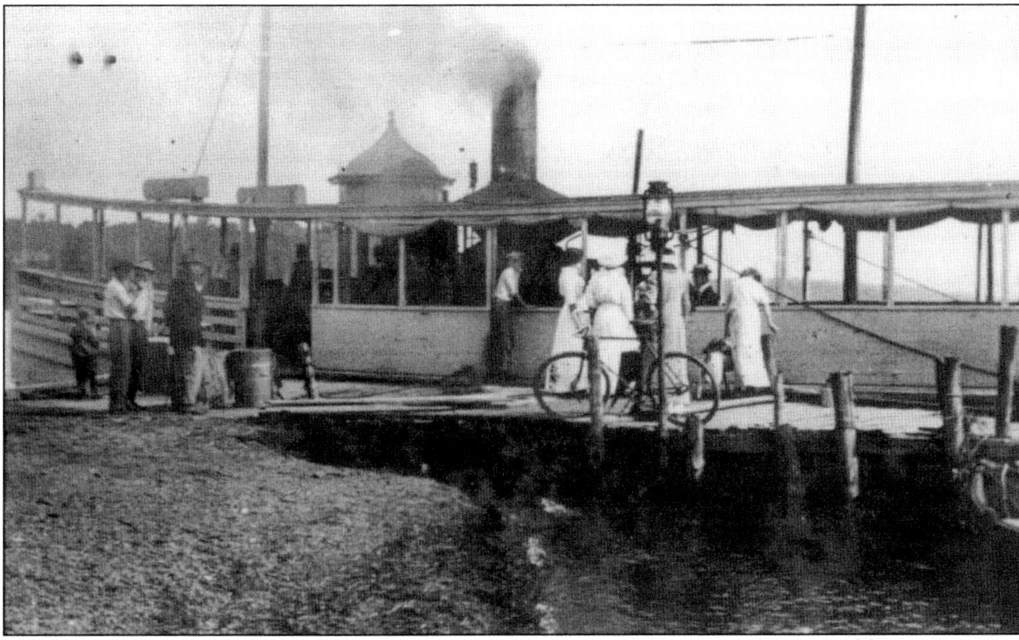

During an outing to Conesus Lake, George Corby photographed friends getting ready to board a steamboat for a tour of the lake. Crewmen watch from off to the side, while the captain gets a good head of steam going.

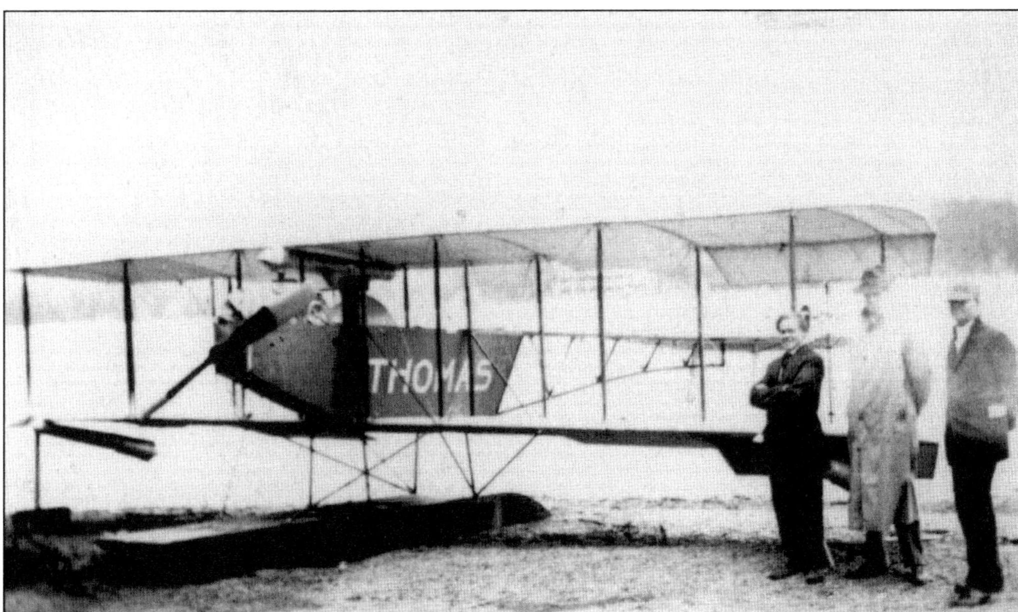

This hydroplane flew regularly on Conesus Lake. It was a real attention getter at a time when airplane flight was in its infancy. Six days after this photograph was taken, the plane crashed in the lake and the pilot drowned.

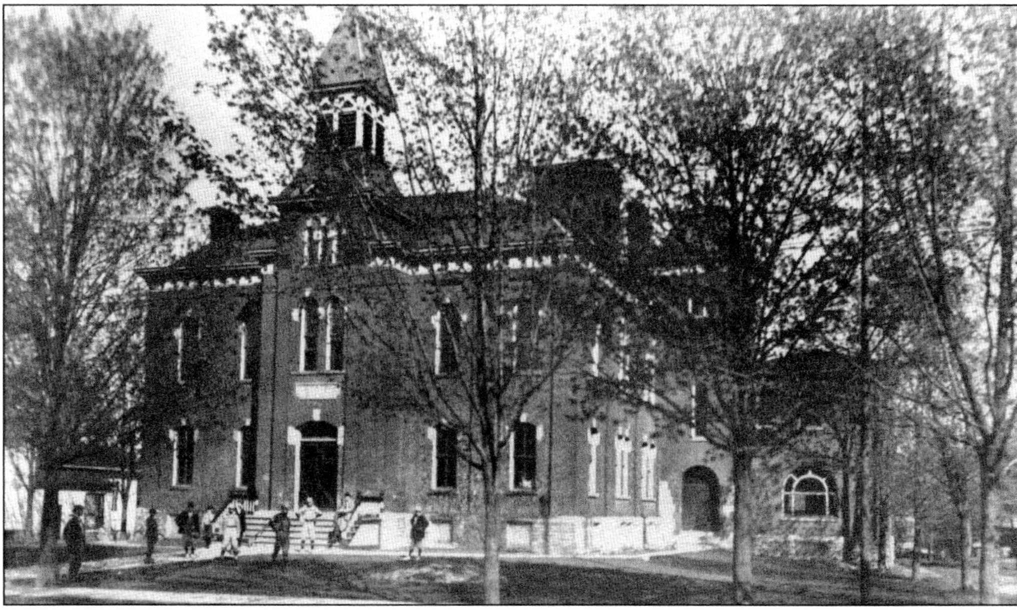

Student baseball players practice on the lawn of Honeoye Falls Free Union School in Harry Allen Park. The school was built in 1879 and served students until 1927, when a more modern school was built on East Street. The school systems of Honeoye Falls and Lima were eventually combined.

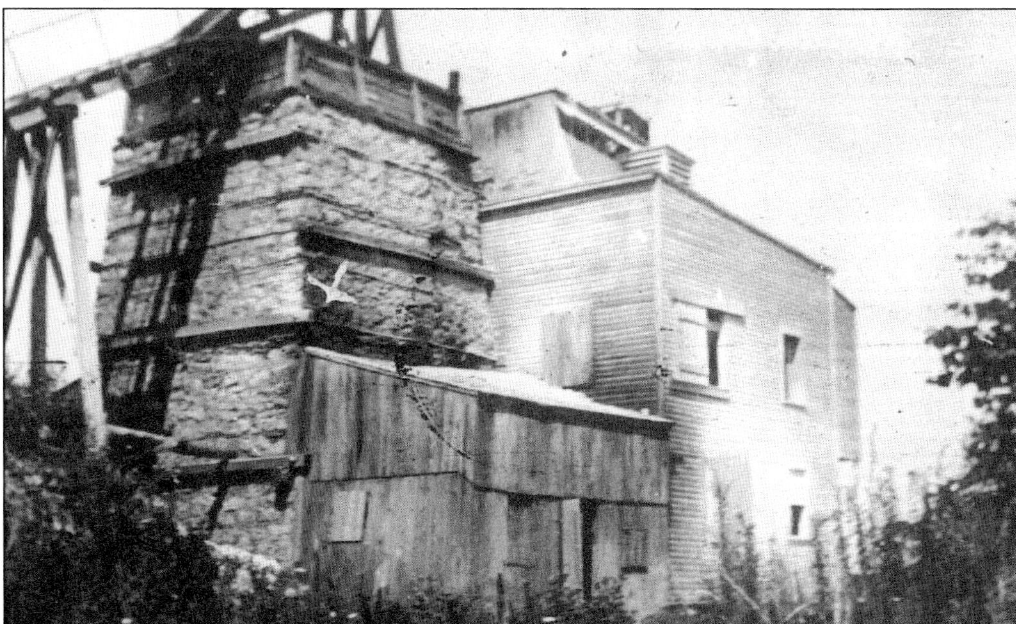

Both the elegant and rugged were worthy subjects to the budding photographer. George Corby had to wander back off Dalton Road in Lima to get this picture of the Genesee Lime Kiln. Limestone fragments were burned in the chamber to produce quicklime, a byproduct essential to lime mortar. Many of the lovely cobblestone homes in this area used lime mortar from here. There are more cobblestone buildings in a 70-mile radius of Rochester than anywhere else on earth. A portion of the kiln was preserved and incorporated into a residence.

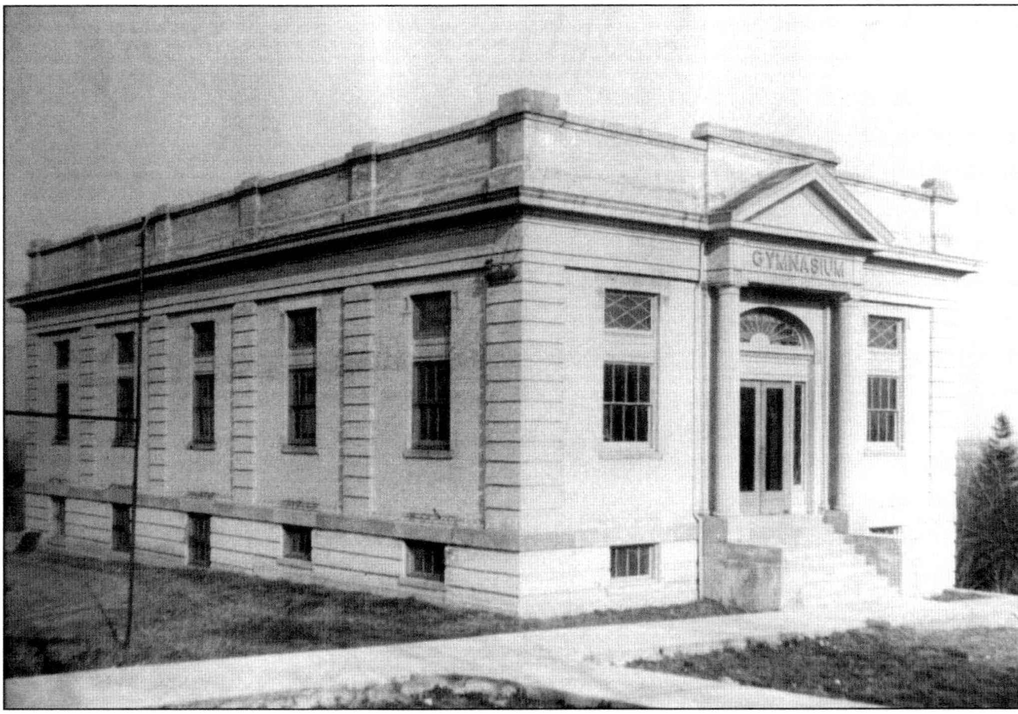

The gymnasium at Genesee Wesleyan Seminary looked fairly new when student George Corby photographed it *c.* 1914.

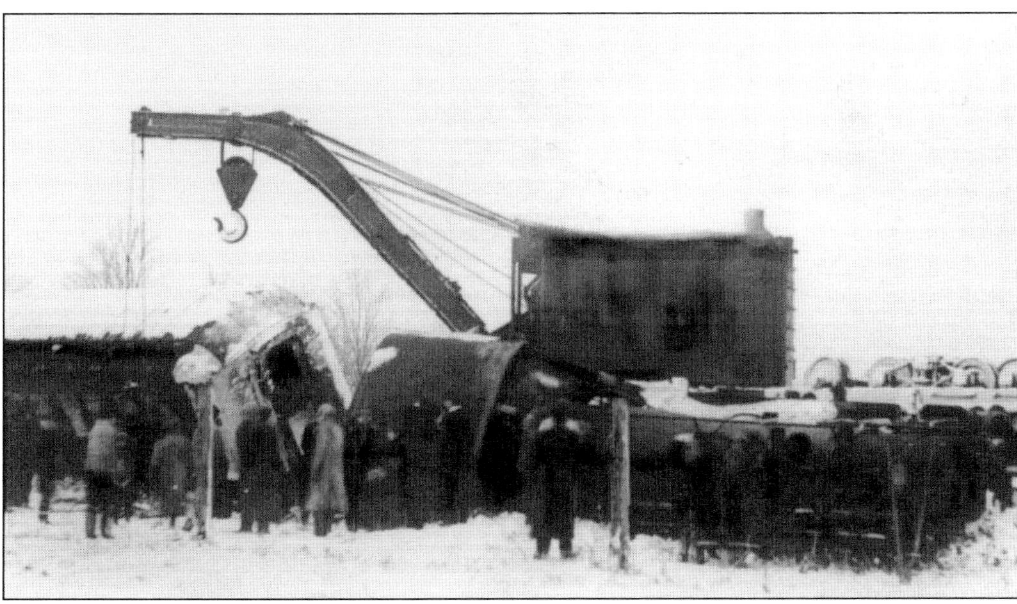

On January 4, 1913, a Lehigh Valley passenger train jumped the track at Palmer's Crossing, outside Lima. A work crew with a powerful steam crane was dispatched to jockey the toppled passenger cars and locomotive back on track.

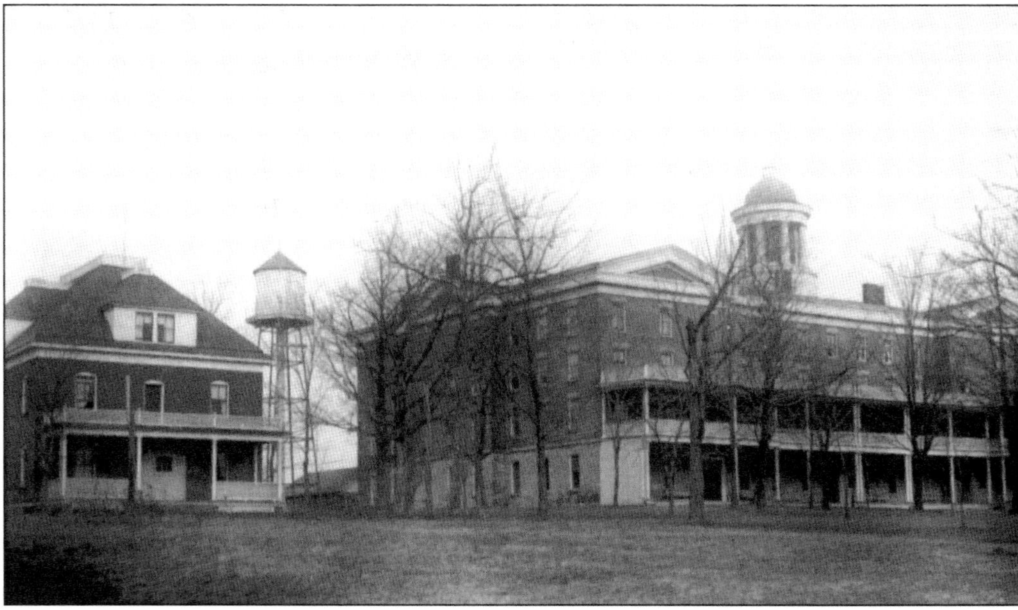

Pictured are the dormitory (right) and Faling Hall (left) at Genesee Wesleyan Seminary. George Corby took numerous photographs of the campus while he was a student. He usually rode his bike back and forth to school.

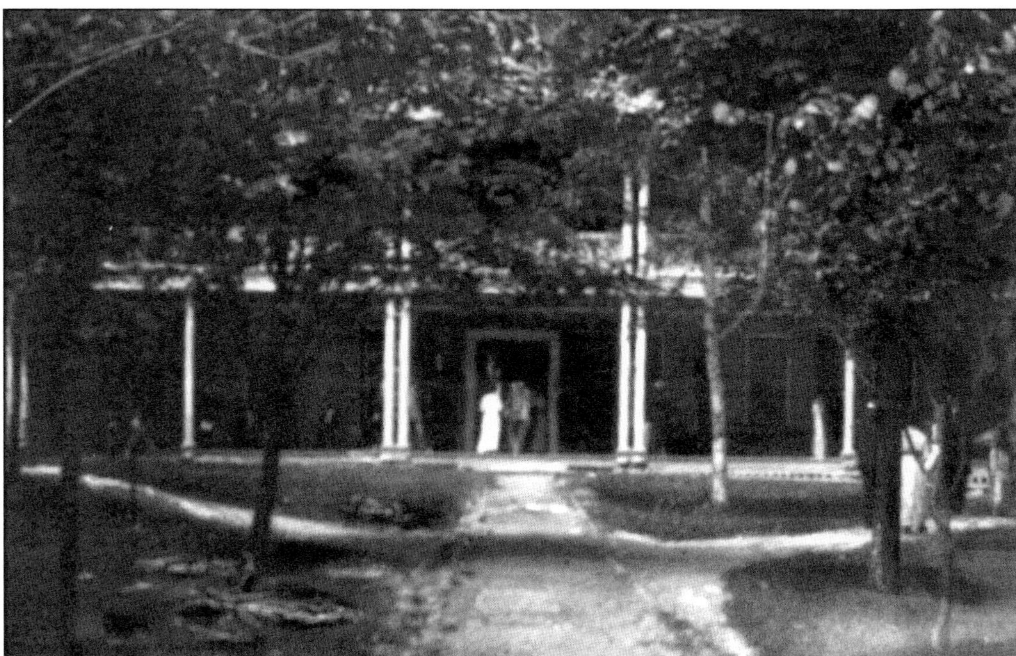

In a view entitled "The Ending of Social Hour," students stroll down campus lanes to return to their dormitories. Social hour was at dusk. It was meant as a time for exercise, meditation, gentle conversation, and prayer. It was more often a time for pranks, kidding around, and potent snowball fights in winter. The students here are not going back to television programs or lengthy telephone calls but, rather, to Latin and alchemy homework and long letters to family and friends.

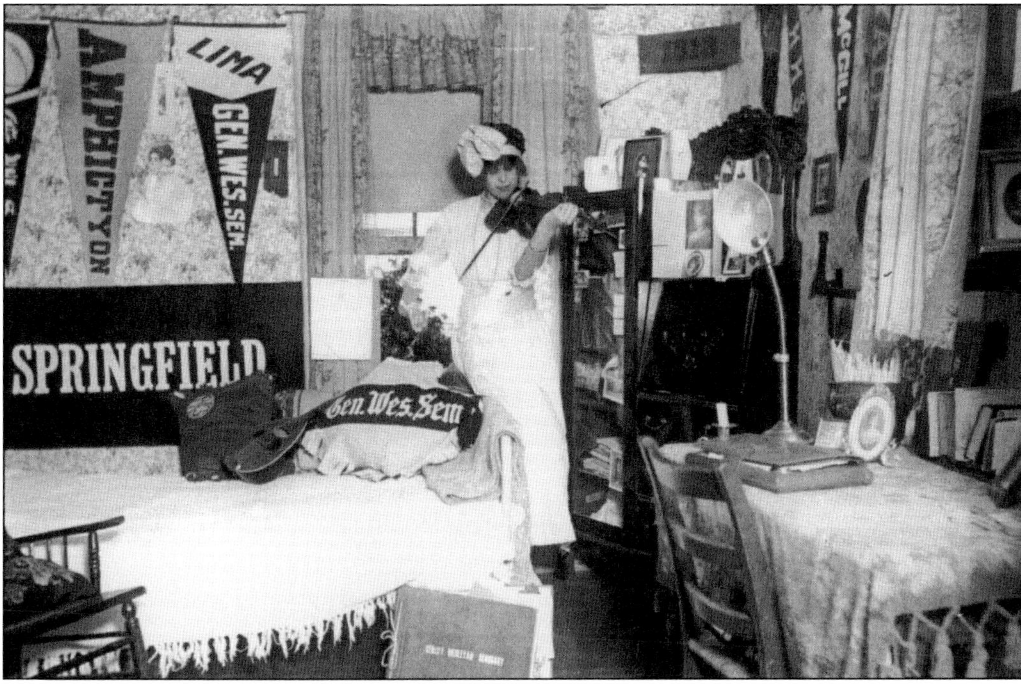

Ruth Williams, a good friend, plays the violin in her dormitory room, surrounded by lace, fringes, and an abundance of what appears to be the campus rage: pennants. It is not known how photographer George Corby managed to get into the girls' dormitory, but he provided a rare glimpse of campus life.

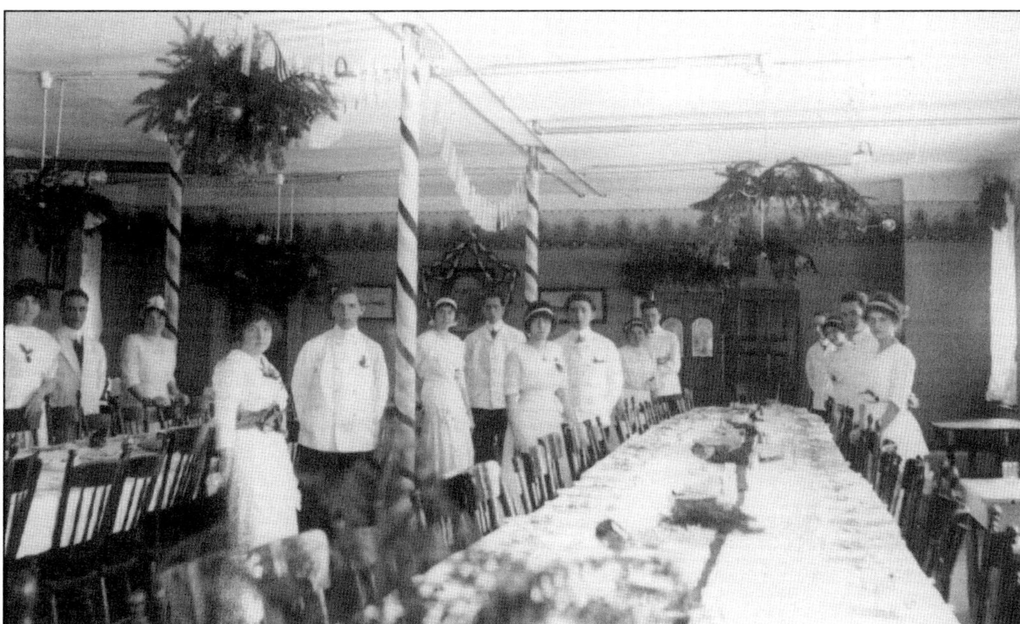

Neatly attired students prepare to attend guests coming to a Washington's Birthday Banquet held in the school dining hall.

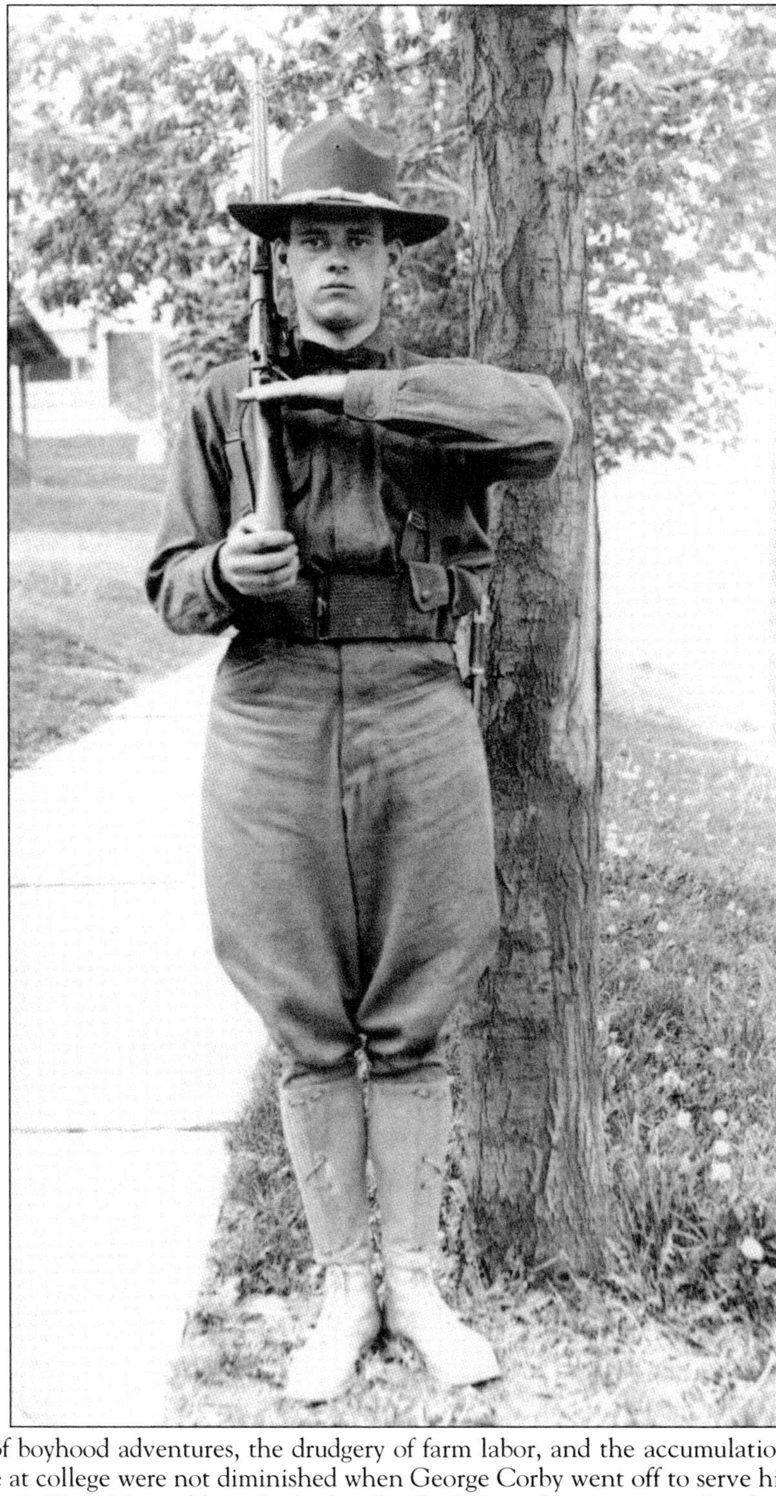

The joys of boyhood adventures, the drudgery of farm labor, and the accumulation of worldly knowledge at college were not diminished when George Corby went off to serve his country in World War I. His spirit could not be broken by the horrors he encountered as long as he had his camera. Here, Private Corby displays the salute "right shoulder arms."

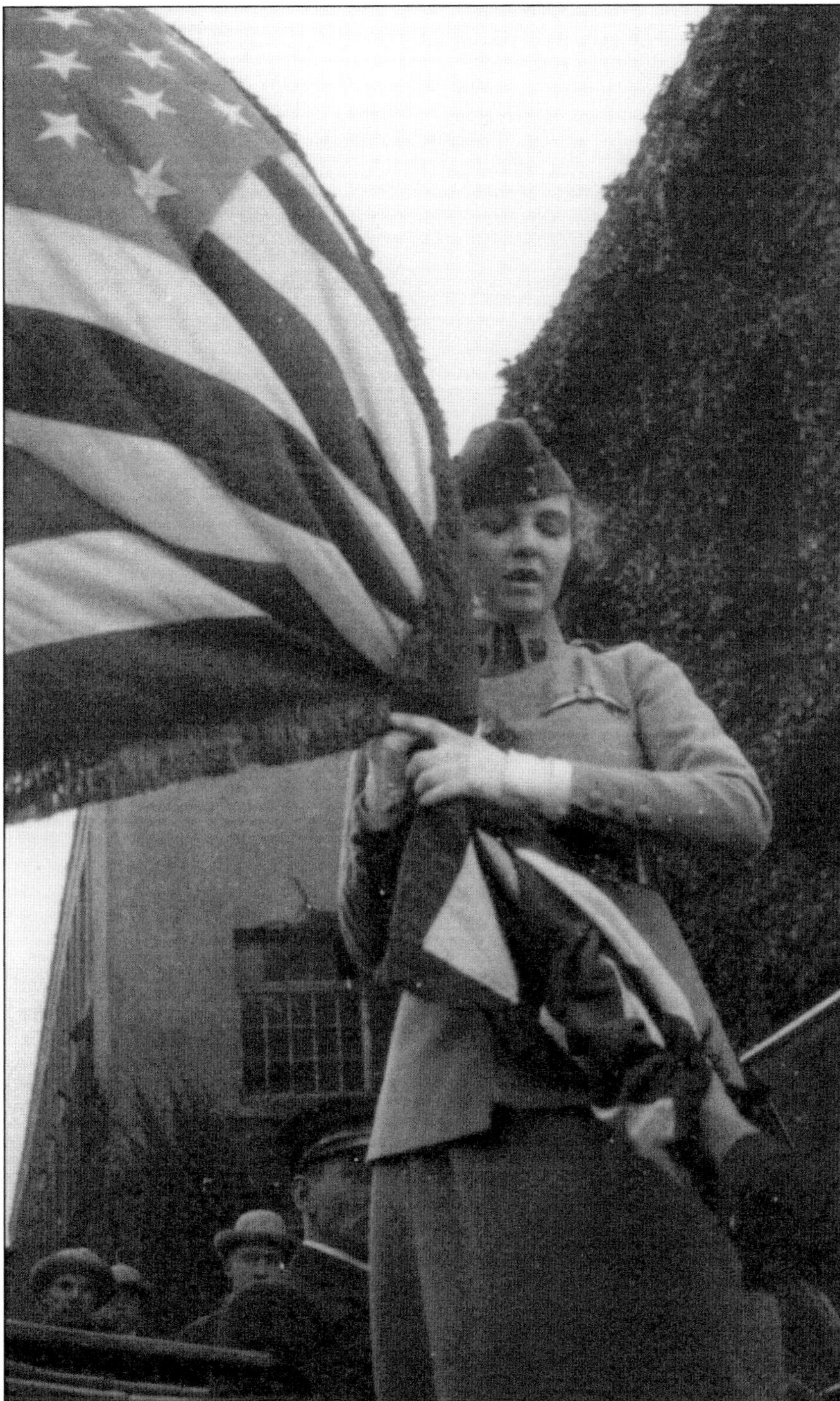

Taken at the time of the armistice, this photograph shows a patriot with gloved hands grasping an American flag, which almost appears to be billowing from her heart. Pvt. George Corby brought back to his small town a record of the war with its battles, parades, triumphs, and tragedies. In many ways this singular image may have captured it all.

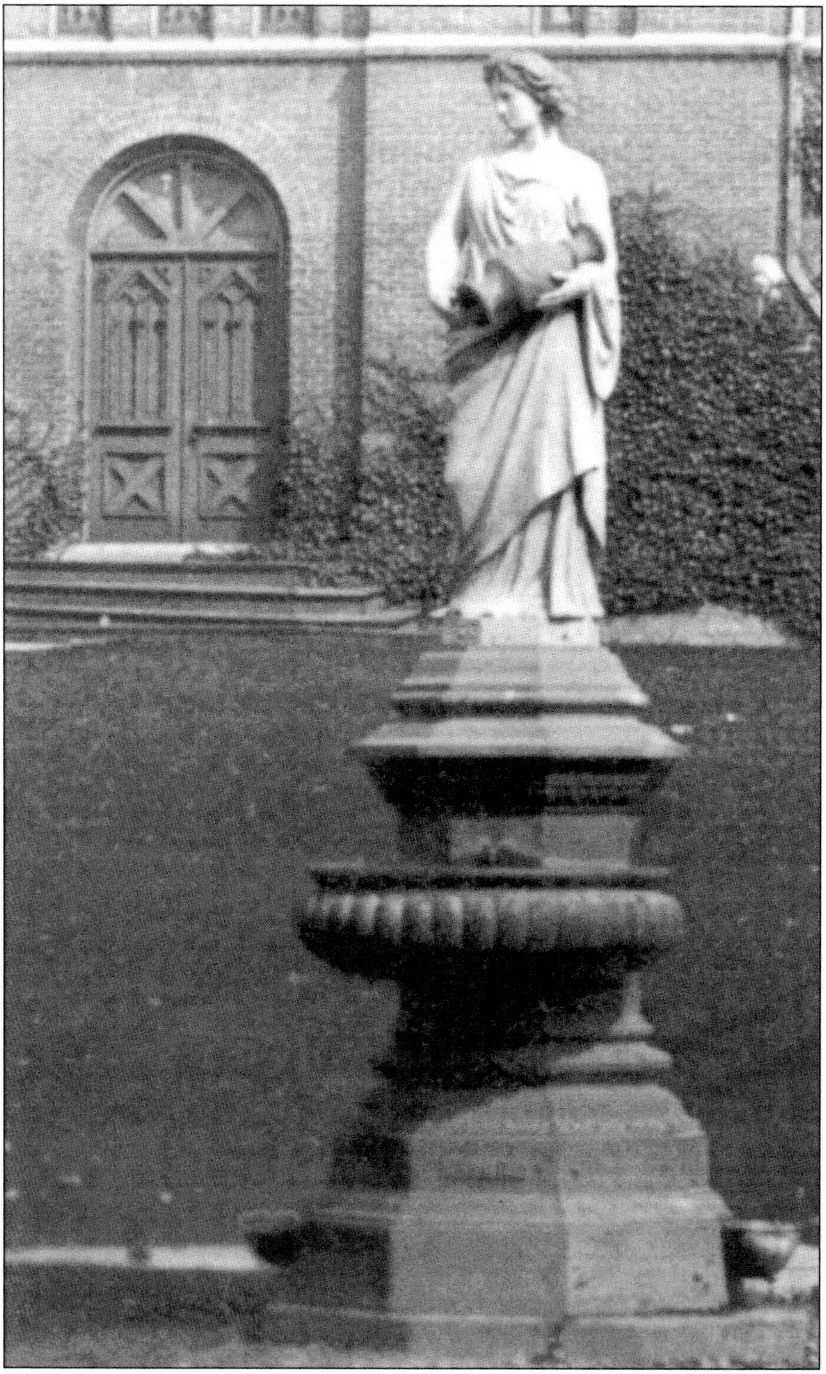

Rebecca at the Well resided for many years in front of the Presbyterian church in Lima. This full view shows that she was set appropriately west of the crossroads. Even her gaze, though downward, is to the west. Near this place Seneca children sang beside longhouses, pioneer wagons rumbled by, and soldiers returned home to loved ones. Lima remains a home to the hardworking and joyous—the adventurous. The gentle curve of *Rebecca*'s lips tells us it is probably best just to take it all in stride.